THE DOCTORS
WHO'S WHO

THE DOCTORS WHO'S WHO

CELEBRATING ITS 50TH YEAR

THE STORY BEHIND EVERY FACE
OF THE ICONIC TIME LORD

CRAIG CABELL

JOHN BLAKE

Published by John Blake Publishing Ltd,
3 Bramber Court, 2 Bramber Road,
London W14 9PB, England

www.johnblakepublishing.co.uk

www.facebook.com/Johnblakepub   facebook

twitter.com/johnblakepub   twitter

First published in hardback in 2010
Subsequently published in paperback in 2011
This revised edition published in 2013

ISBN: 978 1 78219 471 2

British Library Cataloguing-in-Publication Data:

A catalogue record for this book is available from the British Library.

Design by www.envydesign.co.uk

Printed and bound in Great Britain by CPI Group (UK) Ltd

1 3 5 7 9 10 8 6 4 2

Papers used by John Blake Publishing are natural, recyclable products made
from wood grown in sustainable forests. The manufacturing processes
conform to the environmental regulations of the country of origin.

Every attempt has been made to contact the relevant copyright-holders,
but some were unobtainable. We would be grateful if the
appropriate people could contact us.

'If you knew Time as well as I do,' said the Hatter, 'you wouldn't talk about wasting it.'

The Mad Hatter
Alice's Adventures in Wonderland
Lewis Carroll

Special Introductions

Furies Over Korea – The Story of the Men of the Fleet Air Arm, RAF and Commonwealth Who Defended South Korea, 1950–1953 by Graham A. Thomas

Firestorm, Typhoons Over Caen, 1944 by Graham A. Thomas

Terror from the Sky – the Battle Against the Flying Bomb by Graham A. Thomas

The Dan Brown Enigma by Graham A. Thomas

ABOUT THE AUTHOR

CRAIG CABELL WAS a freelance reporter and columnist for 20 years, writing most notably for *The Independent*.

He has travelled the world from the Middle East to North and South America for Government services. His previous books include military history and biography, exposing nuances previously unexplored, including the covert work of crack commandos during the Second World War (*The History of 30 Assault Unit*) and covert operations by specially formed spitfire squadrons (*Operation Big Ben – The Anti-V2 Spitfire Missions, 1944–45*, with Graham A. Thomas). His previous books for John Blake include *Ian Rankin and Inspector Rebus*, *Terry Pratchett – The Spirit of Fantasy* and *Killing Kennedy*. He lives in London.

For Samantha, Nathan and Fern.

ACKNOWLEDGEMENTS

OVER SOME CONSIDERABLE time members of the *Doctor Who* family spoke to me casually, wrote to me, or agreed to be interviewed by me, all of which helped me in the writing of this book. I would like to thank: Patrick Troughton, Jon Pertwee, Tom Baker, Peter Davison, Colin Baker, Sylvester McCoy, Louise Jameson, Sarah Sutton, Janet Fielding, Mark Strickson, Anthony Ainley, Nicola Bryant, Sophie Aldrid, John Nathan-Turner, Dick Mills, Tony Burroughs and Nicholas Courtney.

Thanks are also due to my father Colin, Dave Bush, Brian Aldrich, Deborah Charlton, Barry Burnett, Iain Banks, Christopher Lee, Ray Harryhausen, the proprietor of Pleasures of Past Times (Cecil Court), John O'Sullivan, Moira Williamson and to Miranda Hart for an Eric Morecambe gem I could have overlooked – and of course for including Peter Davison in her excellent show.

I would also like to thank some of my friends and family who have shared their *Doctor Who* experiences with me over the years, namely Nicholas Skinner, Richard Ball, and of course, Anita, Samantha, Nathan and Fern. Extra thanks to

Fern Lavinia for helping scout out extra David Tennant clips and Nathan for watching countless *Doctor Who* episodes time and again.

Sincerely, many thanks to all.

CC

CONTENTS

PART TWO: THE LEGACY

AUTHOR'S NOTE

WE OWE A DEBT of gratitude to the Doctors.

After 50 years of *Doctor Who*, we owe a debt of gratitude to those excellent English and Scottish actors who adorned strange Edwardian – for the most part – costumes, took to the controls of the TARDIS and made television history. How many times have we watched William Hartnell in *Carry On Sergeant*, Patrick Troughton in *The Omen*, Jon Pertwee in *Worzel Gummidge*, Tom Baker in *Blackadder*, Peter Davison in *All Creatures Great and Small*, Colin Baker in *I'm a Celebrity... Get Me Out of Here!*, Sylvester McCoy in *The Hobbit*, Paul McGann in *Hornblower*, Christopher Eccleston in *The Second Coming*, David Tennant in *Broadchurch* and Matt Smith in *Womb* and said 'He was Doctor Who'?

No matter what else those actors did (or do), they will always be known as the Doctor. A man – an actor – instantly recognisable, instantly trusted by parents with their children, because he plays such a unique character in television history.

It is fitting that during the 50th anniversary of *Doctor Who* there is a book that looks at the careers of these special actors who have played the Doctor, to give something back to them and to acknowledge the wider parameters of their acting skills. This was something I originally undertook several years ago in the first edition of this book, *The Doctors Who's Who*. The success of that book has made it possible to revise, update and significantly add to it for the 50th anniversary, in order to celebrate the actors' careers alongside the programme itself. No book has done this before. Of course, each *Doctor Who* actor has released an autobiography or had a biography written about him; but this snapshot overview paints a picture of the programme's influence on each Doctor and shows the impact those Doctor Who actors have had on British culture since around the time of the Second World War.

Doctor Who has had an influence on the supporting cast too. Actors who have appeared in a short scene in a single episode way back in time are still asked for autographs by fans and requested to attend conventions or contribute to DVD documentaries approximately half a century later.

Think about some of the key supporting actors who have passed away (in 2011 and 2012 alone): Nicholas Courtney, Elisabeth Sladen, Caroline Johns and Mary Tamm. In each case, mention was made of their key role in *Doctor Who* alongside the headline announcement of their sad passing; but surely the 1974 movie *The Odessa File* was far more important to Mary Tamm than *Doctor Who*?

Doctor Who demands to be recognised. It is a career highlight, so it is right that we spare a thought for the other work the *Doctor Who* actors have done throughout their careers and the other people who have touched their lives.

Doctor Who has evolved over the years. Regular cast members have come and gone but as long as a blue police box materialises and dematerialises with a wheezing, groaning sound and the programme's once haunting – now wonderfully menacing – theme tune assures us that the *character* of the Doctor is unchanged, the programme will continue to cast its spell over legions of fans across the world for many years to come.

Doctor Who isn't a cult TV programme. Approximately eight million regular viewers per episode make it something more, especially when you couple that figure with overseas franchises, DVDs and the ability to watch the show later via BBC iPlayer. The final head count proves that after 50 years *Doctor Who* is more popular now than ever before, and its reputation will continue to grow over the next half century.

The Doctor's journey is far from over and more actors will have their lives unrecognisably changed by taking on the iconic role.

'I realise that I have been very lucky in that I have had three massive successes in my career to date: *The Navy Lark, Doctor Who* and *Worzel Gummidge*. These have kept me in the public eye for far longer than many of my contemporaries.'

I Am the Doctor – Jon Pertwee's Final Memoir

PART ONE
WHO WERE THE DOCTORS?

'The Doctor is always on the side of the good and he must always win in the end. And, of course, I just adored doing it. It is a unique and magical experience to be able to live out a public fantasy on a gigantic scale and get paid!'

Tom Baker

"DOCTOR WHO AND THE TRIBE OF GUM"

by

Anthony Coburn

EPISODE ONE "An Unearthly Child"

F.I. CAM

Opening Sequence

SUPOSE CAM   Title:

"Doctor Who and the Tribe of Gum"

by
Anthony Coburn

The title page to a draft script of 'An Unearthly Child' by Anthony Coburn, the first ever *Doctor Who* story.

CHAPTER ONE

DOCTOR WHO?

Doctor Who: Who are you?
Chesterton: I'll ask the questions, Buster.

From a draft script of *Doctor Who and the
Tribe of Gum*, Episode One 'An Unearthly Child'
Anthony Coburn

WHO IS RESPONSIBLE for creating *Doctor Who*?

It's not an easy question to answer. A TV show has many people who play a major role in creating it, from its initial idea through to the first transmission; but Sydney Newman must be recognised as the catalyst, the person who laid down the fundamental building blocks for *Doctor Who* and, most importantly, the main character.

Sydney Cecil Newman was born in Toronto, Canada, in 1917. He was educated at Ogden Public School and the Central Technical School, Toronto, where he studied painting, stagecraft and industrial and interior design. His skills were put to work as an artist, designing posters for cinemas and theatres in Toronto, but he soon branched out.

In 1938, Newman decided to go to Hollywood, where he was offered a job by the Walt Disney Company, which was impressed by the young man's skills as a graphic designer. Unfortunately, he couldn't obtain a work permit and had to return to Toronto where, in 1941, he secured employment with the National Film Board of Canada as an assistant film editor.

Later, Newman returned to America to study their film techniques. He would incorporate what he learnt into the ever-growing Canadian broadcasting industry. In the 1950s, he moved across to Britain and became Head of Drama at ABC (former Thames Television), where he created Science Fiction (SF) show *Pathfinders in Space* and cult TV series *The Avengers*.

One of Newman's strengths was his ability to gather the right team of individuals together to make a quality TV series. This was quintessential to his success and, ostensibly, the individual show's success too.

In 1962, Newman moved from ABC to the BBC. Again Head of Drama, he was given the task of trying to fill the gap between *Grandstand* and *Juke Box Jury* on a Saturday afternoon. For the time slot, the show had to be for children. Traditionally, the spot had been filled with a classic serial, such as *Oliver Twist* or *Kidnapped*, but it was felt that it was time for something different.

Donald Wilson was appointed Head of Serial and Series and began to forge the initial ideas of what would become *Doctor Who* with Newman – but what would the show be about?

A report concerning the development of the programme was written in July 1962. It stated that 'bug-eyed monsters' were out but time travel was in. The show continued to be developed and, in March 1963, a second report proposed a 52-week serial featuring 'scientific troubleshooters', with a time machine. The characters would include a handsome young man, an attractive young woman and a 'mature man' somewhere between 30 and 40 years of age, with some kind of twist to him.

Sydney Newman wasn't totally happy with the report – he didn't like the 'scientific troubleshooters' bit. He wanted the show to be different and, for a SF show, educational. Also, he wanted to include 'a kid' who would get into trouble, perhaps somebody the young audience could identify with.

Newman developed the idea further himself, writing a three-page document about 'Dr Who' (Who is this man? Nobody knows – 'Dr Who?'). 'Dr Who' was 'a frail old man lost in space and time…' but apart from that nothing else was known about him. From here, the show really started to take shape.

The script unit was now brought in. C. E. Webber (aka 'Bunny Webber') was the first to try and make sense of this unusual programme. It is unclear if Webber wrote a script or an extended treatment based upon Newman's idea of the regular characters being shrunk to the size of a pinhead and exploring a school laboratory. What is clear is that the script/treatment was rejected and David Whitaker brought in as story editor and Australian writer Anthony Coburn as scriptwriter. Coburn wrote the first useable script, after several drafts had been tweaked by Newman. Around this time, Newman and Wilson decided to find a producer. It was Newman who suggested a young woman from his former employer, ABC Television: Verity Lambert.

Lambert was called 'out of the blue' and asked what she knew about children. The 27-year-old stated that she knew nothing about them. Undeterred, Newman asked if she would mind coming over to the BBC for an interview. She agreed. Newman and Wilson interviewed her and almost immediately she was offered the job of producer of the new programme, which she accepted.

In later years Lambert confessed that the leap from being a production assistant to producer was a huge step. She recalled her first day at the BBC as being somewhat nerve-wracking as she had to go into a meeting with other producers from the Drama department, all middle-aged men, who were amazed that a young female like her held such an senior position. She said that the initial atmosphere affected her for about six months, until she really got her feet under the table.

Lambert was assigned a director, Rex Tucker, who was experienced in making classical serials for the BBC, but his way of doing things didn't sit well with Lambert and, after several artistic disagreements, Tucker asked to be removed from the show.

Lambert was given a new director, Waris Hussein, who was about her own age and who soon came to share her vision for the show.

Lambert and Hussein started to shape the programme and cast the main roles. To begin with, Lambert cast a friend of hers, Jacqueline Hill, as schoolteacher Barbara Wright, while William Russell, a somewhat dashing young lead actor with a strong BBC pedigree, was cast as schoolteacher Ian Chesterton. The casting of teenage schoolgirl Susan Foreman was slightly trickier. Hussein watched Carole Ann Ford while casually visiting a set one day, and was struck by the way she presented herself on and off camera. He instantly asked Lambert down to the set, who agreed that Ford was exactly what they were looking for and soon offered her the part, which she duly accepted.

Ford remembers the chance meeting: 'I was doing one of *The Wednesday Plays*, when Waris Hussein, the original director of *Doctor Who*, spotted me. He was up in the control box and I was on the set – screaming. I think they chose me because they wanted a good screamer. I certainly did an awful lot of it!'

Casting the Doctor was a more difficult affair. Both Lambert and Hussein had their own ideas, which included Cyril Cusack and Leslie French, but the actors weren't interested. William Hartnell became the next choice. Hartnell was an actor concerned about being typecast. He had played an army sergeant in the movie *The Way Ahead* and the TV series *The Army Game*; he also appeared as one again in the very first *Carry On* movie, *Carry On Sergeant*. It seemed that if there was a soldier or hard-man role, he would be typecast; but the role of the Doctor presented a new challenge. He was offered the part despite Lambert and Hussein's concerns that a mature actor wouldn't want to take on a single role for 52 weeks (i.e. a whole year), but their fears proved short-lived, as Hartnell accepted the part and delighted in telling all his friends that he was to star in a children's television series.

The main elements of what was to become the longest-running SF TV series ever had now been gathered together. Newman, Wilson, Lambert, Hussein, Whitaker and Coburn were the main people who devised the show and then brought the vision to screen for Hartnell, Ford, Hill and Russell to captivate their weekly audience. The first *Doctor Who* family had been created.

It was essentially Newman who shaped the lead character of the Doctor on paper during the early reports, but David Whitaker was not a sleeping partner in this process. In fact, his original idea of introducing the Doctor at the end of a road in a swirling fog (titled 'Nothing at the End of the Lane'), while not used on screen, was later used at the beginning of the first novel spawned from the show: *Doctor Who in an Exciting Adventure with the Daleks* (Muller, 1964). Slightly different from the TV show, Whitaker wrote the first *Doctor Who* novelisation introducing the characters in the way he had originally visualised them for screen, and then he amalgamated the show's second broadcast story, which introduced the Daleks, as the main story. So the writer had strong ideas that he could see through to their natural conclusion, albeit in a slightly different medium, and combined with Terry Nation's Daleks – creatures that were not developed until the late summer of 1963 – he could create a strong, one-off novel, which would influence the likes of future *Doctor Who* writers, such as Neil Gaiman.

Newman certainly liked to have tried-and-trusted people around him. Verity Lambert was a known entity, as were David Whitaker and Anthony Coburn. And that cascaded down. Lambert found a like-minded director and cast a friend, Jacqueline Hill.

Coburn wrote the first episode, the initial draft of which was completed by the end of April 1963 before Lambert was hired from ABC. The script was 43 pages long and entitled 'Doctor Who and the Tribe of Gum', subtitled 'Episode One "An Unearthly Child"'.

Early drafts of this script have only recently surfaced and are some of the most important documents in our understanding of how *Doctor Who* was developed. One specific draft used in research for this book showed that the characters were still far from fully formed. Although the script was essentially what later became the first ever episode (not a shooting script but an early out-sourced script of Coburn's), it had some very different dialogue to that seen on screen. Firstly, the script did not mention the TARDIS by name. The Doctor's ship was indeed a police telephone box but no reference was made to its name, unlike the final version of the script. Additionally, in order to pilot 'the ship', as it was referred to, the Doctor had to sit down at the control panel and strap himself in, so some traditional 'rocket-ship' ideas had not been ruled out at the time of the draft script; but Newman was later keen to have all clichés taken out.

There is another interesting point about the draft script. Barbara Wright's character is called Miss Canning. It is made clear that the reason she wants to talk to fellow schoolteacher Ian Chesterton about the bright but strange 'Suzanne Foreman' is because she is new to the school and wants to confide in another teacher and not bother the head teacher about the pupil. In the copy of the draft script used in research for this book, the first time Miss Canning's character is mentioned her name is crossed through and the name Barbara Wright is inserted in pencil.

It was after this draft that Miss Canning was developed into Barbara Wright, and 'Suzanne' became 'Susan'. It seems that Newman wasn't 100 per cent happy with other areas of the script. There was an expensive element to it to begin with: when the two schoolteachers jump into 'the ship' it is still a police box, it was only when the door was shut that it transported them into the main control room. It was decided that this piece should be kept simple, losing an extremely eerie moment in which Suzanne's favourite music is being played in the empty police box but the schoolteachers cannot see where it is coming from. Suzanne later explains this:

Suzanne: You've read stories about space and time machines… When you shut the door and felt everything spinning around you, you were being adjusted to a new relationship of space and time.

In the draft script the Doctor says that in Earth language his name is translated as 'Doctor Who'. This is important in regard to the final six-page synopsis of the show, which was sent out to actors and writers by Whitaker when offers were made to take part in it. That document clearly stated that the companions refer to the Doctor as 'Doctor Who' because they know nothing about him, which is indeed what happens in the first ever TV episode. Also, Miss Canning is suddenly Barbara Wright. This is very important because it is clear that Carole Ann Ford didn't read the draft script (where she is 'Suzanne', not 'Susan') – that was only sent out to writers before casting, and as an aide-memoire of how to write for the show. The version received by Ford was the final version of the script with the names changed and plotlines and main character developed (in line with the six-page synopsis). This is a great shame because if she had read the earlier script she would have found out what her character's relationship to the Doctor was originally intended to be (one of the show's greatest mysteries).

The nuances of the early script of 'An Unearthly Child' have only recently been appreciated. In the original draft Suzanne explains that her parents are dead and her world is gone; all she has left is her grandfather and the ship. Little insight perhaps until the Doctor refuses to let the schoolteachers leave the ship. Suzanne tries to help them understand her situation but they are worried about her welfare and argue with the Doctor, whom they believe to be deranged.

It is here that a very sinister sequence starts, which was changed dramatically (and quite rightly so) in the final version of the script. To begin with Suzanne states, 'I'm trying to save you both,' implying that the Doctor wants to kill them. She goes on to say that '…if you both behave like… like primitives. If you insult him… he won't listen to me.' So it seems Suzanne was scared of the Doctor and, more importantly, it is clear that he considered human beings below him and, if they provoked him, he would destroy them. In fact, that's what he says: 'We must destroy them [Suzanne].'

This was far too scary for children, moving the Doctor character away from a potential hero and into the realms of a potential murderer, or abductor at least. The final script could be interpreted as a tussle at the controls that sends the two schoolteachers, the Doctor and Susan on their journey through time and space but this is not the case in the first draft, where the schoolteachers are clearly abducted. The rest of the dialogue is also lost, where Suzanne's history is explained to all: who she was, where she came from, her relationship to the Doctor, and the reason for them being in London in 1963, i.e. all the things that we – and Carole Ann Ford – wished to know and have been a mystery for the past 50 years.

The Doctor calls Suzanne 'Findooclare'. He explains that if he let the schoolteachers go now that they had seen the ship, they would tell people about it, and although many people wouldn't believe them, the enemy would.

Doctor Who: Everywhere he listens. He searches for you Findooclare… for you. His victory is not complete until he destroys you. He would listen to these primitives. The wilder their talk, the more he would listen.

Here, parallels with David Tennant's story, 'The Family of Blood', begin coming into the equation. It becomes clear that Suzanne is being hunted.

Ian Chesterton believes that they (the Doctor and Suzanne) are both mad:

Chesterton: ...I'll have a few words to say to the Head about this. A child like her left in the care of a doddering old fool like that. An old man who steals police boxes! (to Doctor Who) Where are her parents? I demand to see her mother and father.

Suzanne then explains that her parents are dead, her world is dead and all she had was what the schoolteachers saw before them: her grandfather and the ship. The Doctor elaborates: 'Findooclare would rule! Findooclare would be Queen in a world greater than any your minds could dream of. But her people are enslaved by the Palladin hordes.'

It is at this point that one of *Doctor Who*'s greatest secrets is explained away in one sentence from Suzanne: '[Findooclare] It's a name he has for me. I was a baby when the Palladins attacked our world and he saved me. We got away in this machine... It was the first our people made.'

If one were to put this into context of the present *Doctor Who* mythology, it would suggest that 'the ship' was indeed a TARDIS, which would make both the Doctor and Susan [Suzanne] Time Lords, maybe at the time of the Time Wars. What it concludes, answering one of the great unexplained questions of the show, is that the Doctor and Suzanne are *not* related and she is simply another companion, albeit an important one, and indeed one that feels so incredibly thankful and affectionate towards him, because he managed to save her while the rest of her race – also the Doctor's *own* race – perished.

So the Doctor's first ever companion is a fellow Time Lord? Yes, and an important one too. If we follow the draft of the script, Suzanne is the one who is hiding and, following 'The Family of Blood' idea, it is she who has taken human form to hide from the enemy, the enemy that needs a Time Lord and a

TARDIS. So what important Time Lord was Suzanne and why did the Doctor eventually let her slip away into obscurity (in a later story, 'The Dalek Invasion of Earth')?

The simple answer is: she may well have been the Queen – not the President – of Gallifrey, and the Doctor decided to let her stay human and find love (see 'The Dalek Invasion of Earth') to protect her; or at least to leave her safe until it was time to reclaim her throne...

Newman needed the death threats taken out and the whole section about the Doctor and Suzanne's history removed. He didn't want to set the Doctor up as a bad guy, nor did he want his past – and that of Suzanne – explained: he wanted it left unknown. Who is he? Doctor Who? And it has remained that way for 50 years. Although we know what planet the Doctor came from (Gallifrey), we still know precious little about his youth.

Tony Williamson was sent a six-page story/character breakdown, along with a copy of the draft script of 'An Unearthly Child', by Newman. He had written for *Coronation Street* and would later write for *The Avengers*, among other projects, but decided not to take part in *Doctor Who* because of other work commitments. He preserved the script until his death and ten years later his widow sold it to a private collector, whereupon it was used in the research for this book.

Once the script was rewritten (with the character names changed), it was sent out with a six-page brief of the show. And there the great mystery began: the aliens' history had been taken out. We learn that the Doctor and Susan are exiles from their own planet and they travel in a TARDIS, a name Susan claims to have created out of the phrase 'Time and Relative Dimensions in Space'. All this came later and truly justified

Newman's decisions regarding what material was cut and what was added.

So who is Doctor Who? And what relationship does Susan really have with him? That was the liquid gold that captured children's imaginations. The intrigue and legend had begun and it is fitting that only now, during the 50th anniversary of the show, we find out the original intention as to the Doctor and Susan's relationship and, as far as the modern *Doctor Who* TV series is concerned, what they now consider to be the worthy origins of the Doctor.

> 'Orders are changed. Do not capture, repeat, do not capture Thals. Exterminate. Repeat… exterminate.'
>
> *Doctor Who in an Exciting Adventure with the Daleks*
> **David Whitaker**

The Daleks are a major part of *Doctor Who*'s success. After the introductory pilot, the first story, featuring cavemen, received poor viewing figures – between two and three million people – a disaster by BBC standards. And although 4.4 million sat down to watch the first ever episode, the following three episodes, 'The Tribe of Gum', lost some of those viewers as the story progressed. Verity Lambert confessed that the drop in viewing figures was the result of a poor choice of opening story. In interview, she stated that she would never have commissioned a caveman story, but the decision was not hers to take at the time (Anthony Coburn's script had already been accepted before she became producer). When looking at the original six-page synopsis, we find that Coburn had been selected to write the second story too. Set in the 30th century, it would feature a world only inhabited by robots, and where humanity had 'died away'. The Doctor and his companions would discover that the robots had created a superior robot capable of 'original thought' – but not before they accidentally brought it 'to life'.

Thankfully this second story was not commissioned for production. Instead a work by former comedy scriptwriter Terry Nation introduced the Doctor's most fearsome enemies, the Daleks. Suddenly viewing figures soared to between eight and ten million viewers. Children in playgrounds the length and breadth of Britain started shouting the word 'EXTERMINATE!' and Dalekmania gripped the nation for the first time.

Newman was outraged. The show had very quickly fallen into the 'bug-eyed monster' category that he was so keen to avoid back in his original notes. Lambert denied the accusation, saying the Daleks were humans who lived inside protected casings in the future. It was a good effort but Newman wasn't happy.

Hindsight is of course a wonderful thing and, to his credit, Newman eventually admitted that the Daleks were what made such an enormous success of the programme – and they've continued to wreak havoc ever since.

Terry Nation, not unlike Russell T. Davies, was an influential Welshman, who almost missed out on the chance to write for *Doctor Who* in the first place. When Whitaker approached Nation through his agent, the writer was in Nottingham writing a stage show for comedian Tony Hancock. Hancock apparently joked, 'How dare the BBC approach a writer of your calibre to write for children's television?'

That should have been the end of it, but that night Nation and Hancock had a huge row and the writer found himself on a train back to London the following day with no job. Remembering the offer made through his agent, he called her and asked if she had turned the job down yet. She said that she hadn't had a chance to do so – so he changed his mind. He wrote a treatment for Whitaker, who loved it, and history was made.

Although, in actual fact, it wasn't. Donald Wilson didn't like the original script and asked if they (Lambert and her team) had anything else ready to make instead. They hadn't. In later years Lambert confessed that she had been made to feel so bad about the first Dalek story, that if they'd had anything else ready, they would have definitely made that instead. The Daleks would never have existed.

Although Terry Nation came up with the idea of the Daleks and wrote clear instructions as to what they would look like, it was Raymond Cusick who would design the first Dalek. However, his idea was too expensive to make, so he sat down with two other designers, Jack Kine and Bernard Wilkie, and between them they created the armoured pepper-pot much loved by *Doctor Who* audiences for the next 50 years.

Lambert said that when the first Daleks hit the studio floor, there was something magical about them. Everybody wanted to get inside one – including the producer herself – and she truly felt that they were onto something.

Surely though, the success of *Doctor Who* wasn't just down to the production team and writers? What about the star himself – Doctor Who?

William Hartnell relished the part of the Doctor and made Newman's 'crotchety old man' a mystical and compelling being that even Colin Baker, decades later, would use as a blueprint for aspects of his own interpretation of the Doctor. It must be stressed that, unlike other Doctors, William Hartnell was given a character to play; he wasn't allowed to shape it to his own specifications. Although Hartnell would make the role his own, the Doctor was very much part of Sydney Newman's vision.

Along with Verity Lambert and the original *Doctor Who* family, Newman had another major success on his hands. Yet again, he had created a quality team of individuals. The blend of young and old; the experienced and the young and innovative, was magical. It has never been forgotten and the decisions made in 1963 by the original *Doctor Who* family are still at the core of the programme's success today. In fact, when David Tennant made his final farewell as the Doctor on 1 January 2010, the Doctor is seen attending a book signing of a female descendant of a woman the Doctor nearly married when he was made human (like Suzanne?). The jacket of the book shows that her name is 'Verity Newman'.

Doctor Who was a joint effort from many different talented people, not just the programme makers, but one cannot underestimate the influence of the great William Hartnell.

Hartnell was the first ever star of the show, the man who would convince the viewing public to suspend disbelief for a while and travel through the universe with him in his time machine. That gentle mocking smile, that knowing twinkle in the eye, belonged entirely to Hartnell, and many of the first fans of the show will maintain, to this day, that he was the very best Doctor Who. Indeed, he was the most mysterious. But how did *Doctor Who* change Hartnell's life, both personally and professionally?

An interesting question, and one that requires a detailed answer.

'I leapt at the old man and we fell heavily to the ground. I could hear him snarling at me to let him go and not meddle in his affairs, but the words didn't make too much impression on me because all I could think about was that whatever it might look like from the outside, I knew perfectly well that this was no ordinary police box on Barnes Common.'

Doctor Who in an Exciting Adventure with the Daleks
David Whitaker

CHAPTER TWO
WILLIAM HARTNELL

'Space travel? Quite honestly, it scares me to death. I haven't the slightest wish to get in a rocket and zoom through the stratosphere. Somebody else can be the first man on the moon. It doesn't interest me at all. I do, however, believe that there is life on other planets – and that they know we're here but haven't got the technology to get through.'

William Hartnell

WILLIAM HENRY HARTNELL was born on 8 January 1908 at 24 Regent Square, South Pancras, London. His mother, Lucy Hartnell, was a commercial clerk. To his dying day, Hartnell never knew who his father was, or from where he had originated. His mother came from Taunton and Hartnell maintained a love of the West Country throughout his life. This may explain why he lied about his birthplace on *Desert Island Discs* in 1965, claiming he came from Seaton in Devon.

Hartnell's formative years were in a tough, working-class environment. His illegitimacy would have caused him some embarrassment and, as a young boy, he would get into scrapes.

If we are to believe a journal he left behind after his death (written in the early 1920s and mentioned in his grand-daughter's biography, *Who's There?* (Jessica Carney, Virgin, 1996)), he was fostered by a family called Harris while his mother took up employment as a nanny in Belgium. *Who's There?: The Life and Career of William Hartnell*, states that Hartnell would again live with his mother in Holborn some time later, but he continued to be a wild-card into his teens, until of course he had to choose a profession.

At the age of 16 (1925), Hartnell went into theatre, but not as an actor. He joined Sir Frank Benson's Shakespearean Company as an assistant stage manager, property manager, assistant lighting director and general dogsbody. It was a two-year apprenticeship in theatre and classical acting skills, with the occasional opportunity of a walk-on part. As Hartnell explained, it was tough work: 'It was good training, not only in Shakespeare, but in keeping fit. Sir Frank Benson believed in keeping actors in good health and we were organised into hockey teams and cricket sides.' Benson was in his late sixties by then, so there was little chance of him exerting himself too much.

Hartnell's early performances were minor parts in Shakespearean plays; but he also performed in *School for Scandal* and *She Stoops to Conquer* before taking a part in *Miss Elizabeth's Prisoner* in 1928, where he met Heather McIntyre, whom he married the following year.

By the age of 18, Hartnell was touring the country as an actor, the bug to perform finally consuming him. He no longer wanted to hide away; he wanted to be out there on stage, in front of an audience, and to pursue his love of comedy. For six years, he would tour in comedy and song and dance shows, understudying respected actors like Bud Flanagan (from the infamous Crazy Gang). From this, he progressed to understudying in London's

West End; but would take the main role when the production left London and toured the provincial cities.

Slowly, Hartnell built his skills and became quite well known in the acting world as a player of farce. This progressed to short comedy films in the 1930s, such as *I'm an Explosive* (1933). Although only a 50-minute feature, this was one of Hartnell's favourite roles. He plays Edward Whimperley, a man who drinks an explosive liquid and causes chaos as a consequence. The film was directed by Adrian Brunel and, despite being low budget and short in length, became very popular with audiences on its release. The pay-off is that Whimperley finds he hasn't drunk explosive liquid but not before suing the government for a lot of money. He then decides to marry his sweetheart with the proceeds and lives happily ever after. Contrived, but funny and endearing, Hartnell scored high with his first leading role.

Comedy was a love of Hartnell's as he later confessed, 'My real guiding light was Charlie Chaplin. He influenced me more than any other factor in taking up acting as a career.' A lot of actors adopt an initial love of comedy before settling down to another genre – for example, horror icon (and one time Doctor Who) Peter Cushing had an early role opposite Stan Laurel and Oliver Hardy in their movie *A Chump at Oxford* (1940) before he moved into more mainstream roles and eventually a string of highly popular Hammer Horror movies. Hartnell played in over 20 films before the outbreak of the Second World War, not all of them comedy, but many quite short character roles with his respective parts fairly minor.

Hartnell's career was hindered by the war. He was drafted into the Tank Corps but very quickly had a nervous breakdown and was invalided out after 15 months. 'The strain was too much,' he said. 'I spent 12 weeks in an army hospital and came out with a terrible stutter. The colonel said, "Better get back to the theatre. You're no bloody good here!"

'I had to start all over again. I was still only a spit and cough in the profession and now I had a stutter which scared the life out of me.'

Hartnell worked hard to overcome his illness, which he did with gusto. In 1942, he had an uncredited role as a German soldier in the Will Hay classic, *The Goose Steps Out*. Although his part in the film was very minor, Hartnell was working with a major comedy star of his day, which gave him considerable exposure. In fact, his cold image in the film, set against Hay's chaos, is noteworthy and a taste of what was to come. As Hartnell's roles grew larger, they also grew colder, and *The Goose Steps Out* really shows the beginning of this transition from comedian to hard man, something he would grow to loathe.

His first real praiseworthy role was in a movie called *Sabotage at Sea* (1942), where he played a villain under heavy make-up and moustache. This was a crucial role in his growth as an actor. Hartnell learned that you didn't need much make-up to be a sinister character. A normal-looking man with an expressive face could appear just as cruel; something he demonstrated to enormous credit in *Brighton Rock*, five years later.

In 1943, Hartnell was approached by film producer Sir Carol Reed to play an army sergeant (Ned Fletcher) in the film *The Way Ahead*, alongside David Niven and a young John Laurie (later Frazer in *Dad's Army*). Hartnell's role was extremely tough and gritty. The film depicts a group of conscripts and how they deal with military life. It opens in 1939 with Chelsea Pensioners stating that if war was declared Britain would be in trouble because 'young men can't fight'. As the film was made in 1943, one could label *The Way Ahead* as a propaganda movie, with just enough flag-flying to show young conscripted men that they were doing the right thing in going to war; but Eric Ambler and Peter Ustinov's script is better than that, with a down-and-dirty edge that far from glorifies war. Hartnell's gung-ho sergeant, counterbalanced by David Niven's over-privileged commanding officer, enhances the film further, with subtle interaction showing the divide between classes.

The Way Ahead is a film that explains much about its time and is one of the highlights of Hartnell's career. His character is a stern, no-nonsense regular soldier, not a conscript, who has to whip the new boys into shape, anticipating facets of roles to come (including *The Army Game* and *Carry On Sergeant*). Hartnell really made an impression in the film, with his hard, piercing stare and cast-iron personality.

His first scene is in itself a show of strength: heckled by a man at a railway station, he holds back, says nothing, but looks dangerous. As it turns out, the man becomes one of the sergeant's conscripts; but Hartnell's character never mentions it or shows any extra animosity towards him, which displays an impressive depth of character (and in complete contrast to a similar situation Clint Eastwood finds himself in during the movie *Heartbreak Ridge*).

The Way Ahead is an accurate account of how the different walks of life came together in the barrack room during the Second World War; and how they were brought together as a credible unit by their screaming sergeant, something Hartnell does an awful lot of in the film. It showcases Hartnell in his prime: a robust young actor with a resonant voice and much stage presence. He works perfectly with David Niven, especially when Niven questions his discipline of the men, but perhaps that discipline was based on his own experiences 18 months previously during his army service. This strongly suggests that Hartnell was a better actor than a soldier but, in a way, perhaps the tough army roles allowed him to cope with his wartime experiences; for research purposes, he visited a real-life army sergeant to model his role in the film – surely an uncomfortable experience.

The Way Ahead was a big success and Hartnell became a popular actor, albeit now typecast as a tough straight man.

In 1947 he appeared in the movie *Escape*, starring Rex Harrison and Peggy Cummins. Hartnell took the main supporting role as hard-nosed police inspector Harris. Cyril Cusack (a man considered by Verity Lambert for the role of Doctor Who) took a part, along with future Doctor Who Patrick Troughton, who had his first-ever movie appearance in a small role as a shepherd called Jim.

Escape isn't one of Harrison's finest roles – or more importantly, William Hartnell's – and is only noteworthy today because of the inclusion of the first two Doctor Whos and a man offered the part of the Doctor before Hartnell.

It is probably fair to say that it was Hartnell's unforgettable portrayal of super-cool gangster Dallow against Richard Attenborough's Pinkie in *Brighton Rock* (1947) that truly typecast him. A powerful role in a popular film does tend to do this, and throughout the 1950s Hartnell resigned himself to playing the hard man or army sergeant, even though he wasn't a tall or strongly built man.

Dallow was a dangerous character. His stern face, slightly gruff voice and probing eyes made a menacing presence on screen alongside Attenborough's psychotic character, Pinkie. Both actors turn in commanding performances, but one does get the impression that Hartnell's character is the boss. His sharp suits and cool exterior, set against the cavalier antics of Pinkie, certainly suggest authority.

Brighton Rock is a strange film, based on Graham Greene's

iconic novel of post-war gang fights in Brighton. Centring on the fact that a wife cannot be made to give evidence against her husband in court, it is typical of the quirky one-off movies Britain is famous for and has delivered successfully over the past 70 years.

Despite success in the movies, Hartnell's love of the theatre continued. In 1950 he starred in *Seagulls over Sorrento*, with John Gregson, Nigel Stock, Bernard Lee and Ronald Shiner. Hartnell was Petty Officer Herbert in this nautical farce. The play tells the story of a group of volunteers in a disused wartime naval fortress, where secret peacetime radar experiments are going on. Although a comedy, yet again Hartnell played the straight, no-nonsense military officer, and audiences began to know what to expect from him when he came on stage. *Theatre World* said of the production, '…although the play has many serious moments (for all the men have their own reasons for volunteering), it is undoubtedly for its rich comedy that it has achieved such outstanding success.'

An interesting fact about *Seagulls over Sorrento* is that Hartnell started halfway down the bill, but after a while – and a few changes in personality – he found himself top of the bill. It was a role he stayed with and enjoyed for a quality run, and one that earned him the praise of actor and one time Doctor Who Peter Cushing, who wrote to him and eventually played in the production sometime after Hartnell.

Hartnell longed to do more comedic roles, but the type-casting had taken over completely. In 1951, he took a role as a recruitment sergeant in *The Magic Box*, a movie made to celebrate The Festival of Britain, which showcased many great British character actors. The film was a biopic of the life of dreamer and pioneering inventor William Friese-Greene and included talent such as Joyce Grenfell, Margaret Rutherford,

Joan Hickson, Thora Hird, Sid James, Richard Attenborough and even Laurence Olivier in a cameo role as a policeman.

One little-known fact about *The Magic Box* is that one of London's most notorious gangsters, Ronnie Kray, made a blink-and-you-miss-it appearance as an extra. Along with a group of East End kids, Kray was selected as an extra, and is clearly seen for a split second. Albeit in his teens at the time, it was something the fame-seeking killer would dine out on throughout his life. He even managed to obtain a still of himself, in profile, from the film, which he placed in one of his autobiographies.

In 1953 the paths of two future Doctor Whos would cross again – in a more obvious way – in the movie *Will Any Gentlemen...?* Starring a bewildered George Cole and an impossibly young Joan Sims, the story centres around a mild-mannered bank clerk who becomes wayward after being hypnotised. Fast-talking Jon Pertwee tries to help out but only adds farce to the already chaotic situation. Then along comes Hartnell as the smart detective, the straight man to Pertwee's clown, in a film that is both endearing and satisfying for any fan of the Doctor Whos, or for that matter, classic British comedy.

In a way, the hints of slapstick and farce are the rough edges that would be refined in great British comedies from that time onwards. The classics were just around the corner, such as *Two Way Stretch*, *School for Scoundrels* and *The Ladykillers*. Even George Cole would carve himself a piece of British comedy legend as Flash Harry in the *St Trinian's* movies. Clearly there were great comedy films before then, such as those featuring Will Hay and his sidekicks, but they were few and far between until the 1950s.

Hartnell did return to more mainstream comedy, albeit as an army sergeant yet again, in the TV comedy series *The Army*

Game (1957–58, 1960–61) and the first *Carry On* film, *Carry On Sergeant* (1958); itself a pastiche of *The Army Game* (and with parallels to *The Way Ahead*). He was really creating for himself the niche role of over-serious officer with a bunch of dead-enders to sort out; and the laughs in *Carry On Sergeant* would once more be generated not by him but by the dead-enders. However, the film's pathos emanates from Hartnell's character. Late in their training, the platoon realise that their lenient sergeant is leaving the Army with them, his trainees, bottom of the heap. Realising that he's not a bad man, or as tough on them as he could be, they change their ways and make him the winning platoon sergeant for the first and last time in his career. The end scene is one of recognition and fulfilment, which made the very first *Carry On* a great 'feel-good' movie and the sound basis for future *Carry Ons* to build upon, with outstanding performances from Kenneth Connor, Hattie Jacques, Kenneth Williams and Charles Hawtrey, who would all become familiar *Carry On* regulars.

Meanwhile, the tough roles continued for Hartnell. In 1957, he appeared as Cartley, the bespectacled, hard-nosed manager of Hawlett Trucking in *Hell Drivers*, another great British movie and one that highlighted excellent young talent, such as future James Bond Sean Connery, Stanley Baker, Gordon Jackson, David McCallum, Herbert Lom, Sid James and Patrick McGoohan in one of his finest roles.

An interesting aside here is the fact that Sean Connery's career was given a boost by Jacqueline Hill; she married director Alvin Rakoff, but not before recommending Connery for the starring role in the TV drama *Requiem for a Heavyweight*. Hill felt that Connery's rugged good looks would make the programme popular with female viewers. It was to be Connery's first starring role, and the production would also feature Warren Mitchell and Michael Caine (the latter in a smaller cameo role). From there Connery's career took off.

Hell Drivers opens with Stanley Baker's character – Tom – approaching Cartley for a job. Cartley is quick to lay down the law, which Tom, with no other option open to him as an ex-con, accepts without question.

The Hell Drivers are the fastest road-haulage carriers around, and the faster they go, the more money they make. There is much fighting and competition between them, causing high tensions, but no one of importance cares. These men are outcasts with nothing to lose; they are ostracised by the locals and even by their own families, but for some of them, there is a crumb of pride – there is friendship. When Tom learns of a shady deal between Cartley and his reckless foreman (McGoohan), the plot quickens in pace towards a fatal accident, which leaves Tom crying out for revenge against the money men who have exploited him and his friends.

Hell Drivers is a passionate film, with quality input from McGoohan and McCallum – with their seldom-heard Scottish accents – but Connery, Baker, James and Lom are all excellent too, as are the female leads: Peggy Cummins, Jill Ireland and Marjorie Rhodes.

Although Hartnell appears only at the beginning and the end of the film, his hard-man presence as the company boss is felt throughout, making *Hell Drivers* a milestone in his career, as well as a classic, gritty and tough British movie. Something of a forgotten gem nowadays, it's certainly a film that a typical teenage boy would find of interest, with macho themes throughout it.

Amidst the hard stuff, Hartnell did have a couple of comedy roles though. In 1959, he played alongside Peter Sellers in *The Mouse That Roared*, and he worked with Sellers again in the

Boulting Brothers' comedy *Heavens Above!* (1963), albeit as Major Fowler (back to typecasting?).

In 1963, Hartnell broke the typecasting mould and gave one of his very best screen performances as talent scout 'Dad' Johnson in *This Sporting Life*. The movie starred Richard Harris and Rachel Roberts, both of whom were nominated for Oscars (Roberts eventually picking up a BAFTA).

The screenplay was written by David Storey, based on his own novel and, from the moment the eerie Jerry Goldsmith-type opening music starts (composed by Roberto Gerhard), it is clear that this film is very different.

Roberts's character is a bitter woman who is indifferent to miner Frank Machin and his hard ways. Machin is a talented rugby player, who the kind, gentle and modest 'Dad' takes under his wing to get into big-time rugby. He succeeds and, once he accomplishes this, quietly moves on.

This Sporting Life had some great cameo roles in it, such as those of Arthur Lowe and Leonard Rossiter (Slomer and Phillips, respectively), which enhances the enjoyment by lightening the often depressing storyline. In that respect the film is very much of its day, depicting the tough working classes and their day-to-day plight. It echoes Alan Sillitoe's *Saturday Night and Sunday Morning* and the BBC's *Cathy Come Home* in its unrelenting kitchen-sink realism.

This Sporting Life was instrumental in Hartnell becoming Doctor Who. The show's producer, Verity Lambert, went to see the movie (released in January 1963) and was struck by Hartnell's interpretation of the part. His gentleness and life experience is a perfect counterbalance to Richard Harris's unthinking bullishness, something that greatly impressed Lambert.

Lambert approached Hartnell's agent to see if he would be interested in taking on the role of Doctor Who. She must have displayed much charm in persuading the agent to ask his client – it wasn't his type of work at all. He had started out doing Shakespeare and adult comedy, and then became the tough-guy actor. But perhaps this was why Lambert's offer was so appealing – it was something completely different, something wonderful, like the role of 'Dad' Johnson. The agent made the call and said, 'I wouldn't normally have suggested it to you, Bill, to work in children's television, but it sounds the sort of character part you have been longing to play.' The agent went on to explain that the part was 'of an eccentric old grandfather-cum-professor type who travels in space and time'.

Hartnell wasn't too sure about the part, but did agree to meet Lambert to find out more. He said of the meeting: 'The moment this brilliant young producer, Miss Verity Lambert, started telling me about *Doctor Who* I was hooked.'

Perhaps it wasn't so clear-cut as that, though. Hartnell did go away and consider the offer and perhaps it was the diversity – the break from typecasting – that persuaded him to take it on, as Lambert recalled, '[he] was interested but wary' when first offered the role. However, he soon made a decision and called her to accept.

Hartnell would find the work gruelling. Now in his mid-fifties, he was suddenly working 48 weeks a year, learning a variety of scripts and performing an action role. He admitted that it was 'very hard work' but despite the strain, he 'loved every minute of it'.

The show became a smash hit and Hartnell obviously liked the idea of working for a young audience, as he said, 'To me kids are the greatest audience – and the greatest critics – in the world. You know, I couldn't go out into the high street without a bunch of kids following me. I felt like the Pied Piper.'

This was an impression echoed by his wife Heather, who

used to pick him up from the railway station after a day's filming. She was to recall how he would get off the train and walk down the road with a stream of children behind him – not unlike the Pied Piper.

Hartnell fitted Sydney Newman's perception of the Doctor beautifully. He was the crotchety old man and this behaviour was most prevalent in the opening scene of the fourth *Doctor Who* story, 'Marco Polo'. His rudeness to his fellow companions is almost embarrassing in its childishness and selfishness, but somehow they still respect him.

'Marco Polo' was the first historical adventure story in *Doctor Who*, perfectly showcasing Newman's original intentions for the show. It was informative and engaging, with narration from the Marco Polo character himself (played by Mark Eden, who had appeared in *Heavens Above!* with Hartnell in 1963), promising further adventure and intrigue as the story progressed. It was 'Marco Polo' more than 'The Reign of Terror' (the last story in *Doctor Who*'s first season) that paved the way for the great historical *Doctor Who* stories and showed the quality of the children's entertainment that Hartnell was getting himself into.

William Hartnell played Doctor Who for three years and became quite wealthy on the back of it, earning the equivalent of about £4,000 per episode in present-day money, which was a very good regular salary at the time. Out of the seven stories in his first season, only three have SF connotations: 'The Daleks' (featuring the debut appearance of the Daleks), 'The Keys of Marinus' (featuring the Voord) and 'The Sensorities' (featuring creatures by the same name). The other stories were mainly historical, featuring cavemen (well, historical in idea), Marco Polo, Aztecs and the French Revolution. So there was a strong balance between the educational stories and the more fantastical ones (but even the fantasy had its moral implications).

Hartnell said he quit *Doctor Who* because he didn't see eye-to-eye with the BBC over the use of 'evil' in the show. In a letter to a fan – Ian McLachlan – of 1968, he wrote: 'It was noted and spelled out to me as a children's programme, and I wanted it to stay as such; but I'm afraid, the BBC had other ideas. So did I, so I left.'

In her preface to Jessica Carney's biography of William Hartnell, Verity Lambert said that *Doctor Who* 'emanated from the Drama Department and not, as was the norm, the Children's Department'. This may be the reason why the show started to develop more 'adult' themes and ideas. As the old production staff, including Lambert, moved on, more drama-based staff would take over in order to beef up the darker side of the show. This became more prevalent during Patrick Troughton's time as the Doctor – so clearly the series was naturally progressing through the department it had originally come from (Drama, not the Children's department). This genesis could explain why the show has continued to attract a broad fan-base of people of all ages, not just children. But Hartnell's reasons for leaving do make sense, as some of his later *Doctor Who* stories suggest. Sadly these later stories no longer exist in the BBC archive, so it is difficult to appreciate the visual violence and increasingly adult situations. Looking at the titles, we can infer that a harder edge was being introduced: 'The Massacre', 'The Savages' and 'The Smugglers' leave little to the imagination. Even though these stories fitted Newman's original historical remit, it was clear that the whole direction of *Doctor Who* was pointing towards a darker realism. Perhaps the turning point was the epic story 'The Dalek Master Plan', where two companions are killed off: Katarina, who was introduced in the previous story, 'The Myth Makers', and Sara Kingdon (introduced and killed off during 'The Dalek Master Plan' itself). It was during this story that the first-ever Christmas special, 'The Feast of Steven', was broadcast. Sadly this too no longer resides in the BBC archive. A confusing audio still exists, but unfortunately it doesn't appear to have much of a storyline and is difficult to analyse as a consequence.

Some older fans consider the one-off episode that acted as a prequel to 'The Dalek Master Plan' to be one of the scariest stories ever. Entitled 'Mission to the Unknown', it features grotesque plants and scary monsters and no reassuring Doctor and companions. All of this information vindicates Hartnell's belief that the show was evolving away from the children's programme he'd originally signed up to.

Many critics believe that Hartnell was pushed out of the show because he cost too much money (other regular actors were getting a quarter of what he was earning per episode), but the original six-page treatment clearly stated as a first paragraph that *Doctor Who* was 'an exciting adventure – Science Fiction Drama serial for Children's Saturday viewing'. Again, this vindicates Hartnell's reasons for leaving: the job-spec had changed and he didn't like it.

Hartnell loved children and saw *Doctor Who* as their show. This is reinforced by the fact that in 1964 he came up with an idea of a series called *The Son of Doctor Who*, in which a wicked son would wreak havoc across the universe and the Doctor would have to step in to sort things out. The BBC was not keen on the idea but sometime afterwards Hartnell said, 'I still think it would have worked and been exciting for children.'

One could argue that Hartnell's *The Son of Doctor Who* idea anticipated the new series' story, 'The Doctor's Daughter', in which the audience is given the distinct impression that a spin-off series was highly likely and, above all, had the potential to be successful. In 'The Doctor's Daughter', Georgia Moffett (the real-life daughter of the Fifth Doctor, Peter Davison) would take on the part and play it exceptionally well. Does this vindicate Hartnell's idea? Conversely, does Mary Whitehouse's outrage at the violence in the show, from Patrick Troughton's Doctor onwards, back up his perceptions about the direction of the show? Perhaps not – Mary Whitehouse's intervention caused a lot of unnecessary changes to *Doctor Who*, as well as many headaches for directors and writers such as Barry Letts and Terence Dicks (during Jon Pertwee's tenure as the Doctor).

During his reign as Doctor Who, Hartnell preserved the dignity of his 'grandfather' character. In truth, and with hindsight, his ailing health meant that he couldn't have stayed much longer in the role, even if he had wanted to. A shame really, as four years later the show would be made in colour and Hartnell always commented on the wonderful sets and costumes, some of which can be glimpsed in all their splendour in rare colour photographs of the early years in the BBC archive, especially for 'Marco Polo'. That said, a story like 'Spearhead from Space' (the first Jon Pertwee – and colour – story), in which walking shop-window dummies killed innocent civilians and subsequently attracted the wrath of real-life parents, would have been the final heartbreak for William Hartnell; the fulfilment of his nightmare: the death of *Doctor Who* as a children's programme. Although Pertwee's first season would appeal largely to a more teenage audience, it was quintessential in re-inventing the programme for young and old alike.

When one appreciates how poor and unhappy Hartnell's formative years were, one can understand why he was a little over-sentimental towards children as the Doctor, not unlike the sensitivities Charles Dickens would show his young characters in his novels (he himself had a bad time as a child while working in a blacking factory, and his heart and soul was always with the younger generation). In that sense *Doctor Who* was the show Hartnell had been searching for throughout his whole career. Not hard man roles, not comedy roles; but something else, something different – for children. And *Doctor Who* was exactly that.

William Hartnell left *Doctor Who* at exactly the right time, unaware of the legacy he would create by doing so. The show was still popular, for he had quit while he was ahead. The BBC wanted it to continue, so another actor had to take over; the idea of regeneration took shape and gave the show its own excuse for reinvention. It is widely accepted that Kit Pedler and Gerry Davis came up with the idea of regeneration; indeed, they were writers of the very last William Hartnell *Doctor Who* story, 'The Tenth Planet', also the first ever Cybermen adventure.

Heather Hartnell has said that her husband was happy that Patrick (Pat) Troughton took over the role of the Doctor. Hartnell was familiar with his work, so he believed the future of the show was in good hands.

Hartnell would make one further appearance as the Doctor, for the tenth anniversary story, 'The Three Doctors', playing alongside his successors, Patrick Troughton and Jon Pertwee. He was a very unwell man at that time and had to read the lines for his cameo role from dummy boards, but he did it and enjoyed the experience too, spending some time with Troughton and Pertwee for publicity photographs, although he looked terribly frail.

Within two years of the photo call, Hartnell would be dead from arteriosclerosis. He died on 23 April 1975, aged 67. Until her death in 1984, Heather Hartnell wrote to fans all over the world and attended several *Doctor Who* events, such was the impact and legacy of the first ever Doctor Who.

Today William Hartnell's place in TV history is secured. He was the man who made *Doctor Who* popular – magical – with children all over the world. He was also the star of the very first *Carry On* movie, and appeared in some other truly great British films: *The Way Ahead*, *Brighton Rock*, *Hells Drivers* and *This Sporting Life*. More than that, he was very much a part of the genesis of the British comedy movie, with *I'm An Explosive*, *Will Any Gentlemen*, *The Mouse That Roared*, *Heavens Above!* and, of course, *Carry on Sergeant*.

Perhaps one of the best epitaphs Hartnell could have had, albeit inadvertently, was in a two-page feature in the 1965 *Doctor Who* annual. Entitled 'Who is Dr Who?', the piece talks fondly of Hartnell's time traveller: 'He is mostly very gentle and kind-hearted and he has the utmost respect for life of any kind and his heart is big enough to respect every one of the countless forms life has taken in all the ages and all the worlds.'

Hartnell believed wholeheartedly in *Doctor Who*, so much so, in fact, he lived the part more than any other he had ever played, as he told Jack Bell of the *Daily Mirror* on 23 April 1966: '*Doctor Who* has given me a certain neurosis – and it is not easy for my wife to cope with. I get a little agitated, and it makes me a little irritable with people. In fact, *Doctor Who* seems to be taking over.'

Was this the reason why he left the show, the character taking him over? No, but the irritability was the first sign of his growing illness, something not totally appreciated when he was in the role. He found it difficult to remember his lines; he lost his temper with cast members very quickly, especially new ones. All the original cast and crew had left to pursue other projects and, coupled with his failing health, he began to feel at odds with the show he so deeply loved.

Why did he love it so much? Let us consider that in many of his post-war roles he had played an army officer and, with such a traumatic exit from the war himself (and his love being comedy, not tough-guy roles), a general dissatisfaction is clearly evident regarding the path his career took.

Another reason for his love of *Doctor Who* is encapsulated in a quote from the *Doctor Who Tenth Anniversary Radio Times Special*, where he recalls his lasting memory of the show. He had been asked to open a fête, so he dressed in his *Doctor Who* clothes and turned up in an old car owned by a friend. 'I'll never forget the moment we arrived. The children just converged on the car, cheering and shouting, their faces all lit up. I knew then just how much *Doctor Who* really meant to them.'

Further evidence of the reality of the show for children comes from Hartnell's last *Doctor Who* companion, Anneke Wills, who said: 'My own children got wound-up in it. One day, while I was away rehearsing, they saw an episode in which I got carried off by monsters. They were very worried about whether I was going to come home that night. They didn't realise that the episode they had been watching had in fact been recorded the week before, and they half-believed their poor mum had been gobbled up by the wicked monsters!'

So Hartnell had made a credible character and starred in a show that had a strong young audience, but was there life after *Doctor Who*? If he was a TV icon and had an impressive film career behind him, was he allowed to move on after he left the show?

'No' would be the general answer.

Hartnell was already booked to appear in pantomime that first Christmas after leaving *Doctor Who*. Handbills for *Puss in*

Boots (Odeon Theatre, Cheltenham) highlighted the fact that 'Television's original Dr Who' would be a major star (when in actual fact he was Buskin the Cobbler, looking like Doctor Who). If that wasn't enough, other promotional lines for the pantomime read: 'Meet the monsters from Outer Space... Super Win-a-Dalek Competition'. Clearly Hartnell wouldn't be allowed to forget his greatest role so quickly.

Although the pantomime played to large audiences, it had its fair share of criticism, which stemmed largely from technical problems. Acoustics were a nightmare, with the orchestra too loud and actors, including Hartnell, too quiet when reciting their lines.

Regardless, Hartnell continued to act and, in February 1967, he recorded an episode of *No Hiding Place* entitled 'The Game'. Suddenly he was back in a military role, this time an ex-Indian army sergeant turned rent collector. One reviewer was quick to spot the former Doctor Who, saying that he wished one of the cast would turn into a Dalek, and observed, 'He [Hartnell] is Doctor Who' (James Hastie, *Scottish Daily Express*).

Critics were harsh on Hartnell. He wasn't allowed to truly move on; actors who have since played the Doctor might possibly be wary of typecasting simply because of the way Hartnell was treated after leaving the show. Patrick Troughton was particularly aware of this.

William Hartnell tried to carry on, taking a guest spot in the popular BBC drama *Softly, Softly*, in January 1968. It was here that he seemed to emerge from a low point. Due to the lack of work, harsh criticism and health problems, he had been drinking a great deal, but suddenly he perked up and delivered a great performance.

On 25 April 1968, Hartnell discussed doing a Robert Bolt

play at the Bristol Old Vic. It was called *Brother & Sister* and would co-star Sonia Dresdel, but it appeared that he had problems grasping the nuances of the part. The play ran for four weeks but didn't go on tour thereafter, for unclear reasons. Just a few more TV spots came his way after that, finishing with his return – in colour – in the anniversary *Doctor Who* story, 'The Three Doctors'.

So it appears that *Doctor Who* overshadowed Hartnell's career after he ceased to play the role, but it was his escalating health problems that were the main reason for this, not typecasting or a lack of acting skills. His consequent depression led to more drinking bouts and after brave efforts to restore his health and seriously begin acting again, he fell short of expectations. In hindsight, perhaps he should have retired after *Doctor Who*, but he loved his work and didn't want to give in to illness.

In retrospect, Hartnell had done enough to secure his memory in the hearts of the nation. He was Doctor Who. When he played the part, no one knew who the character was or where he came from; he was exciting and intriguing. Indeed, it was never explained in the original show if Susan Foreman was his granddaughter or not, as Carole Ann Ford explained, 'It was never really explained how she [Susan] came to be with him, but it was sort of accepted that they'd escaped together from another planet.' Was she a fellow alien, or an Earth child – perhaps an orphan? Although Anthony Coburn's draft script of 'An Unearthly Child' explains, it takes nothing away from the intrigue that surrounded the show in its formative years. People didn't know, and that was interesting.

During the Hartnell years, there was a real sense of wonder and eccentricity about the character of the Doctor and his origins. Even the theme music was strange, and its eeriness, coupled with the grainy black and white of the show, helped achieve greater thrills for the expectant audience.

One last thought and, perhaps, final compliment to William Hartnell: when Richard Hurndall took on the role of the first Doctor in 'The Five Doctors' to celebrate the show's 20th anniversary, his incarnation was given much respect by his successors. It was even the Hartnell character who solved the cryptic question set by the great Rassilon himself at the end of the story, which earned nothing less than an admiring shake of the head from the third Doctor. He was *the original* as Hurndall declared, and a great respect for the first Doctor has endured over the past 50 years.

It is clear that William Hartnell left the programme when he knew he couldn't quite meet the demands of a gruelling production schedule any more. He bowed out of show business slowly – painfully – over an approximate three-year period after that, with his only memorable performance being his return to the show seven years later for his very last acting role. He died on St George's Day 1975.

Hartnell was the Doctor of mystery, an eccentric old man and the original interstellar Pied Piper – something his successor Patrick Troughton would build upon.

'All the little boys and girls,
With rosy cheeks and flaxen curls,
And sparkling eyes and teeth like pearls,
Tripping and skipping, ran merrily after,
The wonderful music with shouting and laughter.'

The Pied Piper of Hamelin
Robert Browning

CHAPTER THREE

PATRICK TROUGHTON

'I thought it would be very interesting to have a character who never quite says what he means, who, really, uses the intelligence of the other people he is with. He knows the answer all the time; if he suggests something he knows the outcome. He is watching, he's really directing, but he doesn't want to show he's directing like the old Doctor.'

Gerry Davis, *Doctor Who* story editor, regarding the character of the Second Doctor

PATRICK GEORGE TROUGHTON was born in Mill Hill, London, on 25 March 1920 and educated at Bexhill-on-Sea Preparatory School and Mill Hill Public School. At the age of 16, he went to the Embassy School of Acting at Swiss Cottage, London, which was run by Eileen Thorndike, sister of Dame Sybil Thorndike. He earned a scholarship there and progressed to the Leighton Rollins Studio for Actors at the John Drew Memorial Theatre on Long Island, New York. Troughton was in America when the Second World War broke out. He returned to England on a Belgian ship, but it hit an enemy mine and sank just off

Portland Bill, within sight of England. Troughton escaped by lifeboat and always considered himself lucky to have done so.

On his return to England in 1939 he joined the Tonbridge Repertory Company and acted there for a year. In June 1940, he joined the Royal Navy (RN), undeterred by his close escape from an ocean-going death the previous year. His first duty was protecting the British coastline from enemy submarines in a RN destroyer. He was then transferred to motor torpedo boats based at Great Yarmouth, where he was given his own command after the Allied invasion of Normandy. After an 'E' boat incident, he was mentioned in dispatches: he was part of a team who destroyed one boat by ramming it, and, along with two other ships, destroyed another by gunfire. His decorations included the 1939–45 Star and the Atlantic Star. He left the RN in March 1945, but always retained a fondness for the sea.

Troughton returned to acting and joined the Amersham Repertory Company. From there he was asked to join the famous Bristol Old Vic Company and appeared in *Hamlet* (1947–48) and *King Lear* (1948). He then spent two years with the Pilgrim Players performing T. S. Eliot's plays at the Mercury Theatre, Nottingham.

In 1948 he took his first film role, a cameo appearance in *Escape*, which co-starred William Hartnell. Later that year he appeared in Laurence Olivier's *Hamlet* – based upon his recent work at the Bristol Old Vic.

Troughton also took TV roles in *Hamlet* and *King Lear*, continuing the good practice instigated by Olivier. 'It was the early days of TV,' he remembered later. 'About 300,000 TV viewers in London only… I was never relaxed in live TV.'

As TV techniques grew better, Troughton settled down into more regular character actor roles, admitting in the early 1980s, 'I like to play all kinds of people in all kinds of plays.

I've got a special liking for fantasy and rip-roaring adventures with plenty of action, such as *Robin Hood* and *Kidnapped*.'

Troughton cut his teeth on roles in classic *Boy's Own*-type adventures, burying himself in the work. He was reluctant to give interviews, as he explained in a rare radio interview towards the end of his career: 'It's wrong [for a character actor] to promote their own character too much... the audience get to know you too much, which makes your job harder.'

In 1950 Troughton appeared in the Disney classic *Treasure Island* alongside Robert Newton's infamous Long John Silver, a larger-than-life character actor who had been in the RN with future Doctor Who Jon Pertwee. Troughton's part in the movie was small, playing a ship-hand called Roach. A little appreciated fact is that another British character actor John Laurie (*Dad's Army*) played the part of Blind Pew.

Unfortunately, many of Troughton's early TV performances no longer exist, which makes analysis of this work difficult, but many older people remember him as *Robin Hood*. The six-part show was written by Max Kester and recorded live at the Gaumont-British Studios in Lime Grove, London, between 17 March and 21 April 1953. The 2006–09 BBC version of *Robin Hood* featured Troughton's grandson, Sam, alongside Jonas Armstrong and Keith Allen, and was much more sophisticated than the original BBC TV version.

Some of Troughton's other early roles included Guy Fawkes in *Gunpowder Guy* (alongside future *Doctor Who* producer Barry Letts) in 1950 and *The Scarlet Pimpernel* in 1956. These parts were very modest compared to his film work, which in 1955 included James Tyrell in Laurence Olivier's iconic *Richard III*. Although his was not a major part in the film, it was memorable: being summoned by King Richard and told to murder the Princes in the Tower in a very tight two-shot, before providing a very strong voice-over during the murder scene itself. Troughton was clearly up to the job, with so much experience behind him in such a short space of time. In fact, he adds a truly sinister edge in doing the King's dirty work against his own free will. And there was Laurence Olivier again to give Troughton's career a little boost.

In 1956 he appeared in three episodes of *The Count of Monte Cristo*, which, incredibly, co-starred Burt Lancaster's side-kick Nick Cravat in his usual role of a mute (something Cravat was sentenced to do since the swashbuckling classics *The Flame and the Arrow* in 1950 and *The Crimson Pirate* in 1952, because he naturally swore too much when speaking). Media-mogul Lew Grade co-produced the series. The first 12 episodes were filmed at the Hal Roach Studios (famed for shooting the best shorts and movies of comedy duo Laurel and Hardy) in the USA, while the remaining 39 episodes were shot in the UK.

Troughton appeared in the 2nd episode, 'Marseilles', the 15th episode, 'The Portuguese Affair', and the 23rd episode, 'The Island', as the supporting character Marcel. George Dolenz starred as Edmond Dantes but was constantly upstaged by the charismatic Cravat.

Incredibly the full 39 episodes still exist of this loosely adapted version of the great Dumas novel and were released as a five-DVD box set in the UK in 2010, which is certainly worth a look.

As well as the odd film, Troughton would take various character roles in TV plays and serials up to his time as Doctor Who. One role of particular note was that of Daniel Quilp in the BBC's epic interpretation of Dickens's *The Old Curiosity Shop*, 1962–63, something he mentioned as a career highlight in 1983: 'I did a lot of Dickens... the dwarf Quilp in *The Old*

Curiosity Shop was a big success and a part I look back on with great love and excitement.'

This version of *The Old Curiosity Shop* was a much-loved adaptation of the Dickens novel. Spread over 13 episodes, each one 25 minutes in length, it told the story of how the wicked Quilp heckles Michele Dotrice's Little Nell to an early grave; but not before coming to a sticky end himself. Unfortunately, the adaptation no longer exists in the BBC archive (it's not just episodes of *Doctor Who* that were wiped, other gems have been lost too).

Diversity was the watchword of Troughton's career and next he played the blind man Phineas in the film classic *Jason and the Argonauts*. The movie opens with King Pelias, an evil dictator, receiving a prophecy from a soothsayer regarding a golden fleece. He learns that a baby that will grow into a man will thwart him: Jason, a man with one sandal.

When grown, Jason saves a man – King Pelias – from drowning, and when Jason loses a sandal during the incident, Pelias knows that the events of the prophecy are drawing closer. Indeed, Jason doesn't help himself: he tells the King that he is on a quest to regain his throne and kill the evil Pelias. Knowing that he could never kill Jason in one-to-one combat, Pelias tells him that he's not ready to confront the King and tells him to gather good men and a ship and to prove himself first by capturing the golden fleece. Without knowing who he is, Jason agrees.

Jason and the Argonauts is a well thought-out script with cutting-edge special effects for its day (Ray Harryhausen's revolutionary stop-motion monster effects). When Jason eventually arrives at Phineas's abode and witnesses Harpies (winged demons) stealing his food and tormenting the blind man, the film takes on a mystical edge. Before Jason obtains the advice he seeks from Phineas, he sets up a trap to capture the Harpies, whereby his crew can catch them in a huge net thrown from the top of a ruined temple. The temple used in the scene is a real ancient temple in Italy, and the actors were given special permission to climb on it.

To create any stop-motion animation requires some level of improvisation from the actors involved. There are no model creatures or actors in suits roaming around during shooting, so the actor is left to visualise what is going on and act solo, with the creatures being inserted afterwards. Ray Harryhausen explained the process with regard to Troughton's scene:

> For the Harpies sequence I designed several 'contacts' with humans. The first where the blind Phineas is fighting off the demons and we see his stick and belt yanked from him by the creatures. Both objects were attached to off-screen wires and on my signal a member of the crew pulled them away from Patrick Troughton. Later in the animation studio I would animate the models… as though they were snatching the objects.

Jason and the Argonauts took two years and £3 million to make, but the end result is a magnificent piece of cinema with a great performance from Troughton.

In 1964 he played alongside Peter Cushing and Christopher Lee in Hammer Horror's *The Gorgon*. Based upon the mythological story of Medusa, Barbara Shelley plays a respectable lady who turns into the Gorgon (played by Prudence Hyman) to terrorise her way through 84 minutes of Hammer fun. Troughton has a supporting part as a policeman (Inspector Kanof) in what is nothing more than a bread-and-butter role. Interestingly, *The Gorgon* was released shortly before Peter Cushing took on the role of Doctor Who in the two cinema versions of the TV series. These in turn were finished shortly before Troughton took over from William Hartnell in the title role of the TV adventures.

It was in 1966, while Troughton was filming *The Viking Queen* in Ireland, that he was asked if he would like to become Doctor Who, as he told Peter Haining in *The Doctor Who File*:

> My association with *Doctor Who* began in Ireland. I was there in 1966 filming *The Viking Queen* with Nicola Pagett when the phone started ringing. It was the BBC production office and they were looking for a replacement for Billy Hartnell, who was then a very sick man. 'Come and play Doctor Who,' the voice on the phone said. 'No, no,' I said equally emphatically, 'I don't want to play Doctor Who.' Anyway the phone kept on ringing and I kept saying, 'No, I really don't want to play it.' But they kept phoning and pushing the money up, so that in the end I began to have serious doubts… After about a week of these calls, I decided I must be crazy to keep refusing. It was ridiculous.

Troughton originally felt that Doctor Who was not the right part for him. 'I was astonished that they asked me,' he said later. He had watched the show with his children and really enjoyed William Hartnell's Doctor, but was unsure if it could continue when Hartnell left. 'I thought it would last about six weeks after Billy Hartnell had finished,' he admitted in 1983. 'The whole concept of the Doctor going on was quite a new idea, and one was jumping in at the deep end.'

The BBC's persistence paid off and Troughton became the Doctor, but why were they so keen to cast him? He explained in a 1985 interview: 'I think they cast me because I'd done about 20 years of character acting and so could cope working with something like that.'

His initial thought was to black up for the part, with big earrings and beard, so no one would recognise him. Thankfully, Sydney Newman was having none of that. Newman brought Troughton back down to earth and shaped his interpretation of the Doctor with a throwaway comment: 'Do what you like with him – play him like Charlie Chaplin if you want to.' (*Doctor Who – A Celebration, Two Decades Through Time and Space*, Peter Haining, WH Allen, 1983). This appealed to Troughton and is what eventually happened, but only after other ideas had been thrashed out, as he reminisced on the TV magazine show *Nationwide* (1983): 'First they put a wig on me and I looked like Harpo Marx, then they dressed my hair like a Beatle' – but that didn't work. Troughton had further ideas, such as playing him like a Windjammer captain (very tough and hardy) but Newman wasn't happy with that either.

It's difficult to ultimately say if the Chaplin idea was Troughton's or Newman's. It appears that Troughton went off the idea and Newman asked, 'Whatever happened to the cosmic hobo?' after seeing the Windjammer captain look.

Eventually the clown-like interpretation was agreed, with Troughton playing the part in a very clown-like way to begin with – big baggy trousers and stovepipe hat – but this soon mellowed as he became more established in the role.

What is interesting about this process was the freedom Troughton was given to develop his character. Newman didn't dictate to Troughton – he certainly advised him when he thought he had gone too far – but the final decision as to what he looked like was Troughton's, which is something that has stuck with all *Doctor Who* leading actors ever since.

But it wasn't just the look that was important – what about the character himself? Troughton had to undergo a gruelling planning meeting. It went badly, to the extent that story editor

Gerry Davis threw everyone out of the room apart from Troughton in order to get to grips with the new man. In the end they settled on someone who knows all of the answers but is keen to watch and observe others around him, gently directing them to do what *he* wants. This characteristic was clearly displayed in 'Tomb of the Cybermen', where the Doctor instantly knows what is happening but is happy to let the scientists – and megalomaniacs – find out for themselves, eventually secretly throwing a switch to help them discover the tomb of the Cybermen.

Troughton needn't have worried about being accepted as the Doctor. He was fondly regarded from the off, as highlighted in the *Doctor Who Annual* (1967): 'Our new Dr Who is more "with it"; he is more "switched on", more in tune with the 20th century. There are, of course, still traces of his old personality and, characteristically, he still wears the same clothes, which are a trifle baggy on his new figure'. So the cosmic hobo was thoroughly accepted.

The cast accepted him too, as *Doctor Who* companion Anneke Wills (Polly) remembers:

> We played our little joke on Patrick the first day he started. Michael Craze [companion Ben Jackson] and I ordered some special T-shirts and we greeted our new Doctor with the words: 'Come back Bill Hartnell' blazoned across our chests. It was a ghastly joke, I suppose, but dear Patrick took it very well.

Although the record of Troughton's era as the Doctor has been decimated by the BBC in the 1970s clear-out of old programmes, some gems are still available. The surviving episodes from 'The Abominable Snowmen' and 'The Web of Fear' are dark and eerie, highlighting some of the greatest thrills the black and white series of *Doctor Who* had to offer. Also the return of 'The Tomb of the Cybermen' to the BBC archive in 1991 (from Hong Kong) strengthened the view that tales from *Doctor Who*'s fifth season were some of the strongest and best ever. The Yeti and the Ice Warriors were both introduced during that season, alongside two new Cybermen stories, 'The Tomb of the Cybermen' and 'The Wheel in Space', with the former starting the season in an impressive way.

Troughton always rated his second season (the fifth season) as his favourite; while the first was all about feeling his way and the last season was simply tiring.

Despite being tired, he remembered his three years as Doctor Who with great fondness: 'Of all my years as an actor, I think these were the happiest three years. I particularly enjoyed acting with Frazer Hines, who played Jamie [Troughton's main companion in the series for all but his first story]. We never once had a cross word all the time we worked together.'

Troughton first met Hines in 1964 while filming *Smuggler's Bay*, which was based upon the novel *Moonfleet*. Hines reminisced:

Patrick played an old smuggler. And the day before filming began, I'd actually put my hand through a plate glass window, and I turned up with these great bandages on, and they tried various things to hide it, and they were covered up with an old workers' glove. Years later, when I saw Patrick for *Doctor Who*, the first day of filming he said 'How's the hand?' He remembered. And that was the sort of man he was.

Hines also remembered his time filming *Doctor Who* with great fondness: 'For three years Pat and I had an absolute ball together. I think there's always room for fun when you're working – except, maybe, if it's Chekhov or Shakespeare – and I've always been a practical joker.'

Troughton also got on well with other members of the regular cast and production crew, as he recounts in *The Making of Doctor Who* (Malcolm Hulke and Terrance Dicks, Pan Books, 1972), 'Innes Lloyd [who took over from Verity Lambert], the producer when I started, and Peter Bryant were great to work for. I had a lot of fun.'

Troughton enjoyed the fantasy of the show. He thought it was great that the Doctor could change his appearance, as he explained at the time of 'The Three Doctors': 'We are all different aspects of the same character. Of course it's bound to be a bit of a mystery to us, but in the Doctor's space-time machine the so-called past just doesn't exist.'

Like Hartnell before him, Troughton said that it was difficult to stop being the Doctor when the cameras were off, but, unlike Hartnell, Troughton's Doctor was not a crotchety old man, as he explained: 'When you're playing a part for a long time you certainly take on some of the mental attitudes of the fellow you're playing. Luckily the Doctor was a very jolly fellow and I just bubbled along.'

He would also say that having a young family at the time – three under ten years old – allowed him to keep in touch with the part of the Doctor, as children loved the character so much. So again, like William Hartnell, there was that Pied Piper aspect to Troughton's Doctor, and not just in the pipe – recorder – he played, but also the children who followed him and his travels. Troughton mentioned the younger viewers in 1983: 'It [*Doctor Who*] also gave me great pleasure coming into contact with children, for if I had not been an actor I would quite like to have been a teacher. Children keep one young.' In fact, he also stated that the continuing success of the show was due to new children being born.

Troughton regretted leaving the series 'very much, but you can't do something forever as a character actor'. Three years was a long time for him to be involved in one particular project, as he confessed: 'If I stayed with it too long, I would get stuck.'

Leaving the show was a painful process. Troughton, Hines and Wendy Padbury (companion Zoe), had all decided in secret to leave by the end of the sixth season. Hines was the first to announce his departure and Troughton persuaded him to stay on until the last story of the year, the 10-episode epic, 'The War Games', whereupon all three left with smiles on their faces and the feeling of a job well done.

Some people may consider that the span of a *Doctor Who*'s television life is not that long – roughly three years for most of them – but the gruelling schedule hasn't lightened too much over the past 50 years; the show still restricts the opportunity of appearing in too many other productions.

Troughton and Hines held a mild protest during the filming of one story (Hines recounts it as 'The Mind Robber' in the sixth – their last – season). They argued that they were too tired to keep playing in episodes where only three actors were carrying most of the action. Their protest was heard and the episode lengths cut down slightly with more robots added (Hines's general recollection), so the reason for leaving wasn't just an excuse – they were simply feeling drained.

When Troughton, Hines and Padbury left, it was the break-up of another successful *Doctor Who* family, but the show went on. A new decade was just around the corner and the series would make the transition from black and white to colour, forever changing the mood and pace afterwards. It would be the greatest change in the show's history so far; more so than

William Hartnell leaving. The Doctor of mystery was no more. With 'The War Games' we were introduced to the Doctor's own race, the Time Lords, and learned that he had the ability to continue to change his appearance. The mystery was unravelling, so where would we go to from there?

Patrick Troughton's Doctor is often referred to as 'the monster Doctor' or 'the missing Doctor', to highlight two fundamental aspects of his tenure: great new monsters and the most missing stories from the BBC archive. People who remember the Troughton years rate his stories highly; the Doctor was soon to change into a dashing man of action and the United Nations Intelligence Taskforce (UNIT), introduced in the stories 'The Web of Fear' and 'The Invasion', would become a regular entity in the more Earth-bound stories of the first half of the new decade.

After *Doctor Who*, Troughton took on many more memorable roles, just as he had before playing the Doctor. To him, Doctor Who was just one in a long line of characters and something he was happy to move on from. In 1983, while shooting 'The Five Doctors' on location in Wales, producer John Nathan-Turner and former Doctor Who Jon Pertwee spent some time persuading Troughton to attend the special 20th anniversary convention at Longleat. Nathan-Turner remembered, 'Jon Pertwee and I persuaded him to do it. And then he did cartwheels to get out of it. And [eventually] he said, "I'm not going to get out of this, am I?" and I said, "No!"'

Troughton was a little reluctant to get too involved in the convention circuit, something Pertwee loved and embraced with open arms, but Troughton didn't put *Doctor Who* on a pedestal over his other work. However, always the professional, he did eventually get into the swing of things and set up a comic banter with his successor, as Pertwee explained in one interview: 'We are tremendously fond of each other, but we made out we didn't get along at conventions because Pat's Doctor and mine didn't get on in "The Three Doctors". So it was all an act!' And it was a fine one, too, causing all sorts of fun interaction for the audience to enjoy.

As soon as Pertwee had taken over the TARDIS reins in 1970, Troughton was already hard at work on another major project, *The Six Wives of Henry VIII*, playing the noble part of the Duke of Norfolk. This re-established him as a serious character actor alongside Keith Mitchell's memorable Henry VIII. Although this colour interpretation of the historical accounts has the usual hint of dramatic licence, it still brings home the horror of the plight of the King's wives and made good quality television, which is still enjoyed today.

Fantastical roles always appealed to Troughton and one of his most memorable was as Father Brennan, the tortured priest in *The Omen* (1976). This was a tremendous part and allowed him to adopt an Irish accent and pester Gregory Peck to murder his adopted son, who just happened to be the Devil's spawn.

The Omen is regarded as one of the greatest horror movies ever made, but in actual fact it is a quality thriller, with a choice cast including Gregory Peck, Lee Remick, David Warner and Billie Whitelaw.

Whitelaw was terrifying in the film and proved that the most evil person can be the one who looks normal. But Troughton didn't look that normal in the movie: he had to play a desperate priest, a man with terminal cancer who papered the walls of his home with pages from the Bible and was desperate to tell Peck and Remick the truth about their son Damien. His thick Irish accent, his deathly pale features, inner frustration and desperation to be heard – his inner turmoil – made Troughton's role a truly memorable one, and his death scene is one of the most iconic in movie history. Couple that with a haunting score by the legendary composer Jerry Goldsmith, and you have cinematic history that is impossible to remake with any extra credit.

After *The Omen*, Troughton took a part (wise man Melanthius) in *Sinbad and the Eye of the Tiger* (1977), one of Ray Harryhausen's last stop-motion movies. He had, of course, played the blind man, Phineas, in Harryhausen's classic *Jason and the Argonauts* (1963) before *Doctor Who*, so he was not offered such parts because of his connection with the show. Indeed, he played alongside Christopher Lee in three Hammer Horror classics: *The Curse of Frankenstein* (1957), *The Gorgon* (1964) and *Scars of Dracula* (1970) (taking the small roles of Kurt, Inspector Kanof and Klove respectively). He also played alongside Cushing again in *Frankenstein and the Monster From Hell* (Hammer, 1973), so the role of the Doctor had no ill effect on his career at all; there was a strong similarity in his roles either side of the *Doctor Who* years.

Despite *Sinbad and the Eye of the Tiger* being a Ray Harryhausen movie, the film was quite poor. It was the fourth *Sinbad* movie and clearly ideas were no longer plentiful. The over-dubbing was considered annoying to begin with, and Harryhausen's bony demons were a poor relation to his killer skeletons from *Jason and the Argonauts*, over 15 years previous.

Jane Seymour is the obligatory love interest (just as Caroline Munro was in the previous Sinbad film, *The Golden Voyage of Sinbad*, which starred Tom Baker). That said, the wicked Zenobia (Margaret Whiting), is an unconvincing counterpart to Tom Baker's wizard from the previous film. She physically ages due to her deals with demons and the prince of darkness, but in a more comic than gothic way.

Although *Sinbad and the Eye of the Tiger* gave the appearance of being more expensive in budget than its predecessors, it was an unimaginative story that walked down tried and tested pathways with little additional imagination. But what of Patrick Troughton's performance?

Troughton was an inspired piece of casting. As Melanthius the wise man, he lives with his daughter in a dead city on a desert island. He starts off cantankerous and vain, but manages to muster a sense of wonder and amazement that brings a whole new dimension to the movie, albeit a third of the way through.

While most of the cast appear to try to dazzle the audience with their stunning good looks, Troughton settles down behind his big bushy grey beard with an ever-building sense of humour (which must surely have been as contagious off camera as on). One can probably see a little of the Doctor in his character, especially when an experiment he is conducting goes wrong and explodes, to his immense joy.

To this day, *Sinbad and the Eye of the Tiger* is Sunday-afternoon family fodder – it's unfortunately just a little lazy in its creativity in comparison to other movies in the *Sinbad* series, and especially the Ray Harryhausen canon.

Troughton's love of popping in and out of familiar roles is clearly shown in his strong ties to two particular novels of Robert Louis Stevenson, *Kidnapped* and *Treasure Island*. Despite having a part in the Disney classic of 1950, Troughton returned to *Treasure Island* in the 1977 TV series, playing the part of Israel Hands. His portrayal of the infamous swashbuckler Alan Breck in 1952 and 1956 in TV versions of *Kidnapped* were mentioned as career highlights by Troughton shortly before his death in the 1980s. There were some stories he revisited throughout his career, *Robin Hood* being another one and, of course, *Doctor Who*, to which he returned three times.

Troughton enjoyed dabbling. He even dabbled in the soaps, with a role in the longest-running soap of all, *Coronation Street*, playing the part of George Barton in 1974. So his character actor status was fully appreciated by all sorts of casting directors, not just those associated with action and fantasy.

Troughton continued to work hard, taking on cameo roles in *All Creatures Great and Small* (opposite future Doctor Who Peter Davison in an episode entitled 'Hair of the Dog'), and *The Two Ronnies 1984 Christmas Special* (as a cantankerous judge). He also appeared as concerned Italian father Joe Mancini in the hit TV series *Minder* in an episode called 'Windows'. His performance, alongside regulars George Cole (Arthur Daley) and Dennis Waterman (Terry McCann), was memorable and is one of his finest one-off roles, full of fatherly love and compassion.

Troughton took more of a permanent role in the ITV sitcom *The Two of Us* with Nicholas Lyndhurst in 1986 (on a rowing machine in one memorable scene, despite suffering severe heart attacks in 1978 and 1984 respectively). He was also the first person ever to be murdered in *Inspector Morse* (George Jackson in the very first story 'The Dead of Jericho') in 1987. His last performances were in the TV comedy *Supergran* and *Knights of God*, also in 1987; although *Knights of God* was the last programme to be broadcast (13 episodes in the autumn of 1987), it had been recorded two years previously.

Troughton died on 28 March 1987, in Atlanta, USA. He was attending the Magnum Opus Con II in Columbus, Georgia. While taking part in the panel Q&A, two days after his 67th birthday, he complained of feeling unwell and retired to his room. He suffered a fatal heart attack the following morning after ordering his breakfast at 7.25am and was found lying on the floor. On arrival at the hospital, he was pronounced dead.

Troughton had been warned about over-exerting himself before making the trip to America, but he had appeared to be in fine spirits and was planning a belated birthday party the following weekend after a special screening – at his own request – of his *Doctor Who* story, 'The Dominators'.

When people discuss Troughton's great roles, the part of the Doctor is always there, but his Quilp and Breck, even so long ago, are also considered classic performances. He himself cited Quilp as his very best role, with Doctor Who in second place. His portrayal of Cole Hawlings in the BBC six-part fantasy for children *The Box of Delights* was another memorable part played towards the end of his life, and one for which he was highly praised by *Doctor Who* fans and critics alike.

If we look at the role of Hawlings alongside that of Father Brennan in *The Omen*, and then his roles in *The Old Curiosity Shop*, *Coronation Street* and *Doctor Who*, Troughton's diversity and skill as a character actor is readily showcased and appreciated. Of course *Jason and the Argonauts* is a respected part of cinematic history, as is Disney's *Treasure Island*, with his cameo roles further enhancing his passion for work. Perhaps more should be done to highlight his role as Daniel Quilp in *The Old Curiosity Shop*, but the BBC, and even ITV, keep making new adaptations of classic novels rather than reshowing (or retaining) the old ones, so we are deprived of some of Troughton's finest roles, not just some of his *Doctor Who* stories.

Patrick Troughton was the quintessential British character actor, never staying in one place – or one role – for too long. Perhaps *Doctor Who* fans were initially upset by this, especially the way he would talk about his other parts with equal or more love, but they soon came to understand why Troughton was sometimes shy of public appearances and interviews: he didn't want to give too much of himself away, or for them to get to know his true character. 'You see, I think acting is magic,' he said. 'If I tell you all about myself it will spoil it.'

Like many of the other Doctor Whos, Troughton didn't want to break the magic of the role for children. When confronted by a journalist during his time as the Doctor he said, 'I never give interviews. Just tell them that I am that mystery man of television, Doctor Who.'

Troughton was aware of the power of the role, the command that it had in the acting profession and upon the general public. He treated it with respect but couldn't resist returning to it more times than any other Doctor: first in 1973 for 'The Three Doctors', then in 1983 for 'The Five Doctors' and yet again – because he enjoyed the comeback so much – in 1985, for 'The Two Doctors'. This last appearance – an excellent storyline featuring his faithful companion Jamie alongside current incumbents Colin Baker and Nicola Bryant – showed his love for the role (through one 'dinner party' scene at least, where he is momentarily transformed into a creature with a love of human flesh with a counterpart chef from the same carnivorous race). He also admitted that he loved the Sontarans, great monsters that he had never encountered before.

All of these return visits show that there was a place in Troughton's heart for *Doctor Who* right up until his untimely death, but let us not forget his other, now largely overlooked, roles.

Doctor Who was neither saint nor sinner to Patrick Troughton. What the role of the Doctor has done is to forever keep him in the minds of the young – as the immortality of *Doctor Who* will keep him and his work alive and, perhaps, tempt some people into finding old Troughton gems on TV and DVD. Sadly, there are not many of them remaining to find.

> 'It now seems so long ago that I played the part of the Doctor that there is really very little I can add to what has already been written. And, of course, I've played so many different parts in the last forty years.'
>
> *Patrick Troughton from 'Doctor Who Indulged My Passion for Clowning'*
> **Doctor Who – A Celebration, Two Decades**
> **Through Time and Space, Peter Haining**

Before moving on to the life and career of Jon Pertwee, I wish to underline the fact that Patrick Troughton's life and non-*Doctor-Who* career is dreadfully underrated, maybe because records of so many of his important early TV roles no longer exist, such as *Robin Hood*, *Gunpowder Guy* and *Kidnapped*. In many ways, he is a forgotten actor, let alone the lost Doctor. One thing I want to mention here is his fantastic performance as Adolf Hitler in the Gateway Theatre production of *Eva Braun*. This was in 1950, when feelings about the Nazis still ran high, but he did it and he did it well, avoiding outrage or criticism, and this understanding of his craft, and his instinct for how much he could get away with, was one of his greatest assets.

Patrick Troughton isn't overlooked nowadays, he is still remembered as one of the greatest Doctor Whos; he also has a legacy through his family. His daughter's son is Harry Potter's nemesis Dudley Dursley (Harry Melling). His son David Troughton – apart from being an accomplished Shakespearean actor – appeared in *Doctor Who* during his father's time, in stories 'The Enemy of the World' and 'The War Games', and also played a more substantial role as the dashing King Peladon opposite Jon Pertwee's Doctor in 'The Curse of Peladon', and Professor Hobbes in David Tennant's excellent story 'Midnight'. He even played the second Doctor in two audio *Doctor Who* stories in 2011. David Troughton's brother Michael is an actor and teacher, most notable for playing opposite Rik Mayall in *The New Statesman* as Sir Piers Fletcher-Dervish.

The Patrick Troughton Theatre opened at Mill Hill School in 2007 to celebrate one of its most accomplished former students and, along with his family and many *Doctor Who* fans around the world, Troughton's legacy is somewhat secured. That and, of course, the Eleventh Doctor, Matt Smith, who singled out Troughton as a huge influence on his own interpretation of the Doctor, with bow tie and zany professorial humour.

'I believed totally in the possibilities implied in the series. I never thought of it as fantasy. Far from it – it's all happening. I think space will be conquered through the mind rather than the clumsy medium of space travel.'

'Doctor Who Indulged my Passion for Clowning' by Patrick Troughton
Doctor Who – A Celebration, Two Decades Through Time and Space, Peter Haining

CHAPTER FOUR

JON PERTWEE

'Dr Who is me – or I am Dr Who. I play him straight from me.'

Jon Pertwee from *The Making of Doctor Who* by
Malcolm Hulke and Terrance Dicks

LIKE PATRICK TROUGHTON and William Hartnell before him, Jon Pertwee was one of the great British character actors of the 20th century. An ability to throw his voice and adopt a multitude of characters made him an actor in high demand, especially on radio in the 1940s, 50s and 60s. He was incredibly versatile and as much in demand as Kenneth Williams, or indeed his character acting cousin Bill Pertwee (who Jon nurtured as an actor and who later played Hodges in *Dad's Army*), but it was a great shock to many people when he landed the role of Doctor Who.

Pertwee was not a well-known TV actor; he had cut his teeth as a stage actor, appearing in films and, most notably, through countless character roles on radio. He was selected for the role of the Doctor because of his ability to entertain and be humorous. Unfortunately, Pertwee had decided to play the

Doctor completely straight, to use his own personality and, most importantly, his own voice.

> 'All of my decisions were, as I later discovered, completely at odds with the reason why Producer Peter Bryant had originally wanted me – Peter had *wanted* a comedic Doctor; he liked the fact that I could sing and play the guitar and do all the voices and wanted me to bring those aspects into *Doctor Who*.'
>
> *I Am the Doctor – Jon Pertwee's Final Memoir*

So Pertwee's great triumph was to find himself within the character of the Doctor, which was a novel change for the actor.

John Devon Roland Pertwee was born on 7 July 1919 in Chelsea, London. He was educated at Frensham Heights School, Rowledge and Sherborne School, Sherborne, Dorset.

The name Pertwee is of French-Huguenot origin, actually being Perthuis de Laillevault. He was the son of the famous playwright, novelist and actor Roland Pertwee. Roland's friend Henry Ainley was Jon Pertwee's godfather. His son, Anthony Ainley, would become an actor and play opposite Jon in 'The Five Doctors' as the Master, while Anthony's brother Richard would become Tom Baker's drama teacher while coached as an amateur by William Hartnell.

Jon's father was also good friends with the author A. A. Milne, and Jon was invited to tea one afternoon, where he met Milne's son Christopher Robin. After tea, Christopher took Jon upstairs, where he was introduced to the boy's toy animals: Piglet, Owl, Kanga, Roo and Christopher's favourite – Winnie-the-Pooh. Jon was also allowed to ride on Christopher Robin's donkey – Eeyore.

Despite having a famous father and interesting acquaintances, Pertwee's upbringing was not a happy one. For a start, he didn't see his mother until he was 15. She had an affair when Pertwee was an infant and his father kicked her out of the marital home. She moved away with her lover, and Pertwee and his elder brother Michael were left with a father who was wrapped up in his own world, with little time for them (Pertwee also had a stepbrother called Michael, whom he called Coby, which was short for his surname). The three boys were close but if anyone got left out, it would be Jon.

Jon spent much of his formative years under the care of his uncle Guy, but he was also very close to his grandmother, who helped to look after him.

Despite feeling left out by his father, Pertwee didn't think of any other career but acting. Laurence Olivier was one of his early acquaintances. Towards the end of his life, Pertwee used to tell a story that proved Olivier was indeed the greatest actor that ever lived. He explained that one day he was invited to a party while Olivier was visiting his house. He asked the actor to accompany him, but Olivier wasn't keen. Pertwee refused to take no for an answer and begrudgingly, Olivier went along. Once at the party, Pertwee sat Olivier down with a sandwich and a drink. Believing that he would be all right, he left him alone. He would then explain that Olivier hated anyone creeping up behind him, but unfortunately somebody did. An old lady came up behind him on the sofa, put her hands over his eyes and said, 'Guess who?' Olivier shot up in the air and the poor woman was propelled backwards over a chair. An enraged Olivier stormed over to the host and demanded, 'Who was that woman?'

The host replied, 'That was my wife.'

Seamlessly Olivier declared, 'What an extraordinary woman!'

It's a great showbiz story and must have an element of the truth in it, but Pertwee was always full of such stories.

Acting was the family business, so Pertwee took it for granted that he would follow in his father's footsteps. In fact, Jon had four great-aunts, the Moore sisters, who were also on the stage. He explained during interviews that this complacency about his fated career made him laid-back when it finally came to fruition. During his *Doctor Who* years between takes he was always laughing and joking with the cast, to many a director's chagrin. However, it didn't quite start out that way. At boarding school there was a shortage of young lads who wanted to become actors. His peers considered it to be quite effeminate, so for a while he was picked on.

It wasn't all doom and gloom, though. When he was old enough to drive, Pertwee bought a 250cc SOS trials motorbike and went for a ride. At a T-junction he lost control, went over a wall and into a vicar's garden. 'Well done!' the vicar said. 'You're just in time for tea!' Acting and fast bikes were part of his teenage make-up and neither ever left him.

Some people look upon the above story as a joke, but in fact it wasn't – Pertwee was indeed propelled into the garden and greeted by the vicar. Years later, the actor was passing the same place with his son Sean and showed him the very spot where he hit the wall – it had never been repaired.

Pertwee joined RADA at 18, where he trained alongside Duncan Lamont, with whom he would appear in the *Doctor Who* story 'Death to the Daleks'. His time at RADA came to an end when he was expelled for refusing to play the part of a 'Greek wind' in a production. This caused a bit of embarrassment for his father as he was one of the school governors.

Pertwee then spent some time – while still at school – at a travelling circus, riding the wall of death, which he maintained was very easy to do. What wasn't easy to do – and something he of course refused to do – was to put a real-life lion in the act with him. Because the circus had a very old toothless lion, they thought it would be good for Pertwee to take it for a spin on the wall of death. A preposterous idea, but it was suggested.

The rest of the 1930s saw Pertwee working in a travelling theatre company with the occasional stint on radio, which gave him good grounding for the intensity of radio work he would enjoy after the war. Much of his output from the 1930s and 40s is now lost. Programmes were performed live and too few were recorded on 78 rpm records. At one stage Pertwee was performing 15-minute stints on radio every day for months on end. This made him quite wealthy, but sadly there are only smatterings of this work preserved today.

What we do know of Pertwee's early career is that his father helped him. One of his early theatre runs was in *To Kill a Cat*, which his father wrote. Also, his 1939 movie – *The Four Just Men* – was scripted by his father, who took a small part in it too. The movie has the added distinction of being the first in which Pertwee actually spoke.

Speed was still a passion of Pertwee's: despite his growing popularity as an actor, he competed at Goodwood for the odd motor car engagement. He did this right up until the outbreak of the Second World War and then joined the Royal Naval Volunteer Reserve (RNVR) and became an officer. Like Patrick Troughton, he too escaped death at sea. Pertwee was one of a small group of people who got transferred from HMS *Hood* shortly before it was destroyed in less than ten seconds by the *Bismarck*. '1,762 men went down in one bang,' he told chat-show host Michael Parkinson in 1982. It was a very lucky escape on that occasion, and he experienced several other close calls with death during the war too.

Pertwee and Troughton met several times during the war

years, as he told Peter Haining, '[Troughton] had a strong dislike of the standard issue tin hat that the Navy made the people on motor torpedo-boats wear. So instead he wore this old family tea cosy on his head. It was a gaudy-looking thing and must have annoyed his Commanding Officer no end – but he still went on wearing it!'

Troughton would wear a tea-cosy hat while playing the Doctor in such sea-based stories as 'Fury from the Deep', and for him it became normal sea-going apparel. But he wasn't the only eccentric would-be actor that Pertwee met during the war. There was also Robert Newton, a legendary character in the RN, always managing to acquire quality booze and disappearing to drink it and then sleep it off. Pertwee admired the man, especially the way in which he managed to get away with his insubordination (Newton was, like Pertwee, also expelled from RADA). However, he was eventually arrested and punished by the RN, who sent him on a trawler, but even then he managed to delay the ship's departure in order to acquire smoked salmon sandwiches and quality booze (not easy in wartime), so he and the crew could enjoy a good meal on the ocean waves.

One morning Pertwee woke up after a particularly alcoholic run ashore with his shipmates to discover that he had a large tattoo on his right forearm. To his dying day he claimed that he could never remember getting it done. It is occasionally glimpsed during his *Doctor Who* days, including his very first story, 'Spearhead From Space', when escaping from a hospital in a wheelchair.

A little-appreciated episode in Pertwee's war was when he was transferred to the Naval Intelligence Department (NID) in Whitehall. Towards the end of his life, he toured his one-man show, *An Evening with Jon Pertwee*, in which he briefly mentioned his time in NID, but he gave no real detail about the job. NID was actually the department where Ian Fleming (who would later write the James Bond novels) worked. In fact, the real-life James Bond – Fleming's main inspiration for the character – also worked there: Patrick Dalzel-Job, who, as part of 30 Assault Unit (a crack team of commandos created by Fleming), was instrumental in gathering intelligence concerning V Rocket installations behind enemy lines in Europe. Pertwee remembered that James 'Jim' Callaghan was also there as a 'tea boy' (long before becoming the British Prime Minister), which caused him much amusement years later.

Pertwee wasn't one of the most distinguished officers in NID; during his one-man show he recalled that he had to dispose of Winston Churchill's cigar ends after Cabinet meetings with the Joint Planning Staff (JPS, which included author Dennis Wheatley) and NID. To make a bit of extra cash, he would sell the cigar ends.

Although he eventually landed a desk job in NID, Pertwee admitted towards the end of his life that severe back problems originated from his time in the RN and some of the close brushes he had had with danger. Indeed, his war was not easy, and the tenure in NID shows that he had genuine injuries, but also that his input was still considered vital.

Towards the end of his naval career, Pertwee joined the broadcasting section, where he met Lieutenant Eric Barker, and seriously began his career in radio. This led to two series that made him a household name – *Waterlogged Spa* and *The Navy Lark*. He took on many trademark voices in the latter show, including an eccentric postman that endeared him to the nation, with the catchphrase, 'It doesn't matter what you do, as long as you tears them up' (referring to people's letters).

For a while, Pertwee worked alongside another great mimic

in *The Navy Lark*, Ronnie Barker, who played Fatso Johnson in the show. The two became firm friends. Barker later said of Pertwee, 'Jon was always such fun to work with. We had a lot of laughs and he was always one of the prime instigators. But he was very professional and very talented and I thoroughly enjoyed working with him.' (*Jon Pertwee: The Biography* by Bernard Bale, André Deutsch, 2000).

When Barker left and Pertwee was asked who should take his place to do the other voices he'd done so well, he suggested himself, and went on to do over 100 different voices for the show in the end.

The Navy Lark ran for 18 and a half years, making it the longest-running comedy show in the world at that time (only to be surpassed later by *The News Huddlines*), but it wasn't the only success that Pertwee worked on during that time; he also appeared in the theatre alongside Frankie Howerd in *A Funny Thing Happened on the Way to the Forum*, with which Howerd continued successfully, both on TV (*Up Pompeii*) and film (both *A Funny Thing...* and *Up Pompeii*), Pertwee's role in the movie being taken by Phil Silvers.

Pertwee's first starring role in a film was alongside William Hartnell in *Will Any Gentleman...?* (1953). But this wasn't the only *Doctor Who* connection in the movie. During filming, Pertwee met the actress Jean Marsh, whom he later married on 2 April 1955. Marsh would become William Hartnell's companion in the longest-ever *Doctor Who* story, 'The Dalek Master Plan' (12 episodes). Unfortunately, she was killed towards the end of the *Doctor Who* story and, sadly, her marriage to Pertwee didn't last long either. They separated in 1958, before divorcing in 1960. Pertwee remarried shortly afterwards – to Ingeborg Rhoesa, a German woman he had met on a skiing holiday. The pair married on 13 August 1960 and had two children, Sean and Dariel.

Pertwee's career as a character actor continued on radio (most notably in *The Navy Lark*), television and films throughout the 1950s and 60s. Indeed, there are some forgotten gems, such as *The Ugly Duckling* (1959), starring Bernard Bresslaw as Henry Jekyll and Teddy Hyde, with character actor David Lodge putting in an appearance too.

The Ugly Duckling was made by Hammer Films directly after their iconic *The Mummy*, starring Peter Cushing and Christopher Lee. The movie was a comedy spoof of Robert Louis Stevenson's *Strange Case of Doctor Jekyll and Mr Hyde* and was a vehicle for the immensely popular actor Bernard Bresslaw, who was enjoying great success on TV opposite William Hartnell in *The Army Game*.

Although stills from the movie still exist, sadly a print of the movie doesn't – immensely frustrating for Pertwee and Bresslaw fans.

In Wayne Kinsey's excellent book *Hammer Films, The Bray Studios Years*, Continuity girl Marjorie Lavelly said of *The Ugly Duckling*:

> I thought the script was very good – interesting. It was a happy film to work on with a lovely cast… I seem to remember a lot of gags and laughter. The artists used to have their 'green room' near my desk and some of the anecdotes they told were superb. I know it was not a commercial success, which was a shame as a lot of hard work went into it, but that's life.

Clearly a lot of the laughs would be generated by the two great character actors involved (Pertwee and Breslaw), but David Lodge, a fine supporting actor who worked with The Goons and Norman Wisdom (to name but two), was a quick-witted, seasoned actor, with plenty of anecdotes of his own.

On Sunday, 1 November 1964, Pertwee appeared in the British Forces Broadcasting Service (BFBS) 21st anniversary gala night, at the Victoria Palace Theatre in London. Although he appeared alongside people such as Ken Dodd, Jimmy Edwards, Charlie Chester, Larry Adler, Ted Ray and Tommy Trinder, among many others, the ultimate stars of the show were The Goons (Spike Milligan, Peter Sellers and Harry Secombe), who performed a whole episode of their madcap but ground-breaking show. Though a friend of both Sellers and Milligan, Pertwee would fall out with Spike later in life over who was the bigger fan of the pantomime *Aladdin*.

Pertwee was in his element at occasions like the BFBS gala night, surrounded by talented like-minded people who, despite some dreadful experiences during the war, took a comedic influence from those troubled times and shaped the face of British comedy for the next 50 years. *The Goon Show* started as barrack-room humour and *The Navy Lark* was not dissimilar. Character actors such as Peter Butterworth (who played fellow Time Lord the Meddling Monk, alongside William Hartnell), was actually a prisoner of war in the real-life escape that inspired the 1950 film *The Wooden Horse* – although he didn't get a part in the movie because he 'didn't look convincingly heroic and athletic'.

Butterworth, who was in many of the *Carry On* films with the likes of Bernard Bresslaw, served as a lieutenant in the Royal Navy and was captured in the Netherlands in 1940. He escaped through a tunnel from the prisoner-of-war camp Dulag Luft, near Frankfurt, in June 1941 and then covered 27 miles in just three days before a member of the Hitler Youth captured him. Afterwards, he joked that he could never work with children. Two other escape attempts never got beyond the camp grounds.

Several years after the BFBS gala night, while playing on Broadway in *There's a Girl in My Soup*, Pertwee was offered the lead in a brand-new BBC comedy series. The role was written with his comic talents in mind: it was Captain Mainwaring and the show was *Dad's Army*. But Pertwee turned it down, and the part went to Arthur Lowe, whose interpretation would become legendary. Pertwee later said that he didn't really know what he was being offered back home at the time, that he was too wrapped up in the part he was playing. Suffice to say, if he had taken the part, he almost certainly wouldn't have gone on to star in *Doctor Who*.

Pertwee wasn't sore about losing out on *Dad's Army*, although one of the writers, Jimmy Perry, was annoyed that he didn't take the role. He told Pertwee that an agreement had been made that he would play the part. Where that came from is still a little unclear, but naturally Pertwee didn't want to give up a Broadway show in order to play a part in a pilot comedy.

In retrospect he could see that he had turned down a great part but he also knew that Doctor Who wouldn't have been his next major role had he taken Mainwaring. What's more, he found Arthur Lowe's interpretation of the aloof bank manager absolutely hysterical, praising the little extra expressions the actor added to his character.

In 1970, while filming horror spoof *The House That Dripped Blood* (1971), fellow actor Christopher Lee wanted to know who Pertwee was sending up in his on-screen characterisation. The horror actor told Pertwee that some of the characteristics seemed familiar but he couldn't put a name to who it was. Pertwee told Lee that he was actually sending *him* up! Lee found this hilarious; however the director of the movie cut out much of the fun and the film received indifferent notices as a consequence.

While recording *The Navy Lark* in 1969, Pertwee had a conversation about *Doctor Who* with Tenniel Evans (who would later play Major Daly in Jon's *Doctor Who* adventure 'Carnival of Monsters'). Evans told him that there was a rumour that Patrick Troughton was leaving the show and that he was ideal for the part. Pertwee was interested enough to call his agent, who, although unconvinced that he was the right man, contacted the BBC to see what the situation was. He found that Pertwee was on the shortlist of actors to take over from Troughton and had been for some time.

Pertwee was offered the job. He accepted, and only then were there problems concerning his interpretation of the lead role.

The BBC wanted Pertwee's Doctor to be a bit of a joke-telling minstrel to begin with, building further upon the Pied Piper-like antics of Patrick Troughton. Pertwee explained that although his children enjoyed watching Troughton, he thought his friend had gone a little over the top with his interpretation of the Doctor. He was keen to play the part straight and bring in some real science; he also wanted to incorporate fast cars, power boats, motor bikes and (Venusian) Aikido. After long conversations with producer Peter Bryant, Pertwee got his way and not only did he make the transition from black and white to colour but also attracted a more adult audience into the bargain.

In truth, it wasn't as easy as all that. It was director Barry Letts who suggested to Pertwee that he should play the Doctor as himself. This presented problems for the actor because he didn't quite know who he really was. When his wife started to get him to do various things around the house, he discovered a love for anything mechanical, and for risk taking (as his stuntman Terry Walsh would come to appreciate), which in turn brought him a deeper understanding of the type of thing he most enjoyed doing and, consequently, a greater understanding of himself.

It is true that Pertwee brought in some humorous moments for the younger viewers, but there was always a serious side to his personality too. Just as in life, Pertwee's Doctor didn't suffer fools gladly. He despised ignorance and wanton destruction, displaying a heart-on-sleeve attitude that always showed that he was dedicated to good, not evil. He was constantly at odds with the Brigadier, who always wanted to blow things up but still couldn't help liking him. With a complex group of regular relationships in the new colour *Doctor Who*, Pertwee's interpretation of the Doctor showed greater maturity than that displayed by his predecessors.

So at the turn of the 1970s, *Doctor Who* took a major jump away from its roots, not just from the black and white children's classic to colour family entertainment, but in the Doctor's relationships and interactions with other characters (mainly Earthlings, as many of the stories were set on Earth). Also, by explaining where the Doctor came from, his planet and his people, the show had really opened up. Although Pertwee's Doctor would be Earth-bound, the mystery of where he came from was explained, albeit having its roots in the last ever Patrick Troughton story. He was a Time Lord from the planet Gallifrey, who had his appearance changed (from his second incarnation) and was exiled to Earth because he stole the TARDIS and roamed through time and space as a maverick.

Soon a fellow Time Lord called The Master would became a regular cast member, to be Professor Moriarty to the Doctor's Sherlock Holmes. Roger Delgado took on the role of The Master and the quietly spoken actor became great friends with Pertwee. With his devil's beard, Mediterranean good looks and stern eyes, Delgado was the perfect balance to Pertwee's flamboyance and became an important part of the new *Doctor Who* family, which would include Katy Manning (companion Jo Grant – from Pertwee's second series), Nicholas Courtney (the Brigadier), John Levene (Sergeant Benton), Richard Franklin (Captain Yates), Producer Barry Letts and writer Terrance Dicks.

All of this was a brave move by the BBC. They were destroying the romantic unknown past of the Doctor, which must have been a great gamble on their part; they were explaining the 'Who?' in *Doctor Who*. So would they get away with such a thing? Surely that was an important ingredient in making the show successful, to keep the audience guessing?

There were many changes imposed by Pertwee's Doctor, which back then seemed radical, but are largely taken for granted today. Nowadays, we are used to the Doctor running everywhere and using many gadgets, but it was Pertwee who really started all that off with his dashing interpretation of the title role. His was the 'James Bond' Doctor, but as Pertwee himself said, James Bond only saved the world; he was saving the universe.

Pertwee's love of character acting is sprinkled throughout his *Doctor Who* years. One memorable scene from the story 'The Green Death' has him in disguise as a Welsh milkman in order to get into a high-security establishment. This is a wonderful moment from an actor who had established himself with brilliant comic voices on radio. That said, in a scene from an earlier *Doctor Who* episode Pertwee provided a voice for a radio broadcast, but it was later re-recorded by another actor because his voice was deemed too recognisable.

'The Green Death' was significant for another reason too. It provided the first fragrance of romance between the Doctor and one of his companions, Jo Grant. Jo falls in love with a hip young Welsh scientist and decides to leave the Doctor, go up the Amazon and get married. The Doctor attends the happy couple's leaving celebrations, but is clearly upset at losing Jo, for whom he always had a soft spot. The final scene sees the Doctor sneaking out of the party and, in silhouette, driving his beloved car 'Bessie' away, in what is the greatest unrequited love scene in the show's history.

'I found my way to the bar where Jon [Pertwee] was waiting. He gave me a great big hug, which was his seal of approval to the rest of the cast, I think, like a Roman emperor giving the thumbs-up sign. Relaxed, he said, 'Now, what would you like to drink, Katy?' *Katy?* I didn't say anything – I didn't need to. A second later Jon realised his error. And burst into tears.'

Elisabeth Sladen – the Autobiography

In her autobiography, Elisabeth Sladen (companion Sarah Jane Smith) talks about onscreen chemistry. She mentions that Pertwee shared this with Katy Manning, and he would indeed enjoy working with Sladen too. But before Sladen was offered the part of Sarah Jane, she mentioned that an actress had already accepted the part, but unfortunately it didn't work out. Sladen knew that Pertwee adored Katy Manning, and indeed Manning had fond memories of working with Pertwee too.

Pertwee had really taken Manning under his wing while filming the show, so much so that the affection between them really comes across in every scene they played together on screen. Rumour has it that Pertwee was a little in love with the bubbly young woman, but the relationship was platonic. Perhaps it's this knowledge that adds a little more melancholy to the scene in which Bessie drives away and Sladen's tale of meeting Pertwee in the bar the night before her first day of location filming.

Pertwee enjoyed the more serious storylines, which complemented his interpretation of the Doctor perfectly. He loved the odd pretentious moment too, such as passing comment on a manor house wine cellar while waiting for a 'ghost' to turn up ('Day of the Daleks'). But where Pertwee really succeeded was when he was allowed to get cross at interplanetary narrow-mindedness; then he was in his element. His most serious scenes balanced his more comic ones, so much so that when Tom Baker first took over the role, some young fans found the lack of gravitas an issue.

It is interesting how most of the Doctors were passionate about the underlying messages in the scripts and how their messages could be brought home to the younger viewers amidst all the action, monsters, and the ever-building mythology of the show. A basic theme of good transcending evil has always prevailed in *Doctor Who*, and the Doctor has been a very enigmatic character as a result. To a degree we can thank William Hartnell for laying down some ground rules here, and of course Sydney Newman and Verity Lambert for perpetuating this through the early years.

Returning to Pertwee, it is no surprise that his favourite story was 'Frontier in Space' and the Draconians (creatures from the same story) his favourite foe. This story started off with epic aspirations, being part of a 12-episode 'Space War' story that took the Daleks into the kind of mega-scale story they enjoy in the new series today. Alas, the epic didn't really come off, but what fans reflect upon and enjoy today are two quality stories with a continuity thread from the end of one to the beginning of the other.

The first story said farewell to Roger Delgado's Master,

though not intentionally. Shortly after filming, Delgado went to Turkey to do some filming for his first comedy film role, the never-released *Bell of Tibet*. Unfortunately, he was killed in a car accident, through no fault of his own. When Pertwee learned of his friend's death, he was terribly upset and did all he could to try and get some compensation for Delgado's wife, Kismet. No matter how hard he tried, he couldn't do it. He was appalled by the accident and realised how much he had taken his life into his own hands by playing with so many cars, bikes and powerboats throughout his life.

The impact on the show was catastrophic as well, depriving the Doctor of what was planned to be a grand showdown with the Master, where it would be revealed what relationship they truly had with each other (the consensus of opinion being that they were brothers).

When Pertwee heard that Barry Letts and Terrance Dicks were leaving the show soon afterwards, he decided that it was perhaps time for him to leave too. The latest *Doctor Who* family had really been broken up (perhaps to start with by Katy Manning leaving, but the death of Delgado was significant). Head of Drama, Shaun Sutton, quickly stepped in to ask if Pertwee would reconsider, which he did. He agreed to do two further seasons of *Doctor Who* if the BBC would increase his salary. Pertwee was shocked when Sutton shook his hand and said, 'Thanks for everything, sorry to see you go.' There were no negotiations at all; Pertwee was out of a job. He felt hurt but was told there was no flexibility in the budget, so that was it.

Ever the professional, Pertwee shot the stories that would complete the current season with as much vigour as his earlier episodes. The next story after his resignation was 'The Dinosaur Invasion'. This story introduced the Doctor's space-age flying car 'The Whomobile', which he even drove through Piccadilly Circus one fine day, to the horror of the Metropolitan Police.

During his last season as the Doctor, Pertwee received a touching letter from a mother of a little girl who was a big fan. The mother explained that her daughter was going through a tough time and was emotionally disturbed. Pertwee wrote to the child and sent her a signed photo. The change in the girl's behaviour was amazing – she took the photo of Pertwee everywhere with her and it was comforting to her. Both mother and daughter kept in touch with Pertwee for many years to come and, when the little girl grew up and had two children of her own, Pertwee became their godfather.

Halfway through recording 'Planet of the Spiders', his last *Doctor Who* adventure, Pertwee filmed his regeneration scene. He lay still on the floor for what appeared to be an extremely long time, to be replaced by – transformed into – Tom Baker. Many of the cast and crew said that Pertwee was a different man afterwards. He didn't join in with the jokes on set, but took himself away to read and reply to his fan mail instead. Ever the professional on screen, Pertwee knew that he was at the end of his tenure as the Doctor, and was doing nothing more than preparing himself to move on. He had no idea at the time that the part would never leave him – for all the best reasons – he really thought it was the end. Like his predecessors, he didn't entirely want to go, but knew it was the right thing to do for his career.

When asked years later by Terry Wogan if he missed the Doctor, Pertwee said, 'I miss *Doctor Who* from time to time, but I enjoy Worzel too.'

And, of course, Pertwee had another enormous success following *Doctor Who*: *Worzel Gummidge*. Based on the novels by Barbara Euphan Todd, Pertwee took a country accent

The 12th Doctor -
Peter Capaldi.

Above: The First Doctor, William Hartnell (*left*), with Richard Attenborough and Harry Ross in a still from the classic 1947 film *Brighton Rock*.   © *Rex Features*

Below left: A rare signed 10x8 photo of William Hartnell from *Brighton Rock*.

Below right: One of the first – and rarest – books released to accompany the series: *Doctor Who and the Invasion from Space*.

Above left: For Hartnell, there was no escaping the role of the Doctor.

Above right: Patrick Troughton, pictured here in a 1971 episode of *The Persuaders*, replaced Hartnell in Doctor Who.

Below: Troughton in one of his numerous roles in classic horror films.

Above left: Pertwee hosted the Cluedo programme *Whodunnit?* shortly after portraying the third Doctor Who.

Above right: A poster for *Doctor Who – The Ultimate Adventure*, which was staged at the Wimbledon Theatre, London in March 1989. Jon Pertwee starred in the first half of the run and Colin Baker in the second.

Below left: Another of Petwee's much-loved characters: Worzel Gummidge.

Below right: Pertwee pictured at a London book signing shortly before his death in the mid-90s.

Above left: Tom Baker, one of the most popular Doctors ever, played the iconic role for 7 years. He is pictured here with his barbarian assistant, Leela, famously played by Louise Jameson.
© *Rex Features*

Above right: Publicity shot from 1980.
© *Rex Features*

Below: Baker returned as the Doctor for the five-part *Doctor Who* radio special, *Hornets' Nest*, in 2009.
© *Rex Features*

Above: Old friends? Baker at the *Doctor Who* Exhibition in Earl's Court, London, 2008.

© *Rex Features*

Below left: The great Laurence Olivier, who gave so many young careers a boost, including Patrick Troughton, Tom Baker and Peter Cushing, as well as being friends with Jon Pertwee and his father.

Below right: The Doctor and the Master: Tom Baker and Sir Derek Jacobi, friends from the theatre in 1970 to their association with *Doctor Who* in the Millennium.

© *The Stamp Shop*

Above: Peter Davidson was cast as the fifth incarnation of the Doctor (*left*). He has gone on to star in many of Britain's best-loved television series, including *All Creatures Great and Small* (*right*).   © *Rex Features*

Below: Pictured with some of the actresses who have played the Doctor's assistant over the years: (*from left to right*) Louise Jameson, Carole Ann Ford, Caroline John, Sarah Sutton, Elisabeth Sladen and Janet Fielding.   © *PA Photos*

Above: John Nathan-Turner, the show's longest serving producer, who cast Peter Davison, Colin Baker and Sylvester McCoy in the role of the Doctor. © *The author*

Below: The Sixth Doctor, Colin Baker, pictured with two assistants, Nicola Bryant and Janet Fielding.

© *Rex Features*

and a lot of make-up to become the eccentric scarecrow of Scatterbrook Farm and won the hearts of children all over again. Worzel Gummidge was always an acting highlight for Pertwee, indeed as a child he had loved the original stories of Worzel and the delights of the countryside and had also listened to the radio series after the war.

Worzel Gummidge was produced by Southern Television for ITV and written by Keith Waterhouse and Willis Hall. It co-starred Una Stubbs as Aunt Sally and Geoffrey Bayldon (who had also been shortlisted for Doctor Who, but was better known for his role in the hit children's TV show *Catweazle*).

The show lasted four series in its original format between 1979 and 1981, 30 episodes in total (season two cut slightly short by industrial action, as Pertwee was keen to point out during interviews).

There were many guest stars in the series, including Billy Connolly, Barbara Windsor, Bill Maynard, Joan Sims, Bernard Cribbins and Pertwee's cousin, Bill Pertwee.

There was one Christmas Special entitled *A Cup O' Tea and a Slice O' Cake*, and Pertwee and Stubbs performed a musical version of the series in 1981 at the Birmingham Repertory Theatre.

Two new series were commissioned by Television New Zealand, but only Pertwee and Stubbs agreed to fly across to film the episodes (22 in total). Pertwee didn't like the scripts very much but then again Keith Waterhouse wasn't involved.

One interesting point about these last two series was the early credited contribution from Peter Jackson (*Lord of the Rings*, *The Hobbit*) who worked on special effects, but of course this meant little at the time.

Like *Doctor Who*, *Worzel Gummidge* spawned TV tie-in paperbacks, Christmas annuals, toys, games, videos and even records, and was an enormous success, but this time no one else was associated with the role: Worzel was Pertwee and Pertwee was Worzel, and it's been that way ever since – some 30 years.

What made Worzel Gummidge so endearing? Pertwee had much to do with it. His ability to mix both extreme humour and pathos in one scene, and chaos and heart-warming love in another, reflected the personality of every child in the country. Children could identify with the character, mainly due to the brilliant scripts but also Pertwee's love of the role. Indeed Pertwee took the role to heart so much that in one famous scene he even cried real tears on cue.

Pertwee continued *The Navy Lark* through his *Doctor Who* years, and from 1972 to 1978 (i.e. just before *Worzel Gummidge* started) he hosted *Whodunnit?* with Patrick Mower. *Whodunnit?* was a celebrity quiz show not unlike *Cluedo*, where the panel would see some visual clues and a piece of film and decide who killed whom and in what capacity. However, with the word 'Who' in the title, there was the natural tie-in to the longest-running SF show. Not only that, but Mower would solve every case, which slightly spoiled things.

Before *Worzel Gummidge* and towards the end of his *Doctor Who* days, Pertwee found it possible to appear in movies a little more. His role in *Against the Desert* (1973) is a bit obscure because it was never released. However, the year after he left *Doctor Who*, he had a role alongside Peter Ustinov, Bernard Bresslaw, Helen Hayes, Derek Nimmo, Joan Sims, Roy Kinnear and Derek Guyler in Disney's movie, *One of Our Dinosaurs Is Missing*.

The film was incredibly successful, and even a little madcap by today's standards, but it is rarely seen. Pertwee played an eccentric colonel, but the plot itself is the most interesting and way-out part of the film: Lord Southmere escapes from China with a microfilm of the formula for the mysterious 'Lotus X', and is captured by Chinese spies who have been instructed to retrieve the microfilm from him. Southmere manages to escape from his assailants and hides the microfilm in the bones of a large dinosaur at the National History Museum, but he is observed doing this and the spies decide to steal the dinosaur. A chase around the English countryside ensues with much comic effect. *One of Our Dinosaurs is Missing* is a wonderful children's movie.

More films followed, including a remake of one of his favourites. *Ask a Policeman* had originally starred Will Hay, Graham Moffatt and Moore Marriott. Pertwee would work with comic duo Cannon and Ball in a more sedate version called *The Boys in Blue*. Again, great character actors worked alongside him in the movie, including Jack Douglas, Eric Sykes and Roy Kinnear. Never a patch on the original, it endures today as a light family film.

Of course, Pertwee played in some of the greatest British comedy films, the *Carry On* movies. He appeared in *Cleo* (1964), *Screaming* (1966), *Cowboy* (1966) and *Columbus* (1992); however, he thought he was being offered a part in a serious movie with the last one and was slightly deflated when he found himself in yet another *Carry On*. Although he always seemed a little embarrassed about being in the *Carry On* films in interviews – my personal opinion – he took his cameo roles extremely well in all of them, playing alongside the likes of Sid James, Kenneth Williams, Jim Dale, Harry H. Corbett, Charles Hawtrey, Joan Sims, Peter Butterworth and of course Bernard Bresslaw.

On 20 March 1994, Pertwee appeared on Noel Edmonds' Saturday-night *House Party*. He was the latest recipient of a

'Gotcha' award. A Gotcha was a spoof award given to a celebrity by Noel after placing them in some embarrassing predicament without their knowing that they were being deliberately set up and secretly filmed. Pertwee's set-up involved him taking part in a spoof radio show in which he was meant to pass comment about his favourite music. However, the wrong music was played, spoof callers – part of a live phone-in – inadvertently insulted him, and the studio started leaking water.

The endearing thing about Pertwee's Gotcha was how amiable he was throughout. When Noel turned up at the very end, Pertwee was oblivious to the fact that he had been set up, and was very pleased to see him. The whole piece – slightly shy of 10 minutes in length – is a delightful insight into Jon Pertwee, the man.

Pertwee's last TV appearance was on Cilla Black's *Surprise, Surprise*, in which he appeared in costume as the Doctor to present a small boy with a life-sized Dalek. Again, he is the endearing elder statesman, who can still perform for his audience, especially starry-eyed youngsters.

Pertwee died aged 76 in his sleep of a heart attack. He was on holiday at Timber Lake, Connecticut, with his wife, taking a break from his one-man show, *Who is Jon Pertwee?* Following instructions in his will, he was cremated with an effigy of Worzel Gummidge attached to his coffin. The story goes that when the coffin was placed in the fire the effigy of Worzel fell off – but then, Worzel never liked fire!

Pertwee managed the first great transition for *Doctor Who*, taking the programme into colour TV, giving more insight into the Doctor's own race of Time Lords and bringing in more adult content. For many people, he is the 'definitive' Doctor, embodying the lust for adventure and serious intent that was at the very heart of the show and still prevalent today in the new series, as Tom Baker, who considered Pertwee a great friend, illustrates: 'I was a great admirer of such a stylish actor. He was not only a great performer but he was so good to work with. He made everyone feel at home.' (*Jon Pertwee: The Biography* by Bernard Bale, André Deutsch, 2000.)

Baker first met Pertwee during the regeneration scene in 'Planet of the Spiders'. He mentioned that they met over the years at conventions and while doing voiceovers in various studios. Baker stated that Pertwee was a generation older than him and that probably explained why Pertwee found him a little peculiar; Baker would indeed tease him that he made more money than him through voiceovers, which apparently didn't go down too well.

Jon Pertwee remained to his dying day one of the most popular Doctor Whos. His numerous parts in radio, TV and film are largely overlooked today, with the probable exception of TV's Worzel Gummidge. He embraced *Doctor Who*, even after leaving the programme, loving conventions, responding to fan mail and thoroughly enjoying his comeback in 'The Five Doctors'.

In November 1982, Pertwee summed up his interpretation of the Doctor against the backdrop of his whole career quite succinctly: 'The impact it made on my career was immense. I saw the Doctor as an interplanetary crusader and it was this dashing Pied Piper image that appealed to me. I could spread my cloak, take the Earth under my wing and say, "It's all right now, I'll deal with this."'

CHAPTER FIVE

TOM
BAKER

'I was working on a building site, broke, and with no prospect of work when I was offered the part of the Doctor. It was just the most extraordinary thing…'

Tom Baker

WHEN TOM BAKER shook his curly hair, flashed those bright white teeth and opened those big staring eyes, a new Doctor was born.

Well, not quite. It took at least Baker's first story, 'Robot', for him to win over the faithful, i.e. for the fans to get used to this new eccentric character. Like Jon Pertwee before him, Baker embedded a little humour into the scariest moments and, like William Hartnell, he ensured that fans never saw him – the actor Tom Baker – doing anything as human as smoking or drinking. He was almost angelic in that respect. He instinctively knew the importance and power of the role – the Pied Piper's enigmatic characteristics so crucial to the Doctor's make-up (where did he come from? where did he go to? what was his motive? how did he come to be the creature he was? why did he not do human things? and what magic power did he possess in that long multi-coloured – pied – scarf?).

There was a natural fun about Tom Baker and this fitted nicely into his interpretation of the Doctor. But who was Tom Baker? Where did he come from?

Thomas Stewart Baker was born in Scotland Road, Liverpool, on 20 January 1934 to a Jewish father (John Stewart Baker) and a Catholic mother (Mary Jane).

Being in the Navy, Baker's father was hardly home, but he did instil his Jewish values into his son, while his mother brought him up as a staunch working-class Catholic. No wonder then that he left school at 15 to become a monk and live a monastic life for six years.

Baker said in an interesting video-only documentary, *Just Who on Earth is Tom Baker?*, that fantasy was very much part of the atmosphere of the house he grew up in; fantasy in a religious sense. From about the age of five he was made very aware of the omnipresence of God: no matter what he did or where he was, God was watching him, and he found this very inhibiting. But it still didn't stop him from becoming, as he describes it, a 'professional liar'. Every Wednesday morning he would go to Confession and every Wednesday morning, he would come up with a pack of lies that took him through the process. He later highlighted that as a major influence on him becoming a professional actor, citing many good actors are professional liars by trade.

Baker was a liar because he had to create a sin he had committed at an age when he had no sin to admit, but this didn't turn him away from religion; he embraced it. He joined a monastery because it was something heroic, something that could take him away from the numbing boredom of working-class life in Liverpool. But it wasn't to last: he would leave and National Service soon followed.

Baker served in the Royal Army Medical Corps between 1955 and 1957. Some say it was here that he got the acting bug, but he believes that the acting spirit was there back in the confessional of his youth.

In the early 1960s, he fell in love and married Anna Wheatcroft. The marriage lasted five years and produced two sons. He would later lose contact with his first family, but acting soon became his main passion and he took many small roles as animals (or *parts* of animals, such as the back of a cow). Baker's success was not overnight.

Most of his work in the late 1960s was on stage, but he did secure roles in two episodes of BBC's *Dixon of Dock Green* and a film version of *The Winter's Tale*, which seems to have faded into obscurity, or maybe mediocrity.

In 1971, bored with playing parts of animals on stage – to Laurence Olivier's amusement – Baker turned down the opportunity of a tour of America, believing that he could get better parts in the UK while everyone was abroad. Indeed, the opportunity soon arose, playing alongside Laurence Olivier, Joan Plowright, Derek Jacobi and Jeremy Brett in *The Merchant of Venice*. Baker was desperate for a speaking role and found the only part open to him was that of the Prince of Morocco. Unfortunately, the director wanted a dwarf to play the part, but an undaunted Baker strode in to the audition and said, 'Sorry about the height, I was brought up a Roman Catholic.' And suddenly the Prince of Morocco was a taller man.

Baker has fond memories of working with such great actors as Olivier and Brett. He admitted in his autobiography *Who on Earth is Tom Baker?* (HarperCollins, 1997) that they made him more extravagant as an actor. Olivier persuaded him to take risks in *The Merchant of Venice* and developed a bit of a soft spot for Baker, later telling him that his eyes were perfect for the stage, that they could penetrate the back rows of any theatre. In *The Musical Murders of the 1940s* (Greenwich Theatre), nearly 15 years later, it was obvious when he was on stage during darker moments; when cast in shadows, there was only one actor in the company who towered over everybody else, and that was Tom. His height, teeth, hair and eyes gave him much character on both stage and screen and he really came to public prominence in 1974 when he became Doctor Who.

Elizabethan plays have been a staple in Baker's career. 'A marvellous Elizabethan play' (Baker's words) is *A Woman Killed with Kindness*, in which he starred alongside Derek Jacobi after *The Merchant of Venice*. But it was Olivier who suggested Baker for his first film role, as Grigori Rasputin in *Nicholas and Alexandra*. Olivier took a part himself, but it was Baker who stole the film. His performance begins humble but sinister. The eyes say it all, exposing a chilling depth behind a calm exterior. But then he becomes more passionate and angry. 'I spent two years in a monastery and then I walked home again,' he states in the movie, and one cannot fail to spot the connection with Baker's own life. Indeed, his intensity and conviction of beliefs clearly come from a deep understanding of religion. The role of Rasputin was perfect for Baker, and Olivier was absolutely right to suggest him for the part.

This powerful role led to Baker being nominated for two Golden Globe Awards, one for Best Actor in a Supporting Role and another for Best Newcomer.

So, after sacrificing a trip to America, Baker had created an opportunity to play alongside some of the cream of British acting, with plaudits too.

It is interesting, but not necessarily surprising, that Laurence Olivier had a hand in two Doctors' fledgling acting careers, Patrick Troughton and Tom Baker, as well as being a good friend of Jon Pertwee. Olivier was always good at spotting young talent and getting the best out of everyone, and one can see a very positive move in the right direction when he gets involved with Troughton and Baker (and also Peter Cushing – another Doctor Who – as we will later examine).

Baker's next key role in cinema came in 1973: *The Golden Voyage of Sinbad*. He played Prince Koura, a black-hearted wizard who attempts to thwart Sinbad in his quest. 'Every voyage is a new flavour,' Sinbad says, and *The Golden Voyage* is one of the most memorable adventures in *Sinbad* film history. Although the plot is basic, the movie is a classic piece of fantasy. Lavish locations, sets and costumes provide a magnificent backdrop to Ray Harryhausen's wonderful stop-motion animation.

Caroline Munro is the beautiful love interest alongside John Phillip Law's excellent Sinbad who, through their heroic deeds, make Baker appear even more black-hearted and sinister.

With the use of vintage trick photography, Baker's serious, intelligent performance enhances the impact of the overall movie. 'He who is patient *obtains*,' he tells his sea captain as they pursue Sinbad towards the fabled Fountain of Destiny.

Prince Koura is one of Baker's most sinister roles, and one that endures and captivates children to this very day. In fact, being only a year before he took over the part of Doctor Who, *The Golden Voyage of Sinbad* captured the magic of Baker's acting skills that were quintessential to his interpretation of the Doctor. He never overplays or camps the role, keeping enough back to be plausible.

One scene is of particular note, which nicely blends Baker's acting skills with Ray Harryhausen's stop-motion creations: it is where Koura employs his sorcery in making a ship's female figurehead come to life to do battle with Sinbad and his crew. Throughout the suspenseful scene, Baker uses mime and his own physical props (large piercing blue eyes) to show his character's inner turmoil. When the scene is over, Baker's character has physically aged; such is the price of summoning the demons of darkness.

In another scene, Baker plays with a tiny winged demon that he has brought to life with drops of his own blood. Using mime and the playful way one talks to a pet budgerigar, he makes the incredible seem plausible. Perhaps all of this helped convince the BBC that Baker could be the next Doctor.

The Golden Voyage of Sinbad is a film that encapsulates the dying embers of the out-and-out swashbuckling movie, which the first Douglas Fairbanks Jnr movie in the series so blatantly was. With an early appearance from Martin Shaw (from TV show *The Professionals*), *The Golden Voyage of Sinbad* is an important milestone in fantasy cinema, as it highlights the best of model-making monster techniques.

If the part of Prince Koura prepared Baker for the role of the Doctor, it certainly wasn't the most important factor. That fell to his inclusion in an earlier BBC Play of the Month entitled *The Millionairess* (1972). Baker worked alongside Maggie Smith in this production, blacking up for the part of an Egyptian dignitary (not unlike the Arab Prince Koura, perhaps). But it was the director Bill Slater who would become crucial to Baker's future success.

One Sunday evening, a couple of years after *The Millionairess*, Baker wrote to Slater and asked him if there were any regular parts going at the BBC for an actor like him. He posted his letter that Monday morning, the same day as Slater, soon-to-be head of series, had a meeting with *Doctor Who* producer Barry Letts.

Baker didn't know that Jon Pertwee had quit the show and that other actors were being considered for the part (in his autobiography, Baker mentions that Graham Crowden and Richard Hearn had at least been considered).

The casting meeting between Letts and Slater drew no conclusions, so they decided to reconvene later that week and, because of Slater's workload, that meant Wednesday.

On Tuesday, Baker's letter arrived at the BBC. After several late meetings, Slater went home with Baker's letter and read it before getting into bed with his wife, Mary Webster. It was 11.15pm. Having discussed his day with his wife over supper, it was suggested that perhaps Baker would be a good choice as the Doctor. Mary suggested that Slater call Baker, despite the time. He did. Baker answered. Slater asked if he could get to TV Centre for a 6.30pm meeting the following day. Baker said he could. That was it. Everybody went to bed.

The following morning Slater had his casting meeting with Barry Letts. He suggested Baker for the role and told Letts that the actor was coming in at 6.30pm.

When Baker walked in – on time – Slater took him to head of drama Shaun Sutton's office, where Slater, Sutton and Letts talked things over with the nervous actor. After nearly an hour, Slater said, 'We've got an idea, you see, Tom. Do you think you could come back and see us tomorrow?'

Baker agreed. The following day, he went to work on a building site and then went home and got changed, had something to eat and turned up slightly late at the BBC, but soon found himself back in the same office with the same people. There was a brief silence before he was asked, 'Would you like to be the new Doctor Who?'

Baker had been so depressed and cash-strapped that he had written a begging letter to Slater, who was now offering him the biggest role in television. All he could do was nod, and nod again, and again. And then he was asked to keep his joyous news a secret for ten days, which somehow – fearing the part might be taken away from him – he managed to do, until, of course, he walked into the BBC Headquarters at Wood Lane with a friend as chaperone to attend a press conference announcing him as the new Doctor. Everybody wanted to touch him or shake his hand and he just rode the crest of the wave, knowing that he could now pack in the job as general labourer. Instead, he was suddenly a renegade Time Lord.

None of his predecessors had enjoyed so much celebrity on taking the part, but the show had built up a huge fan base over the years, and the announcement of a new Doctor was big news.

While celebrating in the West End with his friend, Baker picked up the second edition of the *Evening Standard* and saw his face plastered over it. 'Oh bliss. Fuck off anonymity, hello everybody,' he declared in his autobiography, and the relief was that joyous.

Although Baker had played some great roles and acted with some of the most important professionals of the 20th century, work had dried up, he had become depressed, he had taken a labouring job and then – *Doctor Who*.

'And this whirligig of activity went on for all my time as Doctor Who. Suddenly the crowd who'd found me boring found me fascinating…'

Who on Earth is Tom Baker? An Autobiography
Tom Baker

Although Baker would make the part of the Doctor his own, with his jelly babies and floppy hat, his multi-coloured over-long scarf came about by accident. James Acheson, the costume designer, had provided too much wool to the knitter, Begonia Pope, and she used it all up. It was Baker's wish to use the final ridiculously long scarf, which is now the most iconic piece of *Doctor Who* costume in the show's history. If you refer to somebody's scarf as 'a Doctor Who scarf', you quickly get the impression of something colourful and a little too long.

When Baker finally took to the controls of the TARDIS, he found that Barry Letts – who had effectively given him the job – had wanted to leave the show with Jon Pertwee. Letts did, in fact, stay for a while, directing the Baker story 'The Androids Invasion'. Elisabeth Sladen, who played Pertwee's feisty journalist companion, Sarah Jane Smith, was still very much part of the show, which must have pleased Baker (it wasn't a mass exodus after Pertwee's exit). Also, for his first season, Ian Marter became the Doctor's companion and the three actors developed a great rapport, both on and off camera.

Baker even went to Italy to write a *Doctor Who* feature film script with Marter and film director James Hill. It was provisionally titled 'Doctor Who Meets Scratchman' or 'Doctor Who and the Big Game'. The premise was that the Doctor would come face-to-face with Scratchman (an old name used to describe the Devil). Unfortunately the film didn't come off due to lack of funding, which was a shame as the end scene had the Doctor fighting the Devil on a huge pinball machine, with the holes being portals to different dimensions.

On joining the TV series, Baker was keen to meet the show's iconic monsters. Sladen had reminisced about her time with Pertwee and the Daleks, and it was soon known that the infamous pepper pots were due to make a comeback in a six-part story called 'Genesis of the Daleks'. This was to become one of the greatest stories in the show's history, introducing the Daleks' creator Davros, so brilliantly played by Michael Wisher, who had cropped up in small parts during Jon Pertwee's Doctor (such as the excellent 'Ambassadors of Death') and provided the voice of the Daleks too.

Baker soon became very absorbed in the character of the Doctor. The fan mail poured in and he met children walking down the street who all accepted him as their friend; and this seemed fine by their parents too. The Doctor was no stranger to children, he was a man to be trusted and Baker became firmly aware of this, almost to the same extent as William Hartnell.

Baker felt as though the role placed him in a protective bubble, away from suspicion, accusation and scorn: if you are the Doctor, you are a friend to all children. And, as a certain Marvel movie so aptly states, 'With great power comes great responsibility.' Baker became another man. He refused to be seen doing anything remotely human-like when children were around – he wouldn't eat or drink, smoke, anything like that. He would only sign autographs 'The Doctor', knowing that the children saw the character, not the actor and so, like his predecessors, he turned up at various events in costume and played to the younger audiences who poured nothing but total love upon him in return.

For one story – 'The Deadly Assassin' – Baker was concerned about the violence of a fight scene and, on his way back from a *Doctor Who* exhibition in Blackpool, he found himself watching the show with a young family in Preston. He simply knocked on the door and asked, 'Do you watch *Doctor Who* here?' Whereupon he was let in with a big smile to sit and watch the show with the family, which included two young lads who were simply amazed that the Doctor could be in two places at once – on screen and in their front room. 'What a wonderful hour or so that was,' Baker reminisced years later. Once again, proof of the unique power of the Doctor.

Baker freely admits that, by the time the story 'The Stones of Blood' was screened (four years into his career as the Doctor), he was arguing with the director. At that stage, he was by far the most important person in the show, as all of his peers had left, and he was keenly aware of the responsibility he had to the younger audience.

Hartnell had quit *Doctor Who* because he felt the children's element was going out of the show. This was managing the expectations of millions of children, while deeply understanding the expectations of the fans. Baker, like Hartnell, took that to heart and battled his corner against any change in focus.

And so we can see a very important connection, something shared by the actors who play the Doctor. And it's there from the original series to the new series: the Doctor has a responsibility to the youngest of viewers, those who live and breathe the show; who believe he is real. In some cases, children know the names of the Doctor Who actors, but that doesn't mean that the character isn't real to them as well. In their young minds, the Doctor lives his adventures on screen, a separate person to the actor associated with him. Almost instinctively, the actor playing the lead role knows this, but the changing *Doctor Who* family always find themselves on a learning curve, proving that being part of the show is being part of a show like no other.

'Doctor Who was innocent. He was uncorrupted. And that was a fantasy of mine… to recapture the innocence of childhood. And so I did think he [the Doctor] was rather God-like. And it really got to me. I was invited to the bedsides of dying children and parents were very grateful, and I was humbled by what I saw. And therefore I wouldn't tolerate any adult or disappointing behaviour [on set].'

Just Who on Earth is Tom Baker?
Tom Baker

Certain scenes needed tempering and Baker was able to do that instinctively. Indeed Patrick Troughton always used humour during scary scenes so that the children didn't get too frightened; Pertwee would ham it up during action scenes, or when a particularly menacing monster came wandering in, Baker could defuse tension by offering a jelly baby, and so it goes on. In fact, in one famous scene, Baker's Doctor was to hold a knife to the throat of an attacking savage, but Baker thought this too excessive and so decided to hold up a killer jelly baby instead. Because the scene made the director laugh, it stayed in the final episode.

After Elisabeth Sladen left the programme, Baker explained that he didn't want a companion in the show at all. He managed to get his own way for one story, 'The Deadly Assassin' – a story that was quite dark and violent (it was this very story that prompted Baker to drop in on the family in Preston that memorable night: he thought one particular scene was too explicit).

All too soon the Doctor had a new companion: Louise Jameson, who played the savage in animal skins, Leela.

In the press Baker described her as 'beautiful', but, to begin with, their acting relationship was not terribly smooth. Many years later, Baker admitted during a documentary interview that perhaps he was a little aloof because he wanted something he couldn't have – a romance with his companion – something that would come later with Lalla Ward.

A friendship has grown between Baker and Jameson since their *Doctor Who* years, but it doesn't disguise the fact that the pressure of the role became immense at times. Each story was different, a combination of different location shooting and studio work. A good example of this was the story 'The Talons of Weng-Chiang', where Baker swapped his iconic scarf and hat for a Victorian Sherlock Holmes-influenced costume, and location shooting took place in Northampton and the chilly River Thames.

'The Talons of Weng-Chiang' is an incredibly atmospheric story with swirling fog and sinister characters. It also allowed the beautiful Louise Jameson to dress up in Victorian clothes, shedding – for the only time – the animal skins that turned on most of the watching adult male population.

We have observed that, as a very young man, Baker married Anna Wheatcroft, but the marriage fell apart after five years and the actor-to-be lost touch with his young family. Towards the end of his reign as the Doctor, Baker married his co-star Lalla Ward on 13 December 1980 at Chelsea Register Office – a quiet affair and very cold weather by all accounts. The marriage lasted two years and the break-up of this second marriage is something Baker still feels guilty about and, although Ward has now happily remarried, the two never see each other – not even at *Doctor Who* signings or exhibitions.

Baker's third marriage was successful, though, in the respect that it has so far lasted approximately 25 years. Sue Jerrard worked on the production team of *Doctor Who* and Baker became friends with her before he married Lalla Ward. After the marriage failed, he found solace in the company of Jerrard.

By the time Baker called it a day with the Time Lord (seven years in total, making him the longest-serving Doctor Who to date), he was a household name. Although a respected actor beforehand, he was now so much in the public eye that he was instantly recognisable, but not necessarily typecast, as time would prove. Perhaps playing other parts at the same time as starring in *Doctor Who* helped this situation somewhat.

The Book Tower was a long-running children's programme made for the ITV regions (ATV). In accompanying a narrated story with dramatic scenes and music, it aimed to encourage more children to read. And the programme became extremely successful.

The eerie theme tune was based upon Bach's Toccata and Fugue in D Minor, which was arranged by no less a figure than Andrew Lloyd Webber. Over the years the programme was presented by different people including one-time *Carry On* star and former Ice Warrior, Bernard Bresslaw. But it was Tom Baker who started the ball rolling on 3 January 1979, presenting the first 22 episodes. Baker brought his own charm to the part, along with the mystery of the Doctor.

Of course, with Baker as the ever-popular Doctor, children who probably wouldn't normally watch such a programme were tuning in and fulfilling the show's original remit of introducing them to books. *The Book Tower* would endure for over 10 years, with 11 seasons, before finishing on 30 May 1989.

Although he admitted once on a BBC news item that he had 'no immediate plans' after quitting *Doctor Who*, Baker went on to say that he had done the best he could with the part and that it was now someone else's turn.

His resignation from *Doctor Who* came two weeks after the announcement that robot dog K9 would be leaving. Asked if the show could go on without them both, Baker said, 'It will just go on and on and on.' He commented that *Doctor Who* had changed his whole life and created some of the fondest memories in his acting career. But one cannot help but marvel at another mass exodus: just as Barry Letts and Terrance Dicks had wanted out after Pertwee quit, suddenly Baker and co-star/wife Lalla Ward would leave together, with the only continuity being three companions introduced into the series at the end of the season and, of course, producer John Nathan-Turner. That said, Baker's final scene will go down as one of the most visually stunning – and slightly poignant – regeneration scenes ever; then again, the whole of his final story ('Logopolis') was extremely good, not unlike Jon Pertwee's swansong in that respect ('The Planet of the Spiders').

Tom Baker returned to the theatre, first at the Mermaid playing Long John Silver in *Treasure Island* and then in *Feasting with Panthers* at the Chichester Festival. Although perfectly suited to the theatre, he came back to the BBC to play Sherlock Holmes in the four-part adaption of Sir Arthur Conan Doyle's *The Hound of the Baskervilles* (1982), thanks to Barry Letts who produced it; then he was back in the theatre for *Hedda Gabler* and the 1982–83 RSC production of *Educating Rita*.

In 1984 Baker starred alongside comedy legend Eric Morecambe in *The Passionate Pilgrim*. It is a significant work as it was the last screen appearance of the brilliant Morecambe. The short film is delightful. Although shot in colour it is played out like a silent movie with John Le Mesurier (best known as Sergeant Wilson in *Dad's Army*, who also died shortly afterwards) providing the narration.

The film was shot on location at Hever Castle and tells the story of a love-sick Lord (Baker) trying to enter a castle to win the love of another Lord's (Morecambe) lady (played by Madeline Smith). Baker's wide-eyed antics are not dissimilar to those of Peter Seller's Clouseau, trying to enter a castle in *The Pink Panther Strikes Again*. An amusing little film, it was shown in cinemas with the James Bond film *Octopussy*. It was due to be expanded, with Beryl Reid playing Morecambe's mum, but sadly the master comic's untimely death prevented this. However, the film is available on DVD and well worth watching.

A couple of odd one-offs occurred in 1986 for Baker, when he took small roles in *Roland Rat: The Series* and *The Kenny Everett Television Show*. However, there was one role of note: his part in *Blackadder II*. Although only in one episode of the hit comedy, entitled 'Potato' (Season 2, episode 3), his part is memorable. Baker plays the legless (physically and alcoholically) Captain 'Redbeard' Rum, a mad old sea captain who pledges his heart to Nursie before venturing off with Blackadder, Baldrick and Percy to sail around the Cape of Good Hope.

Rum is a drunken charlatan who cannot even find the coast of France, let alone the Cape of Good Hope! He does, however, manage to run Blackadder and his trusty side-kicks aground on a volcanic island with cannibal natives. Rum's fate is to be put into the cooking pot, not dissimilar to that of Captain Cook and his crew after discovering Australia. Indeed, Blackadder brings a boomerang back from his travels for Queenie (played so brilliantly by Miranda Richardson), implying that he got to Australia many years before Cook.

Baker took on the role of Captain Rum with red-faced relish. His blend of humour and eccentricity fitted the series perfectly, which was in complete contrast to the old sea captain he played some time before in the horror *Frankenstein – The True Story*.

Years later, Baker mentioned his role in *Blackadder* while narrating an episode of *Little Britain*: 'With nothing on telly but repeats of *Doctor Who*, *Medics* and that episode of *Blackadder II* I'm in, Lou and his friend Andy choose a video tape.'

Baker's cameo in *Blackadder* is proof that even the smallest roles can be indelible on the minds of a watching audience. In one respect, Captain Rum was the quintessential Tom Baker role: loud, eccentric – slightly hammed – and enormous fun.

Some would think that after *Doctor Who* Baker's career started to wind down, but series' such as the revised *Randall and Hopkirk (Deceased)*, with Vic Reeves and Bob Mortimer, showed his continued value as an actor.

Baker played Wyvern against Reeves (Hopkirk) and Mortimer (Randall), with Emilia Fox (Jeannie). The show ran for two seasons (2000 and 2001) and had many small tie-ins to the original 1960s TV show of the same name (including, in episode one, Spooner Drive, in praise of former scriptwriter Dennis Spooner, who also penned some early episodes of *Doctor Who* and *The Avengers*).

Baker had noticeably aged since audiences had last seen him on screen, but he was wonderfully over-the-top and cherished his friendship with the comic duo immensely.

Comedy was the watchword for him around this time, and he soon became the regular narrator for Matt Lucas and David Walliams' TV series, *Little Britain*.

With his own quirky sense of humour, it shouldn't come as a surprise that Baker got on well with characters such as Reeves and Mortimer, Lucas and Walliams, and indeed the whole of the *Blackadder* cast too. There's something of the alternative comedian in Baker. Even *Private Eye*'s Ian Hislop was a little surprised by his comments when he appeared on the BBC's *Have I Got News For You*, again something he took to quite naturally.

Another quality acting role came along shortly after

Blackadder, in the acclaimed TV drama *The Life and Loves of a She-Devil*, but that's where the serious stuff seemed to dry up for Baker.

He returned to a semi-regular role in *Monarch of the Glen* for several series, even managing to once again grace the cover of the *Radio Times*, but having assumed the dubious mantle of the oldest living Doctor Who, he decided to slow down a little.

And what about big movie roles? Baker was offered a part in Peter Jackson's *Lord of the Rings* trilogy, but not the role of Gandalf, as some people suggest. However, when he learned that he would have to spend time away in New Zealand, he turned down the opportunity, something the jobbing actor on a building site would never have dreamt of doing years before.

'… I'll give you a tip. The tip is well meant so don't get all upset. It's just between you and me. It's a tip that spells power, like the tip of a wand, if you know what I mean.'

The Boy Who Kicked Pigs
Tom Baker

As well as his autobiography, Baker wrote a macabre children's novel entitled *The Boy Who Kicked Pigs* (Faber and Faber, 1999). Filled with dark humour, the story is about Robert Caligari, an evil 13-year-old who kicks pigs because of an unfortunate experience with a bacon sandwich. The slim tome is illustrated by David Roberts, and in size and style of illustration is reminiscent of Eric Morecambe's children's classic, *The Reluctant Vampire*.

Nowadays, threatening retirement, Baker is still known as the voice of *Little Britain* and regarded as a British institution. If he was perhaps a little 'precious' while playing the Doctor, then he must be forgiven, for he *was* the man children would instantly trust, and follow without question – the Pied Piper of children's TV. He was – and still is to many – the quintessential Doctor Who and a man who encapsulates the individualism and eccentricity that only the very best British character actors can muster. Louise Jameson summed up the Tom Baker she knew in the series as opposed to the one she knows today:

> Things weren't too brilliant between us to begin with. He was unsympathetic to writers and actors, but he lived, ate and slept the programme. He took it very seriously. He felt a great responsibility towards the children who watched the show and never smoked around them or anything like that.

The tension – the pressure to deliver – is highlighted clearly. She went on to discuss Baker's overall presence:

> You know when he's in the room even when he's not showing off, and that voice of his is beautiful. He's mellowed over the years, and I'm grateful for the friendship we share nowadays. We go out and have lunch, or take a walk in the countryside. He's a great friend and a great actor and, if anyone thought he was awkward, I ask them to meet up with him today.

For Baker there was redemption. He has apologised to actors, and even the odd director over the years, for his behaviour while on set as the Doctor. He explained that he felt under terrible pressure to always do the right thing, and he makes many comparisons with Ebenezer Scrooge and the Dickens classic *A Christmas Carol*, noting that it is a great story of redemption. Looking back at *Doctor Who* he says that 'it was all such fun'; but it was serious fun.

Baker visited many sick children in hospital. He recalls one particular visit where children had been maimed by drunk drivers and other road accidents. He saw crushed limbs and kids at death's door (he had been asked to go there as Doctor Who). I think it is very clear where Baker's responsibilities lay during his time in the TARDIS and the reason why he was such a perfectionist. Like Pertwee before him, he was asked to approach children in extreme physical and mental anguish, and pretend for them as they coped with the terrible pain of reality.

He responded beautifully to his responsibilities. The role gave such emotional fulfilment to Tom Baker, just like his predecessors.

'Scrooge was better than his word. He did it all, and infinitely more; and to Tiny Tim, who did NOT die, he was a second father. He became as good a friend, as good a master, and as good a man, as the old city knew, or any other good old city, town, or borough, in the good old world. Some people laughed to see the alteration in him, but he let them laugh, and little heeded them; for he was wise enough to know that nothing ever happened on this globe, for good, at which some people did not have their fill of laughter in the outset...'

A Christmas Carol
Charles Dickens

CHAPTER SIX

PETER DAVISON

'I was Peter Davison's wife in *Molly* [1995]. And Peter is great fun. Not quite serious enough!'

Louise Jameson

PETER DAVISON WAS born Peter Moffett on Friday, 13 April 1951 in Streatham, London, son of Sheila and Claude, an electrical engineer from British Guyana.

Any time the youngster got into trouble his mother would always blame the fact that he was born on Friday 13th, but there were no behaviour problems with the young Peter, who appears to have been as sincere as many of the character roles he has since taken on.

Davison moved from Streatham with his parents and sisters (Barbara, Pamela and Shirley) to Knaphill in Surrey where he was educated at Maphill School and, later, Winston Churchill Secondary Modern School. It is noted that he failed to excel in anything until he wrote a speech on philosophy – which he knew little about – and won a Rotary Club public-speaking contest normally won by grammar school children.

Peter's headteacher then recommended that he should go on to stage school.

Throughout his youth Davison adored music, even making up a song about his retiring headteacher at secondary school. He would later get a band together, which he enjoyed, but they failed to make the big time; he did, however, make it onto *Top of the Pops*. While at drama school Davison made a blink-and-you-miss-it appearance in the audience, head-banging to a Dave Clarke number.

Davison didn't just go to drama school and concentrate on an acting career; he had to support himself along the way, taking a string of jobs that included roles such as a mortuary assistant and clerk for the Inland Revenue. In a very endearing moment during his *This is Your Life* programme (discussed later), his former colleagues from the Inland Revenue came on stage to congratulate him on his successful acting career, reminding him that they bought him a pen when he left the office so he could sign autographs when he was famous. He was keen to point out that he still owned the pen, delighted to see his former colleagues.

Davison started his drama career as a member of the amateur dramatics society The Byfleet Players, and managed to secure a place at the Central School of Speech and Drama. In 1972, he acquired his first job at the Nottingham Playhouse. His work wasn't all acting, which was just as well as he suffered from first-night nerves and forgot his lines. He soon found his feet though, and went on to spend a year with the Edinburgh Young Lyceum Company, working up to a series of Shakespearean productions including *Two Gentlemen of Verona*, *Hamlet* and *A Midsummer Night's Dream*. It was in the latter that he met American actress Sandra Dickinson. The two were lovers in the play and soon real-life imitated

Shakespearean romance, but there was much work to do before the two were married.

Davison first changed his name from Moffett so he wasn't confused with Peter Moffatt, the actor and director with whom he would later work, and moved back to England after his flirtation with Shakespearean theatre.

In 1975 he appeared in an episode of the Thames TV children's SF series *The Tomorrow People*, entitled 'A Man for Emily' – the spoilt Emily character being played by Sandra Dickinson, no less.

When one looks back at this role today, one cannot be anything other than deeply shocked. With big white curly wigs and screechy Southern American accents, the episode can best be described as horrific. The couple were married on 26 December 1978.

Davison and Dickinson would play opposite each other again – albeit briefly – in Douglas Adams's *The Hitchhiker's Guide to the Galaxy* (1981), with Peter playing a heavily made-up Dish of the Day that tries to sell bits of itself to his clients (Dickinson and others) at The Restaurant at the End of the Universe. When John Nathan-Turner called Davison to ask him if he would become the new Doctor Who after Tom Baker announced his departure, Dickinson was very supportive of her husband, even to the point of requesting that she be one of his companions. Clearly their relationship was a strong one to begin with.

Davison and Dickinson composed the theme song to the children's programme *Button Moon* (eight series, 1980–88) and had a daughter, Georgia Moffett, who was born in 1984 and would grow up to be the Doctor's daughter (not just Peter Davison's, but Doctor Who himself, during David Tennant's stint as the Time Lord). But it was not all plain sailing for

Moffett, as her parents split when she was eight and then divorced in 1994. Moffett would have a child at 16 and did not appear to have another serious relationship until she fell in love with, and married, David Tennant after appearing in 'The Doctor's Daughter'.

Davison's first major TV role was as Tom Holland in the 13-episode London Weekend Television *Love for Lydia* (written by H. E. Bates), starring Jeremy Irons. Davison featured in 7 of the 13 episodes amid a young cast, which also included Mel Martin (Lydia) and Christopher Blake. This was followed by the highly successful *All Creatures Great and Small* (1978–90), a programme that focused on the lives and work of a group of vets in North Yorkshire, based on the books by James Herriot (played by Christopher Timothy in the series). The programme also made a household name of Robert Hardy who played the pompous Siegfried Farnon; his younger and much-maligned brother Tristan was played by Davison.

Davison brought his natural sensitivity to the role, which made him endearing, but it is difficult to see a future Doctor Who in him at that time.

All Creatures Great and Small was the turning point in Davison's career, not only in giving him a regular job, but also allowing him to develop a character in a popular BBC show. This was enhanced when Timothy had a car accident and was restricted from doing location work for a while. Davison's character was given these scenes instead, which added to his experience as an actor. *All Creatures Great and Small* is considered a classic British TV series, but perhaps Davison's next role was slightly less memorable.

The trials and tribulations of brotherly love in *Sink or Swim* (1980–82) was part of Davison's flirtation with sitcom. *Sink or Swim* was a very popular situation comedy in its day but is almost forgotten today. Davison played the lead role, Brian Webber, a man desperately trying to make his way in the world while living in a flat above a petrol station. His opinionated girlfriend (Sara Corper) is a vegetarian who is concerned about ecology, which causes some frustrations for Webber but then his northern brother Steve (Robert Glenister) turns up and adds greater problems. Suddenly Davison's character is the sensible older brother to a troublesome but endearing younger sibling.

The title music to the programme was The Hollies' 'He Ain't Heavy, He's My Brother', which summed up the programme well. *Sink or Swim* lasted three years, with the latter two years overlapping Davison's time as Doctor Who, which caused some shooting problems. The programme was written by Alex Shearer, who later went on to write *The Two of Us* starring Nicholas Lyndhurst.

The 1980s had many easy-viewing situation comedies, including another one starring Davison, this time for the ITV regions, *Holding the Fort* (1980–82). The programme was written by Laurence Marks and Maurice Gran (*The New Statesman*, *Birds of a Feather*). Three series were broadcast (20 episodes) over three years.

The basic situation for this comedy was role reversal. Davison was a passive house-husband looking after the baby, while his wife (Patricia Hodge) was a captain in the Woman's Royal Army Corps. Matthew Kelly completed the regular cast and was there to encourage Davison's character's love of football, drinking and pacifism, leading to utter chaos. It was mild stuff, but that was 1980s sitcom. Gone were the gritty situation comedies of the 1970s, such as the brilliant *Steptoe and Son* and *Porridge*. Even cop dramas grew more sedate: after *Callum* and *The Sweeney* came *The Professionals* and *The*

Bill, lightweight in comparison. And dare I suggest that football players had a little less blood and muck on their shins in the 1980s than the previous decade, which has led to the overprotected (and overpaid) cry babies on the field of play in the new millennium? Artistically, the 1980s were a passive response to the high-cholesterol 1970s.

'A man is the sum of his memories, a Time Lord even more so.'

The 5th Doctor
'The Five Doctors'

It was during *All Creatures Great and Small* that John Nathan-Turner, then just a production unit manager, recognised Davison's talent and noted him as someone to watch. When Tom Baker decided to leave *Doctor Who*, Nathan-Turner (now producer) decided upon Davison as a good choice for the next Doctor.

Davison stated that his intention was to make the Doctor 'vulnerable and perhaps flawed, and that he would sometimes make things worse before he made them better.' His research for the role included looking at videos of all his predecessors and hoping something would stick. He didn't consciously take things from the previous Doctors but instead tried to pick up on a moral thread, which he could then make his own.

Davison was only 29 when he became Doctor Who, the youngest person ever to play the Time Lord at that time (Matt Smith would later land the role at the tender age of 26) but his maturity shone through, quickly endearing him to both young and old viewers alike.

Unlike many of his predecessors, Davison didn't have much say in his costume. In one interview he claimed that he chose the cricket sweater as he was asked to pick something that denoted action and eccentricity, but the Edwardian coat, striped trousers and plimsolls were not his. His question mark shirt was the suggestion of John Nathan-Turner, who introduced it into Tom Baker's costume during his last season.

Davison sometimes wore a Panama hat and had a stick of celery pinned to his lapel. The presence of the celery was explained in his very last story, 'The Caves of Androzani'. It was meant to turn purple if the Doctor was subjected to certain gases that he was allergic to. The idea was then to eat the celery, 'if nothing else I'm sure it's good for my teeth,' he would state.

Like the very first regeneration (Hartnell to Troughton), the first Peter Davison story followed the last story in the preceding Doctor's tenure in the role, without a break between seasons. The story was called 'Castrovalva' and was frustrating for many fans, as the Doctor was hardly himself after his regeneration and it was difficult to see how the new actor would interpret the role. However, the story did build into something quite interesting with the presence of the new Master (Anthony Ainley), who was so prevalent in Tom Baker's last two stories.

The next story, 'Four to Doomsday', fared well, as did the period piece 'Black Orchid', where the Doctor actually got to play cricket. 'Kinda' was next – an average story with a brilliant and highly scary new foe, The Mara – but it was the ingeniously plotted Great Fire of London story, 'The Visitation', which really won the hearts and minds of the seasoned Doctor Who fan, a story hailed as a classic to this very day. However, it was not voted the best story of that season by the Doctor Who Monthly faithful; that accolade went to 'Earthshock', which included the return of the infamous Cybermen. The story had a memorable and shocking climax – the death of Adric, one of the Doctor's young and faithful companions. The end credits were silent as a consequence, showing Adric's broken badge for mathematic excellence discarded on the floor. It was a powerful ending and one that has remained in older fans' minds ever since.

Lighter moments in 'Earthshock' included the presence of a spaceship captain (Briggs), played by British character actress Beryl Reid. Reid later said that she thoroughly enjoyed her time fighting the Cybermen, and this clearly comes across in the story.

Unfortunately, the last story in Davison's first season was the most disappointing. 'Time Flight' brought the Master back again, but failed to make any lasting impression on fans and is all but forgotten today as a consequence.

After 'Castrovalva', Davison was accepted as the new Doctor Who. His sincerity and youthful get-up-and-go was instantly appealing and struck the right balance against his evil adversary the Master, who cropped up throughout Davison's era; even in the 20th anniversary story, 'The Five Doctors'.

During his first year as the Doctor, Davison was the subject of the classic TV surprise show *This is Your Life*. Hosted by Eamonn Andrews, the popular presenter pounced on a celebrity when they were least expecting it with a big red book that tracked their life story. They were then whisked off to a TV studio, played embarrassing clips – in Peter's case *The Tomorrow People* – and subjected to embarrassing anecdotes from former stars, co-stars, and teachers from their impressive life.

Sandra Dickinson blazed the trail and was joined on stage by her two brothers (both of whom were Peter's best men at their wedding), who wore *Doctor Who* sweaters. But the highlight was really the cast of *All Creatures Great and Small*, led by

Robert Hardy. It was clear that they were all great friends. Carol Drinkwater (Helen Herriot) brought on some balloons and all of them gently ribbed the star actor. The real-life Tristan Farnon (Brian Sinclair) also came on stage, and stated that he was flattered that someone as tall and handsome as Peter Davison would play him on screen.

Another highlight in the show was when members of the cast of *Love For Lydia* came on stage. Mel Martin recounted a screen kiss with Peter's shy character in the series that caused him to really blush on screen. Indeed it was one of his original drama school teachers who commented on Davison's natural sensitivity, which had been there from the start and really made his many characters believable – but the reality was onscreen for all to see as the *Love For Lydia* clip was shown.

Davison's second season as Doctor Who saw the return of the Brigadier (Jon Pertwee years), played once again by Nicholas Courtney, and the Black Guardian (Tom Baker years), once more played with menace by veteran actor Valentine Dyall. Again there were strong stories throughout, most notably 'Arc of Infinity' (shot in Amsterdam and featuring future Doctor Who Colin Baker as a Time Lord guard), which marked the return of the all-powerful Omega (Pertwee years). However, it was 'Mawdryn Undead' (featuring the Brigadier) and 'Terminus' (the last story for companion Nyssa) that were the most noteworthy stories. It seemed all stops were pulled out to celebrate 20 years of the longest-running Science Fiction show of all time.

Unfortunately, one story that didn't work out so well was 'Snakedance'. It marked the return of the Mara from 'Kinda', but both 'Snakedance' and 'Kinda' were two of the most uninteresting scripts of the Davison era – a great shame, as the Mara were incredibly scary in both stories. What probably didn't help matters with regard to 'Snakedance' was the laughable giant snake that appeared at the climax of the story and was meant to symbolise the Mara's pure evil, when in actual fact it only highlighted the beginning of the programme's diminishing special effects budget. On that basis, it is unfortunate that the Mara haven't made a more memorable comeback in *Doctor Who* since the Millennium return. Who knows what reaction they would get with a half-decent script and special effects nowadays...

The 20th anniversary season concluded with 'The Five Doctors'. The feature-length story was broadcast on Friday, 25 November 1983 (two days after the actual anniversary) as part of Terry Wogan's *Children in Need* charity evening, with a short introduction vignette by Wogan, joined by Peter Davison. For only the second time in the show's history (the first being the Peter Davison story 'Castrovalva') was there a teaser before the opening title sequence. This took the form of a clip of William Hartnell saying his farewell to Susan at the end of 'The Dalek Invasion of Earth', the first ever companion to leave the programme.

It was a wonderful tribute to the first Doctor and perfectly set the scene for the celebration story that followed, which included Carole Ann Ford taking on the role of Susan again; this time as an adult (18 years had passed since her last appearance in the programme). She was splendid, as was Jon Pertwee, who didn't look much older than the day he left the show (already his hair had turned completely white during his reign as the Doctor). It was a treat to see Patrick Troughton as the Doctor in full colour, something that would happen again during the Colin Baker years, in Baker's finest story, 'The Two Doctors'.

'The Five Doctors' showcased all the other Doctor Who actors, Richard Hurndall standing in for the late William Hartnell, and footage from the unreleased 'Shada' compensating for the absence of Tom Baker.

Although the story 'The Visitation' saw the end of the sonic screwdriver as the Doctor's magic get-out-of-trouble tool, Pertwee's Doctor used it in 'The Five Doctors', marking its last appearance in the classic series. As the present incumbent, Peter Davison took the lead and was the catalyst for bringing all the Doctors together for a satisfying end scene. Although technically the star of the programme, Davison provided an almost humble, laid-back style alongside Troughton and Pertwee, which is both endearing and important to the balance of the end scene featuring the four Doctors.

It was a great shame that Tom Baker was not present at the celebration, a decision he claims to regret to this day, and the lack of his commanding presence after seven years in the TARDIS does affect the overall impact of the story. Originally Baker was intended to work alongside Sarah Jane (Elisabeth Sladen) but that pleasure fell to Jon Pertwee, who described Baker's Doctor when reunited with Sarah Jane as 'all teeth and curls'. The special effects held up well through-out the story and, with extra scenes added and additional CGI images on DVD, the 20th Anniversary Special still entertains audiences to this day.

While Davison's stories seldom over-reached the modest BBC budget, towards the end of his tenure there was more criticism of poor special effects. For example, 'Warriors of the Deep' was a great comeback story for the Sea Devils and their cousins, the Silurians, but the impact was lessened by a giant monster that looked like the winning prize in a *Blue Peter* papier mâché competition. The story had great sets (by Tony Burroughs) and a half-decent script, but the poorness of the monsters started *Doctor Who* on a downward spiral that finished with the show's demise during Sylvester McCoy's reign.

Davison would only play the Doctor for three years. This is commonly thought to be Patrick Troughton's fault, who advised the young actor to quit because of typecasting. Both Davison and Troughton did some TV interviews together around the time of 'The Five Doctors' and Troughton did mention typecasting then, so this perception does have some credibility.

It appears that Davison thought that three years was long enough and sentimental headlines said things like 'Dishy Doctor Peter says Ta-Ta to TARDIS!' This headline was the work of *The Sun*, who called Davison a 'heart-throb'. It also stated that producer John Nathan-Turner wanted the next Doctor to be vastly different, perhaps older. *The Sun* took this to heart and had Clarkson draw a cartoon of the next Doctor as an old eccentric based on politician Michael Foot, making him look like William Hartnell.

Nathan-Turner hadn't ruled out the possibility of a woman taking over the controls of the TARDIS, but maybe this was simply the producer being provocative – apparently he also considered getting rid of the TARDIS.

As culture changes the idea of a female Doctor appears more tempting to the production staff of *Doctor Who*. In the new series, River Song is a popular character and at one stage she could have been mistaken for a future Doctor coming backwards in time. Surely any anniversary story featuring more than one Doctor doesn't necessarily have to include the Doctors we've already had so far, it could include a future one? Now wouldn't that be interesting, and the perfect way to trail a female lead...?

'It is very easy for an actor to stay in a safe role, but there's a danger of being typecast.'

Peter Davison

The Sun, Friday, 29 July 1983, on announcing his departure from Doctor Who

Despite being the first young Doctor, Davison created a credible character, deeply moral and sincere, which endeared him to many children. He wasn't an aloof eccentric like his predecessor, but a breath of fresh air, invigorating the role and programme with a strong supporting cast of companions. In fact Davison was the 'companion's Doctor', caring and nurturing them like a some-times exasperated schoolteacher. His lack of flirtation with the more attractive female companions - such as Nyssa (Sarah Sutton) and Peri (Nicola Bryant) - made him appear more like a protective older brother than potential suitor; the Doctor's first kiss with a companion was still years away (Paul McGann's watershed movie version).

Davison probably had the last decent season of the Classic Series, which culminated with the regeneration story, 'The Caves of Androzani'. Not since the Tom Baker story, 'The Deadly Assassin', did we witness the Doctor being blown up, covered in muck and taken to the brink of his physical capabilities. Not only that, but this time he loses the battle and actually dies – well, regenerates.

'The Caves of Androzani' was a pastiche of *Phantom of the Opera* and, during David Tennant's era, was voted the best story ever by *Doctor Who Magazine* readers. It also won a poll on satellite TV and remains one of the most accomplished stories of all time. Written by *Doctor Who* veteran scriptwriter Robert Holmes, it was funny, sad, scary and ultimately heroic, with the Doctor staggering back to the TARDIS with his dying companion in his arms, giving her the elixir that would save her life. Sadly there was not enough left for him, and he died.

It seems that Peter Davison quit while he was still ahead of the game and judging by what happened directly afterwards, i.e. the deteriorating quality of special effects, monsters and scripts, his decision to leave was probably the right one, albeit for different reasons.

Despite rarely being considered the very best Doctor Who, Davison simultaneously fails to get much criticism and was a worthy follow-up to Tom Baker, who was quite a tough act to follow. Perhaps in that respect history later repeated itself, with the young Matt Smith following the extremely popular David Tennant. But then again, Tennant – if we are to believe the *Children in Need* Special 'Time Crash' – had the utmost respect for Peter Davison's Doctor, replicating him with his 'dodgy trainers' and 'make me look more intelligent' glasses, something Davison donned while studying a fascinating piece of gadgetry.

'Time Crash' was the first TV comeback for Davison's Doctor. First broadcast on 16 November 2007, the fifth Doctor meeting the tenth had a bit of the Troughton/Pertwee confrontation about it. Tennant poked fun at the stick of celery on Davison's lapel, 'Look at me, I'm wearing a vegetable', but then settled down to declare at the end that, 'I loved being you' and 'You were my Doctor'.

Although not a major return for Davison's Doctor, he did enjoy the opportunity of once more putting on his cricket sweater and, of course his stick of celery, saying afterwards, 'It is an honour for me to be able to make the connection between the fifth and the tenth Doctor.'

It's a shame a Doctors' reunion story, such as 'The Three

Doctors' or 'The Five Doctors', wasn't forthcoming in the lean years between the 25th and 50th anniversaries. But with more Doctors to accommodate, it was a logistical exercise the BBC were not prepared to take on. Indeed, ideas for a 30th anniversary story were scrapped, even though a script, 'The Dark Dimension', had already been written. Instead, there was a *Children in Need* sketch entitled 'Dimensions in Time' in which Davison's only contribution was blowing up a Cyberman. Not a very satisfying celebration for the actor or the fans.

Doctor Who never affected Davison's career in an adverse way. It has fallen into place beside the rest of his CV. In the summer of 1984 Davison went on tour in *Barefoot in the Park* with his then pregnant wife. For him the show was a very physical one, especially when he had to do two shows a day, as he had to do a lot of running up and down stairs.

Directly after completing his last season as the Time Lord, Davison started work on the show *Anna of the Five Towns*, which was set in the Midlands. Work for this was completed at the beginning of May 1985. He appeared in four episodes of the period piece, in which he played Henry Mynors, a self-made businessman who becomes Anna's romantic interest. Actress Kate Webster (who played Agnes in the programme) recalled Davison: 'I particularly remember that Peter Davison's last episode of *Doctor Who* was screened during the time we were on location and he sat and watched it with us. It was so strange to sit alongside him, he seemed so modest about it all.'

After handing over the keys to the TARDIS to Colin Baker, Davison and his successor appeared on *The Russell Harty Show*. He made it clear that it was time to move on and that he had no regrets. Forward thinking, he was keen to take on more diverse roles, which indeed he did.

In 1986 Davison played Dr Stephen Daker in *A Very Peculiar Practice*, written by Andrew Davies. He seems to be the master of the two/three-year stint at TV dramas, such as *Campion* (1989–90), one of his most popular and critically acclaimed shows. This programme showcased his ability to act the straightest of roles, as well as the more comic ones. *Campion* was adapted from the Albert Campion novels written by Margery Allingham and told the story of a credible detective with very human failings. Two seasons of the show were made by the BBC, starring Davison alongside Brian Glover (as his manservant, Magersfontein Lugg) and Andrew Burt (policeman friend Stanislaus Oates). Interestingly, Davison sang the theme tune to the first season but had it replaced with an instrumental version for the second season. Sixteen episodes were recorded in total. A great shame that Davison wasn't allowed to continue the show and build it into something quite legendary, as it had much potential.

Davison hasn't done too much work in cinema. However, in 1994, he did appear alongside Sean Bean, David Thewlis and Jim Carter in *Black Beauty*. He played the good-natured Squire Gordon, with his delicate wife and beautiful children. Very much the English gentleman, Davison fits this gentle family film perfectly. Although horse-anoraks see some technical flaws in the movie – as any military enthusiast would with a war film – many younger viewers loved the film, with the horse narration throughout echoing the sentiment of the original novel. It was a nicely made film, and a good solid part for Davison; and one does wonder why he didn't get more credible film roles afterwards. There was of course the TV movie *Molly* in 1995, where Davison played alongside Louise Jameson (Leela) as husband and wife, but film roles have been few and far between for the actor.

Lots of bread and butter roles followed, including a part in the sixth *Jonathan Creek* adventure - where he plays the son-in-law of a horror writer shot dead on Halloween - but one of his most popular roles was as Dangerous Davies in *The Last Detective* (2003–07).

Based on the books by Leslie Thomas, *The Last Detective* succeeded where other detective/police series have notoriously failed (for example *Anna Lee* and, to a degree, *Rebus*). Most of this is due to Peter Davison being a very good TV counterpart to the original novels' main character. His natural sincerity meant he could play the role quite lightly and still portray a character with much depth. '[I'm] more a detective than a policeman,' he says, but do people – especially his colleagues – go along with that? Battered by life, Davies walks around with seemingly the world's problems on his shoulders. His melancholy is deeply felt and the show is a memorable and complex one as a consequence.

The Last Detective was not a violent show, which instantly made it, and the main character, endearing. Comedian Sean Hughes's inclusion enhanced the more uncharacteristic laid-back style. The programme is a well-worn shoe, comfortable and reliable, so fantastic TV fodder and a show instantly missed after its demise by its faithful audience – perhaps a lost gem rather than a TV classic.

In 2009 Davison appeared in TV comedy series *Miranda*. He played the part of Mr Clayton, a sexually active French teacher in 'Teacher'. The episode is a little bit of an eye-opener for Davison fans as he scoops up Miranda's pint-sized friend Stevie to rush her to the bedroom. Towards the end he memorably asks, 'Has anyone seen my pants?' and it is clear he's not wearing anything below the camera line!

Later the same year he played Denis Thatcher in *The Queen*.

In this demanding role he quickly showed his versatility. Previously, he hadn't played someone so much in the public eye (apart from Doctor Who!) and he pulled it off well.

Perhaps his most accomplished role since *Doctor Who* has been as Henry Sharpe, the Director of the Crown Prosecution Service in *Law & Order* (2011–13). Davison played in 17 episodes in 2011 and 2013 alongside Freema Agyeman, who appeared as one of David Tennant's companions during his *Doctor Who* years.

Henry Sharpe is a very experienced boss who always takes the broader look when assessing the character of a criminal. He digs into the psychology of the criminal mind and this, coupled with his laid-back style, makes him a well-respected director of the CPS; perhaps the character emanates the seasoned actor that Peter Davison is today. Never boastful or outspoken, he is characteristic of a host of actors who have had their ups and downs while making their way in life. Like Patrick Troughton before him, Davison has been content to work hard at a huge range of roles for television. Yes, he was once Doctor Who, but he was also once Tristan Farnon, Dangerous Davies and a whole list of others characters too, such as Henry Sharpe.

Davison made it very clear – as did Patrick Troughton, Jon Pertwee and Tom Baker before him – that there was life after *Doctor Who*. Every one of them seemed to worry about the typecasting that appeared to plague William Hartnell throughout the remainder of his career, but this was completely unfounded. Hartnell was unwell when he quit playing the Doctor and it was this rather than typecasting that ended his career.

In 2010 Davison starred alongside Jill Halfpenny in the musical *Legally Blonde* at the Savoy Theatre. One could argue that he wasn't suited to this role – especially if people only knew him for his TV parts – but with theatrical credits as prestigious as West End shows *Spamalot* and *Chicago*, one can appreciate that there is more to this actor than initially meets the eye.

Of course with his daughter now associated with *Doctor Who*, it seems logical that the show will continue to be a major part of Davison's life. In recent interviews he claims that Sunday dinner at the Davison household is a *Doctor Who* fan's dream, with two Doctors and the Doctor's daughter around the table and, of course, grandchildren. In that respect, Davison enjoys the most tight-knit *Doctor Who* family; long may it reign.

'I do feel I have managed to distance myself from the character [the Doctor] now – but if I got to the age of 65 and somebody offered it to me then, I'd do it till I dropped. It's a great form of retirement – you just keep going until you keel over!'

Peter Davison in conversation with journalists, 1998

CHAPTER SEVEN

COLIN BAKER

'If you're ever on *Who Wants to be a Millionaire*, make sure Colin Baker is your "Phone a Friend". He has a brain the size of a planet!'

Louise Jameson, in conversation with the author

'I LOVE WORKING with Colin,' Louise Jameson said. 'We do one-off plays together. We toured in a whodunit called *Corpse* with Mark McGann. We also did *Bedroom Farce* [2007] together.

'Back in the seventies, we played darts as a team (post Leela) in Oxford. And Colin had to get a double and a bull to win the game, and I foolishly said to him, "If you get it, I'll sleep with you." And he got it. I shot out of the pub and he chased me.

'Fast forward 30 years and we are in rehearsals for *Bedroom Farce*, and the stage is basically three bedrooms, and Colin said to me, "At last I've got you into bed!"'

Anyone who meets or works with actor Colin Baker adores the man. Intelligent, humorous and adorable with children (I speak as one who has introduced him to two) one quickly forms the opinion that he got the least out of being Doctor

Who, which is a shame as he had been a fan since the very first episode. With declining budgets, unimpressive storylines – for the most part – and the Sword of Damocles hanging over the head of the show, Baker's Doctor had a rocky ride; but he shouldn't be passed off as a lesser Doctor or lesser actor because of the quality of his stories. When I started this project, I thought that there was less to document about Colin Baker than most of the other Doctors, but I was very wrong: his list of credits is extremely long, with much theatre and TV work (see Part Two).

Baker is one of the most experienced jobbing actors in the country and has been working hard since the 1960s. He is one of those actors seemingly taken for granted, but those in the acting profession have great admiration for him, as do his many *Doctor Who* fans.

Colin Baker was born at the Royal Waterloo Lying-in Hospital, London (behind Waterloo station), during an air raid on 8 June 1943. He escaped death while still a baby when a piece of shrapnel embedded itself into the side of his cot. Perhaps the luck of the Irish came in here (his mother being of Irish ancestry). His family moved to Rochdale when he was aged two and he was later educated in Manchester.

His first acting role came about by accident. The mother of a fellow pupil was a casting director and needed a child who could speak good French. Baker soon found himself playing a young French boy in a series called *My Wife's Sister* (1954), starring Eleanor Summerfield, Martin Wyldeck and Helen Christie.

After this flirtation with acting, Baker went on to attend St Bede's College, Manchester. He would appear in the college productions of Gilbert and Sullivan operettas *Yeoman of the Guard* and *Iolanthe* (the latter in the lead role). After seeing an amateur production of the *King and I*, he joined the North Manchester Amateur Dramatic Society.

Although he loved the theatre, he spent five years training to become a solicitor because his father told him that a steady career was better than being an actor. He became an articled clerk but never took his final exam. His father had a stroke from which he never really recovered and Baker, deciding that life was too short to pursue a career he didn't enjoy, auditioned for the London Academy of Music and Dramatic Art (aged 23). He was accepted and studied alongside David Suchet (who would later play the definitive TV Poirot).

Baker left the Academy and spent a short time with a touring company. He then spent three years in repertory theatre. He found the touring company hard work but told Terry Wogan in 1986 that he didn't get much work in rep, making irregular appearances.

Baker made his first appearance on TV in *Roads to Freedom* (1970), which was based on the novels by Jean-Paul Sartre. He played the part of a rapist, and sinister roles have followed him ever since; including the portrayal of some of Doctor Who's blacker moods.

A long list of TV and theatre credits followed, including another period drama based on Tolstoy's *War and Peace*. It was this role that led to his first notable part as Paul Merroney in the TV series *The Brothers*. The producer of *The Brothers* had been the production assistant on *War and Peace* and, knowing that Baker had studied to become a lawyer, thought he'd make him a fictional one.

Paul Merroney was only meant to be a small role, but Baker soon made it one of the leads.

The Brothers was compulsive Sunday-night viewing for many people in the mid-seventies (1974–76), the show clocking up 46 episodes in its two-year life. As a consequence Baker was voted the most hated man in television, something he was very proud of until someone knocked his tooth out with a vicious thump to the mouth! It seemed some people believed the act of being evil on screen meant that you were like that in real life.

The Brothers was a great success and made Baker a household name. Merroney was a very cold, pompous, ruthless individual, an accountant who took hold of a family business and turned it into his own personal plaything to the cost of everyone around him. The public loved to hate him.

In 2002 the cast of *The Brothers* was reunited. It had been over 25 years since some of them had last met. Kate O'Mara (the evil Rani in *Doctor Who*) reminisced that the actors in the show cared an awful lot about each other and used to socialise quite a bit, going out for meals and other social events. It was a very tight-knit team. Like Louise Jameson, the cast talked about the humour and pleasant times they had had with Baker, despite the pressures – and punches! – which came with the show's success.

After *The Brothers*, Baker found it difficult to get work. In fact, *The Brothers* more than *Doctor Who* proved to be his typecasting nightmare. Indeed, when it was announced that he was taking on the Doctor, one newspaper commented, 'Actor Colin Baker, once a J R Ewing-type television screen villain, is to take on the role of one of the small screen's most loved heroes, Doctor Who!'

This was lost on many youngsters who had never heard of *The Brothers*, let alone seen it; but they soon knew of it: 'Colin, 40 – who rocketed to fame as villainous Paul Merroney – replaces Peter Davison, whose final appearance as the Time Lord will be seen in January.'

Typecasting never seemed to bother Colin Baker, not even when he took on the role of the Doctor. He explained on

Breakfast (BBC's morning magazine programme) that he didn't worry about such things and that he'd rather enjoy the experience of being Doctor Who. He never thought he would land the part even though he secretly wanted it after Tom Baker left the series in 1981.

Baker had previously played a role in a hit BBC science fiction programme (ignoring his short appearance in *Doctor Who*). In 1980 he appeared in Terry Nation's *Blakes 7*. The story was called 'The City at the Edge of the World'. Coincidentally, Baker played alongside *Doctor Who* legend Valentine Dyall in the episode. It was about the opening of a sinister vault and Baker was the obligatory bad guy, Baybon the Butcher (a sort of leather-clad Paul Merroney), exploiting the cowardly Villa (one of the regular cast) to open the vault for him.

Baker said of the role, 'Baybon was the second most dangerous man in the galaxy, which caused him great annoyance because he wanted to be the most dangerous. It was a great part, an over-the-top role.'

It's an important fact that Baker has played many 'bad guy' roles, the Doctor being a bit of an exception; perhaps it's his training to be a solicitor that gave him his sinister side – it certainly landed him the part of Merroney.

In 1983, Baker took his first role in *Doctor Who*. He played the part of Commander Maxil in the Peter Davison story 'Arc of Infinity'. At first he was reluctant to consider the part – he wanted to be the Doctor – but he was told that he probably would never be considered so he might as well take a bit part.

It was during the filming of 'Arc of Infinity' that Baker impressed and entertained both cast and crew of the show so much that director Ron Jones would suggest him to producer John Nathan-Turner as the next Doctor when Peter Davison quit.

Just as had happened with the role of Paul Merroney, it was the production staff of the current programme remembering Baker and awarding him the part – but, possibly because he had now played a small role in *Doctor Who*, he thought he had scuppered his chances of landing the lead. As he recalled: 'When I read in the papers that Peter was leaving,' Baker said in 1983, 'and that they were looking for an older Doctor, or even possibly a woman, the idea didn't even cross my mind. So, when John Nathan-Turner rang and asked me to go and see him, I genuinely didn't have a clue what it was about.' Baker explained that he thought he would be asked to open a fête rather than be offered the lead role in *Doctor Who*.

When Baker found out the real reason for the call he was absolutely delighted, as he explained: 'It offers the most tremendous scope to an actor, and it really is in a category of its own. *Hamlet* talked about plays being "tragical-comical-historical-pastoral" – well, if you add "scientifical", you've got *Doctor Who*.'

Like every other actor who had taken the lead role since Jon Pertwee, Baker had to keep quiet about landing the part until the official announcement, which caused more than the odd difficult situation, as he explained in the *Doctor Who 20th Anniversary Radio Times Special*: 'We were having dinner with friends one night and this chap said, "My wife wants to write to the BBC and tell them you'd be perfect as the next Doctor Who. Do you think she should?" I had to keep my face very straight as I said, "No, I shouldn't think so. Knowing the BBC, they've probably already made up their minds."'

Baker got off to a very shaky start as the Doctor with the story 'The Twin Dilemma', one of the very worst *Doctor Who* stories ever in terms of plot and costume design. The fact that his Doctor was a little erratic at the time – having just regenerated – turned the story, or what there was of it, into a bit of a circus and didn't bode well for the future.

Baker had a clear idea of how his Doctor should behave. He was familiar with the show and explained that he 'should have wit with a sharp edge to it, even a touch of anger underneath'. He watched some of the earlier Doctors on video, as Peter Davison had done, and 'realised that they do have their hard moments, when they show an apparent lack of concern for the people around them...'

Baker's interpretation of the Doctor was pretty faithful to this description, but there is a school of thought that believes that he played the role too brashly and his costume (an idea of John Nathan-Turner's) was the least impressive of all the Doctors with its multicoloured (pied) patchwork quilt look. He himself called it 'The coat of many colours' (*The One Show*, 2013) and explained that the remit for the costume was 'something totally tasteless'.

When Baker took over the role, the show was on the rack. It was getting tired and too expensive, and that's probably a major factor in the slippery slope of the original series from then on. It wasn't Baker's fault. In fact, when he sat up at the end of 'The Caves of Androzani', having just regenerated, his pomposity – or is it his self-assurance? – was quite inspiring and interesting. Then again, 'Androzani' was a classic story written by one of the most distinguished *Doctor Who* writers ever – Robert Holmes.

One of Baker's very best stories was also penned by Holmes. Working alongside his 'American' sidekick Peri and Patrick Troughton and Frazer Hines, he took on several different alien species to save the world yet again in 'The Two Doctors'. The story is an absolutely classic *Doctor Who* adventure, with quality location filming (in Spain) and some old enemies (the Sontarans) coming back for a big dust-up.

What was also refreshing was the introduction of the alien chef – Shockeye – who had a taste for human flesh and abducted both Jamie and Peri in order to slaughter and eat them (being thwarted on both occasions). With Jacqueline Pearce (a former *Blake's 7* regular) as yet another evil influence, the classic adventure restored some dignity to the show and really allowed the actors to prove what they could do with a half-decent script and location.

It was a great shame that the BBC had no faith in the track record of the show at that time, because 'The Two Doctors' showed that there was still life in the old boy yet.

Baker had some good times working on *Doctor Who*. With 'The Two Doctors', he was delighted to work alongside Patrick Troughton. It was quickly established that Baker was as keen to play practical jokes as his predecessor. In one scene, the Doctor (Baker) had to wake Peri up by splashing water on her face. The scene went well but Nicola Bryant was asked to do it again whereupon Baker threw a whole jug of water over her. She had a few moments of spluttering before she realised that she had been set up.

Bryant got on very well with Baker, but it was hard to keep a straight face on location in Spain, as Baker confessed: 'There was an awful lot of joking between Pat [Troughton] and I on that Spanish shoot... we were both a bit badly behaved and took the piss out of each other unmercifully. I used to call him a "geriatric" and he got his own back by calling me "fatty".'

It wasn't long before John Nathan-Turner called Baker to tell him that the show was to be suspended. Baker called the news 'pretty devastating' but his wife was about to have a baby and he realised that a job was just a job at the end of the day; the BBC had effectively given him paternity leave. Having lost a baby before to cot death, he recognised that keeping perspective was the most important thing - but worse still was just around the corner.

Doctor Who came to a bitter end for Colin Baker on Thursday, 19 December 1986, when the BBC announced that he was to leave the show. He did not shoot a regeneration story to make way for the next Doctor. John Nathan-Turner tried to persuade him to shoot the scene but he wasn't having any of it; he felt let down and consequently didn't want to know.

The *Sun* newspaper would write some heavy headlines blasting BBC controller Michael Grade, who allegedly didn't want Baker to continue in the role, but life went on and Baker's career moved on to other things.

In 1986, Baker told Terry Wogan that if the budget of *Doctor Who* was inflated to cope with bigger science-fiction shows, it would probably lose its appeal. Hindsight would prove him wrong here, but I would suggest that if somebody at the BBC had perhaps cared a little more then it may have fared better during the latter years of the Classic Series. One could also suggest that despite being a likeable man and the right man at the right time, producer John Nathan-Turner had spent too long in control of the show and may have got a little stale. That said, he had done so much good for the series over the years it is hard to deal out any harsh criticism of the man; he weathered many storms within the BBC and kept the show going as long as he could.

The BBC considered many ways of reshaping *Doctor Who*, from threatening to get rid of the TARDIS to putting a woman in the lead role. In the end, they sacked a perfectly good Doctor because they couldn't work out what they wanted to do and therefore only half-heartedly supported the programme.

Doctor Who was never far away from Colin Baker's life. The stage play, *Doctor Who – the Ultimate Adventure*, opened on 23 March 1989. Initially, Jon Pertwee played the Doctor, but he didn't take it on tour; instead, it was left to Baker, who made a good fist of it after the dust had settled on his TV departure. Although there were problems with some visual effects and certain shows did not sell out, the young fans – the target market – loved it. Daleks and Cybermen terrorised the Doctor but there was enough time towards the end of the play for him to reminisce – in a very sentimental way – about the companions he had left behind and the ones who had gone on to better things. This of course included Sarah Jane Smith (Elisabeth Sladen), who, when she did return in the show in the new millennium, explained to the Doctor that she had waited for him to come back and that she thought he was dead. So rose-tinted glasses from the Doctor there then!

Colin Baker and Sylvester McCoy had the worst of *Doctor Who* because of the problems they experienced with budgets and scripts, but their careers as actors gave them the ability to rise above this and show some Dunkirk spirit in their interpretations of the Time Lord.

In 1991 Baker played in one of his most favourite productions, *Privates on Parade*. He played several roles, including Marlene Dietrich, Vera Lynn and Noël Coward. A video of one of the performances still exists, showing how brilliantly Baker played Dietrich.

In 2004, Baker played alongside Louise Jameson and Peter Duncan in *Corpse*, another favourite role. He loves the stage and once asked Patrick Troughton why he hadn't been in theatre for a while, Troughton responding: 'All that shouting in the evening? It's not for me.'

Baker will state in interviews that he much prefers TV roles to theatre, but he's played in many theatrical productions, some earning quite high praise. For example, in 2005 he played alongside Richard Bremner's lead in *Dracula*, playing the part of Professor Van Helsing. The production was a fine interpretation of Bram Stoker's original story, with spooky sets and quality acting. It enjoyed very good reviews.

Although Baker was free from *Doctor Who* at this time, he was still billed as 'starring former Doctor Who Colin Baker', something that didn't bother him too much. Just like the production's producer, he was keen to see a packed theatre and if the Doctor could draw more people in, so be it. This was in contrast to William Hartnell, who wanted to shake off the Doctor image when he re-joined the theatre after leaving the programme. But *Doctor Who* wasn't an albatross around Colin Baker's neck – he was totally at ease with it.

Like Pertwee before him – someone he holds in high esteem – Baker loves pantomime and is a Christmas regular, happy to dress up as a female and wow his audiences, young and old alike. In recent years, he has attended various *Doctor Who* conventions and signing sessions, where he meets up with old friends such as Nicola Bryant and Louise Jameson, and has taken part in celebrity reality shows too.

His first reality jaunt was on the show *Celebrity Come Dine With Me*. His Christmas Celebrity Special (26 December 2011) included Linda Nolan, Nick Bateman, Bianca Gascoigne and Danny Young. Pantomime was the theme throughout, so Baker was very much at home there. His dinner party was the last of the week, and his episode really complements the calmness and great fun of the man. Before he did any cooking he had to go out and buy his ingredients; he was served by a Cyberman in his local butcher's, which he took well.

Baker cooked Charming Salmon Mousse for starters, followed by One Little Pig's Shoulder of Pork à La Karina with Pommes de Terre Purée, and Berry Chocolatey Christmas Pots for dessert. No one seemed to complain about the food but there was a moment of drama when Nick Bateman seemed like he might walk out of the house after feeling a little too heavily criticised by his fellow guests. It was Baker who brought things to a happy conclusion, getting everybody to ride a fake rodeo bull and being flung onto crash-mats. The laughter and camaraderie meant that Bateman scored Baker a 10 out of 10 card, meaning that he had won the whole week and making him very emotional - although he downplayed the whole thing by saying, 'Frankly I'm overwhelmed. Now I can relax and let my wife do the cooking again!'

Celebrity Come Dine with Me proved a triumph for Baker, even though it was laced with *Doctor Who* references. One pink disaster of a dessert earlier in the week was compared to a *Doctor Who* monster – a Vervoid - and when we returned to Baker in the kitchen during the last episode of the week, the link commentator stated, 'Back at the TARDIS, Colin cracks on with dessert.'

But if *Celebrity Come Dine with Me* ended up being a pleasant experience for Baker, his next venture into reality TV wasn't. In 2012 he agreed to be on Ant and Dec's *I'm a Celebrity... Get Me Out Of Here!*

'I'm Colin Baker and I played Doctor Who in the 1980s,'

from Colin Baker's opening profile in
I'm a Celebrity... Get Me Out Of Here!

For a man in his sixties *I'm a Celebrity...* seemed a bit of a bad choice of adventure to embark upon, especially as Baker confessed to having a fear of heights and spiders. But from the moment his celebrity-filled rowing boat sank at the beginning of the show, he met each jungle challenge with enthusiasm and good humour, endearing himself to his celebrity comrades.

Baker was the fourth of the 12 to leave the show, after a particularly unpleasant bushtucker trial called 'The Panic Rooms', where he had to put his hand in various boxes to retrieve stars (and therefore food for the whole camp) and get bitten, stung or nipped by an assortment of jungle creatures in the process.

He had told everyone that his family was 'ridiculously delighted' that he was on the show, but he said it felt 'remarkably good' to leave. Of course his exit was full of *Doctor Who*-related quotes: 'Colin has been exterminated from the jungle', and 'Buenas TARDIS'. But this didn't faze him one bit, for he had achieved what he had set out to do: lose over a stone in weight.

Baker explained that he adored his food – he could happily give up drink – but one of the worst things about appearing on the show would be the lack of a fridge to raid at night. However, yet again, he fared well on reality TV.

'Children should be scared daily in my opinion.'
Colin Baker from Robert's *Full English Breakfast*

To this day, Baker continues to hold *Doctor Who* close to his heart. He classes 'The Empty Child'/'The Doctor Dances' (Christopher Eccleston story) as one of the best two-episode stories ever, alongside 'the one with angels' ('Blink', David Tennant), explaining, 'They've got it right now.' He also stated that *Doctor Who* was like a Roald Dahl novel and that Dahl got the scare factor 'dead right', when thrilling a child with his fantasy. He is of course, completely right, also stating that when Mary Whitehouse decided to criticise the programme (most fiercely between 1975-77), it had also 'got it right'. And most sensible people are in total agreement with him.

For a while Colin Baker left TV acting to re-join the theatre, and also to become a school governor (and look after the education of his four daughters), but, as time has shown, *Doctor Who* is still a happy part of his life. He continues to embrace the show, even presenting Chris Evans with his multicoloured coat to wear during the last broadcast from BBC Broadcasting House on 22 March 2013 (which also included Sylvester McCoy).

Baker doesn't cling senselessly to *Doctor Who*; he has gathered many other strings to his bow since leaving the series. He is a book reviewer, a lyricist and the writer of a children's musical, *Scrooge – A Ghost of a Chance* (written with composer Sheila Wilson and performed in over 100 schools). He has also contributed regular weekly columns to the *Bucks Free Press*, which culminated in an anthology of articles in his first book, *Look Who's Talking* (Hirst Books, 2009); so not dissimilar to Sir Terry Pratchett there, who was a columnist for the *Bucks Free Press* for a while (before becoming a bestselling author).

Colin Baker will continue to surprise and delight his many fans around the world. His love of panto is well known, as well as his continued love of *Doctor Who* and, with star turns in shows such as *Celebrity Come Dine With Me* and *I'm a Celebrity... Get Me Out Of Here*! he continues to venture into our living rooms when we least expect him.

'A great reason for the programme's continuing success has to be the fact that every four or five years you have a new generation of kids growing up. The time I liked the least was when the Doctor became the person the establishment rang up and said "Help us out, Doctor!"'

Verity Lambert
Doctor Who – A Celebration, Two Decades Through Time and Space
Peter Haining

CHAPTER EIGHT
SYLVESTER MCCOY

'Then up and spoke the Cameron,
And gave him his hand again:
"There shall never a man in Scotland
Set faith in me in vain."'
'The Saying of a Name'

Robert Louis Stevenson

SYLVESTER MCCOY WAS born Percy Kent-Smith in Dunoon, Argyllshire, on 20 August 1943. His father (Percy James Kent-Smith) came from Pimlico, London, and was an acting petty officer in the Royal Navy. Unfortunately McCoy never met him. Within six weeks of meeting his Irish mother, Molly Sheridan (which included a two-week honeymoon in Ayrshire), he was blown up in a submarine in the Mediterranean. McCoy's father was only 23 years old when killed and his mother never recovered from the trauma, receiving medication for the rest of her life as a consequence and, as McCoy would later say, spending a lot of her life in an institute for the emotionally distraught. He spent his formative years being raised by his mother, grandmother and aunts, and he attended St Mun's, a local Dunoon school.

McCoy never started out with the intention of being an actor. His first vocation was the priesthood. Between the ages of 12 and 16 he trained at Blair's College, Aberdeen, to become a priest – the same choice of career as the young Tom Baker and, like Baker, he eventually decided that it wasn't for him. He left and completed his education in Dublin before returning to Scotland for a while. Following this, he went for a holiday in London, where he stayed and worked in an insurance company until it went bankrupt.

It was around this time that he became a hippy and took a job at the Roundhouse Theatre, London, where he was reputedly one of the most unlikely bodyguards of The Rolling Stones, as he explained: 'The Roundhouse in the 60s and 70s was a wonderful place where lots of avant-garde plays were put on, and lots of rock concerts. I was a bouncer for The Rolling Stones one night.' So, more of a fluke than a serious vocation then.

It was at the Roundhouse that McCoy met actor Brian Murphy (later to star in TV comedy *George and Mildred*), who was out of work and selling show tickets. One day a producer came in seeking an actor to replace someone who had let him down, whereupon Murphy suggested McCoy (wrongly presuming that he was an out-of-work actor too) by saying, 'There's a guy in the box office who's crazy...' It seems this particular craziness has followed McCoy ever since, as his most famous roles prove.

The producer was Ken Campbell, and through his wacky road show McCoy began to develop his own unique routine. Another actor who enjoyed the road show alongside McCoy was Bob Hoskins. Murphy also joined the fray and devised the name Sylveste McCoy in a play called 'An Evening with Sylveste McCoy', in which McCoy would stuff ferrets down his trousers and set fire to his head.

The name Sylveste McCoy stuck because journalists thought that it was indeed the actor's real name, and McCoy only lengthened it to Sylvester McCoy (because he favoured a 14-letter name to a 13) much later.

McCoy remembers his tour with the Ken Campbell road show as one where he 'learned to do the impossible with total conviction', and it was surely his apprenticeship to the world of acting.

In 1976 McCoy did a bit of serious acting in *Twelfth Night*, which also starred his future nemesis Davros – actor Terry Molloy. He followed this with *She Stoops to Conquer*, albeit, at that time, still under the name Sylveste.

BBC2's *Big Jim and the Figaro Club* was an early sitcom success for McCoy, although it was only meant to be a BBC Bristol one-off. The club were a group of builders who lived and worked around a seaside town in the 1950s. The show was broadcast between 1979 and 1981 and apparently captured the nostalgic 1950s feel so much that audiences adored it.

McCoy played the deranged 'Turps', a role that brought him his first true character actor plaudits - although, again, he was still billed under the name Sylveste McCoy at the time.

Throughout the 1970s and 1980s, he took madcap parts in children's programmes such as *Vision On* (where he played Pepe/Epep, the man in the mirror) and *Eureka*, as an eccentric professor-type character; it was appropriate then that his *Doctor Who* companion Ace would nickname him 'professor' when he later took the part of the Doctor. His often madcap antics fitted the show perfectly.

In 1985, McCoy played in the six-episode serial *The Last*

Place on Earth. The serial was a dramatisation of Roland Huntford's book *Scott and Amundsen*, which studied, in detail, the historic race to the South Pole.

The programme, like the book, shows where Scott made some vital errors, which caused a bit of an outcry when the book was first published. The mini-series is faithful to the book and a largely overlooked classic nowadays, not unlike Paul McGann's *The Monocled Mutineer*, which was also castigated for the politics of an historic event (but more of that later).

McCoy played the part of the heroic Bowers, one of Captain Scott's most trusted men, and the serial showcases one of McCoy's finest – and most poignant – performances.

In mid-1986, McCoy and Timothy Dalton performed together with Vanessa Redgrave in a season of Shakespearean plays at the Theatre Royal, Haymarket. The duo discussed the rarity of regular quality parts in the acting profession. A year later McCoy was cast as the seventh Doctor Who, and Dalton cast as James Bond in *The Living Daylights* (1987).

> 'And to Koppelberg Hill his steps addressed,
> And after him the children pressed,
> Great was the joy in every breast.'
>
> *The Pied Piper of Hamelin*
> **Robert Browning**

An incredible coincidence is that one of the strongest themes in *Doctor Who* history, *The Pied Piper*, became the catalyst for McCoy getting the part of the Doctor in the first place. *The Pied Piper* was a colourful theatre production written for McCoy by Adrian Mitchell, with a very 1980s 'Pied Piper Rap' in it (performed by McCoy).

McCoy learned that the part of the Doctor was available

again while performing *The Pied Piper* and duly went for it. This wasn't the first time he had gone for the role, as he had done so when Davison had given up the part, but that time he had lost out to Colin Baker.

At the same time as approaching producer John Nathan-Turner, a producer who knew McCoy got in touch with Nathan-Turner and told him that McCoy would be a great Doctor. Although Nathan-Turner suspected conspiracy here – which there wasn't – he went along to see McCoy in *The Pied Piper* (6 January 1987) and came away suitably impressed.

On obtaining the part, McCoy sent out an introductory signed letter to the first fans who wrote to him, along with a colourful flyer publicising *The Pied Piper* at The National Theatre (29 October 1987–20 January 1988) and a one-page biography on *Doctor Who* headed notepaper entitled 'The Real McCoy', where he is asked at the conclusion if he has a favourite Doctor, to which he replies, 'We are all the same person, so why should I?'

An interesting aside regarding McCoy's introduction to playing the Doctor is a low-budget movie called *Three Kinds of Heat*. Mere months before taking on the role, he appeared in the movie, which also included Mary Tamm (companion and fellow Time Lord Romana from the Tom Baker years) and Trevor Martin (one of the few stage Doctor Whos).

McCoy's Doctor Who was not a write-off, despite what some critics claim. Although there was a diminishing budget, some quality stories were made, such as 'The Curse of Fenric', 'Silver Nemesis', 'Delta and the Bannermen' with the legendary Ken Dodd, and 'Dragonfire', with its scary *Raiders of the Lost Ark* melting-face scene.

McCoy certainly brought back much mystery to the part of the Doctor, especially with the notion that he could have been

Merlin the Magician. But it was his token Dalek story that impressed many. 'Remembrance of the Daleks' was the first story to show a Dalek travelling upstairs. It also returned the Doctor to his Earth origins at 76 Totter's Lane, the junkyard in the very first *Doctor Who* episode.

There was much to like about McCoy's Doctor, including his final story 'Survival', which brought the whole original series to a climax with Anthony Ainley's last outing as the Doctor's nemesis, the Master.

McCoy was always thrilled to be Doctor Who. He wrote in his introduction letter to the fans, 'My new appearance takes place on UK TV screens in September 1987 for 14 action-packed episodes. 1988 is *Doctor Who*'s 25th anniversary so there is plenty to look forward to.'

And indeed there was, until the programme was terminated through no fault of McCoy's. The show, in its old incarnation, had simply run out of steam...

...but McCoy's career hadn't. In 1996 he appeared in an episode of *Rab C. Nesbitt*, as would future Doctor Who and fellow Scot David Tennant. McCoy's episode was entitled 'Father', and he played Rab's mentally ill brother Gash Snr to hysterical effect.

McCoy also appeared as Grandpa Jock in John McGrath's *A Satire of the Four Estates* (1996) at the Edinburgh Festival. It appears that he doesn't forget his Scottish roots and it would be great to see the two Scottish Doctors (McCoy and Tennant) in a one-off production.

Another interesting part for McCoy was as Snuff in the dark and macabre BBC Radio 4 comedy series, *The Cabinet of Doctor Caligari*.

In 1997 McCoy appeared as rapist Michael Sams in *Beyond*

Fear. The true story of Stephanie Slater (Gina McKee), an estate agent who was kidnapped, raped and held in a coffin-like box for eight days by Sams. The drama focuses on how Slater and her family come to terms with the ordeal and the resulting court case, with flashbacks to the harrowing events.

It is clear that by using flashbacks the opportunity of greater drama is missed. The main theme is the result rape has on its victims and their families and what they are put through in order to appease the justice system. McCoy and McKee are terrific in what is a drama with an average script.

McCoy has had a series of near-misses in the movies. When Steven Spielberg was planning on directing *Pirates of the Caribbean: The Curse of the Black Pearl*, McCoy was attached to the role of Governor Swann. Also, he was second choice to play Bilbo Baggins in the Peter Jackson *Lord of the Rings* trilogy; but his ship would come in later…

McCoy took the part of the lawyer Dowling in the BBC production of Henry Fielding's novel *The History of Tom Jones, A Foundling*. He also appeared in the RSC's *The Lion, the Witch and the Wardrobe*, as well as *King Lear* (2007), playing the fool to Sir Ian McKellen's Lear, a performance that bizarrely allowed McCoy to play the spoons.

In 2008 he performed *The Mikado* (Gilbert and Sullivan) with the Carl Rosa Company. He only performed with the company briefly, for the show's one-week run at the Sheffield Lyceum. *The Stage* review from 24 September 2008 said: 'Sylvester McCoy as the Mikado delivers the songs like speeches, in stentorian tones. Convincing performances come too from Gareth Jones…' Perhaps it was a shame that he had only a butterfly life in the production as the overall review of *The Mikado* was very good, although a little sting in the tail: 'Such well-known music strikes a happy chord. It just needs the company to gel together a little more and work not as individuals but as an ensemble.' Overall the short tour was quite well received.

The Academy (2009) was a one-off drama starring Sir Ian McKellen as the head of a run-down creative arts academy in Clapham. The academy has seen better days and greater popularity, so it is decided that they form a documentary to raise awareness and funds, but the bittersweet concoction of a famous brother (to McKellen) and a staff that has lost direction is almost a step too far. McCoy plays the disabled Felix in what was a well-suited role for his eccentric sense of fun.

McKellen's presence dominates throughout, but McCoy is thoroughly entertaining in this quirky mockumentary. A little gem that is likely to be forgotten, despite the fact that a spin-off TV series was considered – perhaps *The Lord of the Rings* and *The Hobbit* postponed that decision briefly.

'In a hole in the ground there lived a Hobbit.'

The Hobbit
J. R. R. Tolkien

Although Sylvester McCoy missed out as far as *The Lord of the Rings* trilogy was concerned, he was not forgotten by *Doctor Who* fan Peter Jackson, when he was casting the prequel, *The Hobbit*.

McCoy was cast as Radagast the Brown and soon flew over to New Zealand to film the episodic movie (released from 2012).

He had always brought a tinge of madcap humour to his roles, but with Radagast he threw caution to the wind, playing him as a totally crazy wizard with all the energy of a new millennium *Doctor Who* – even though nearing 70 Earth years of age by this time.

It was during *The Hobbit: An Unexpected Journey* press conference that McCoy explained his Tolkein screen-legacy: 'I was up for the part [the old Bilbo Baggins] all those years ago and got down to the last two actors, and the other one was the amazing Ian Holm. I was a bit miffed, but I was also delighted to be in such company... And then when I met Peter [Jackson] and his team later they said to me, "Well maybe it's a good thing you didn't get it because we've written you a rather interesting part"... and I think maybe they're right.'

In fact they were completely right. Radagast was the perfect vehicle for McCoy's talents. Although there might be some prestige to playing an old Bilbo, it was not the kind of role that an actor such as McCoy could bury himself him to the extent that he did with Radagast. Both roles were eventually cast extremely well.

Sylvester McCoy never started out with the intention of being an actor. Like his hippy beginnings, events in his life tended to happen around him, both impressive and diverse. This theatrical wandering allowed him – like so many other Doctor Whos – to brush shoulders with Laurence Olivier. It was a non-speaking part in the Frank Langella 1979 production of *Dracula*, but, yet again, the great actor had a presence in the life of a Doctor. Perhaps the great 'Larry' was indeed the Doctor that got away.

McCoy hasn't been an over-used actor, but that doesn't seem to bother him. His career has been full and successful and it appears the threat of typecasting in any way has never entered his mind. And even though his *Doctor Who* years are not considered to be the most impressive in terms of visual effects or scripts, his portrayal of the Doctor did hark back to those more formative years of the show, when no one was really certain if he was an alien or even Merlin the Magician.

'After bidding farewell to the second supporting party, Captain Scott and his four companions, Wilson, Oates, Bowers, and Petty Officer Evans, entered on what might be called the last phase of the polar journey...'

No Surrender
Harold Avery

CHAPTER NINE

PAUL
MCGANN

'… but abide the change of time…'

Cymbeline
William Shakespeare

ALTHOUGH HAVING HAD the shortest on-screen reign as the Doctor, Paul McGann has been involved with *Doctor Who* ever since appearing in its first true TV movie in 1996. In fact, because of the amount of work he has done with audio, radio drama and his likeness appearing in comic strips too, there is a school of thought that considers him the longest-serving Doctor.

McGann's Doctor is significant, because he provided some significant milestones in the evolution of the programme. In fact, if it wasn't for *Doctor Who – The Movie*, the new millennium show would not be as developed and therefore as successful as it is. McGann was the first Doctor to kiss a companion, he had the first new TARDIS interior (something in line with the series since Christopher Eccleston's tenure), and the first feature-length one-off episode (OK, it *was* called a movie but it was a continuation of the TV legacy, unlike its earlier movie counterparts).

Many *Doctor Who* fans have wondered why McGann has never been offered an opportunity to do a few seasons as the Doctor. Even now there is nothing to stop him. He wasn't a failure in the role; he signed a contract that was to last longer than his one-off special. And what harm would there really be in going back to the eighth Doctor after Peter Capaldi? As the programme informs us, time is relative and the 13th Doctor is meant to be the last, so only one more actor left after Peter Capaldi... apparently!

'A Time Lord has 13 lives and The Master had used all of his.'
The Doctor
Doctor Who – The Movie

Paul McGann is the Doctor everybody wants to see a little more of, but probably won't get the opportunity. So how has his career been affected by the programme? It is something he once did on screen, much as he once did a film called *Withnail and I*. It was a one-off, but nevertheless one that gave him much prestige.

McGann's interpretation of the Doctor is riveting, even if the story itself wasn't. The Edwardian clothes didn't quite work and Russell T. Davies must have picked up on this. A more modern look should have gone with a more modern forward-looking Doctor; but the movie didn't take that radical step. Strange really, as the TARDIS interior was dramatically changed and the potential of a love interest marked a departure for the Doctor. Well, McGann was certainly heroic in the role, rather than the respectable elder statesman.

Paul McGann was born on 14 November 1959 in Liverpool. He was the third of six children. In 1958, his mother Clare gave birth to twins, Joseph and John, but John died shortly after birth. Joe, along with his three younger brothers, Paul, Mark and Stephen, are all actors. His sister – Clare – works behind the scenes in TV.

McGann's first significant role in television was as Mo Morris in the BBC series *Give Us a Break* (1983). He was the fresh-faced snooker ace in a show that capitalised on the TV snooker boom of the early 1980s, where charismatic players such as Alex 'Hurricane' Higgins and Jimmy 'Whirlwind' White captivated huge TV audiences. The show had its moments as early-evening light entertainment but soon ran out of steam, despite a quality appearance from Robert Lindsay after his *Citizen Smith* days.

In 1986, McGann took on the role that would be a significant milestone in his career: *The Monocled Mutineer*. Based upon the 1970s novel by William Alison and John Fairley, he played Percy Toplis, a vagabond, deserter and criminal.

The show was highly praised at the time and McGann received many plaudits. However, it was blasted by the Conservative Party as left wing in its interpretation of a sensitive action during the war (the Etaples Mutiny), which Toplis was apparently involved in.

The Monocled Mutineer was never repeated on the BBC, although it has since been released on video and DVD. It showcased the very best of the young Paul McGann and, like other BBC series of that time (such as the mini-series *House of Cards*), it is remembered fondly by those who watched it.

McGann is generally known to a younger audience for his part in the classic movie *Withnail and I*. Noted as a student film (i.e. that it is primarily student audiences who watch it), it follows two out-of-work actors, Withnail (Richard E. Grant) and Marwood, aka 'I' (McGann). With drink, drugs and more than a hint of homosexual angst, the film is student self-indulgence to excess. The movie is set in the 1960s and is meant to be based upon the director's (Bruce Robinson) own formative years.

McGann enjoyed making the movie, but only really got to see it 20 years later at the anniversary screening on London's South Bank. He called it 'an extraordinary piece of work', because it is a film of words, a film where the actors have to act and not hide behind props and special effects. To a degree, he is right. To me, the film lacks a little substance in its plot, but that's not to say that the performances are lacking; they are not. In fact Richard E. Grant, who is famously teetotal, was made hideously drunk by Robinson to assist the reality of the part he was playing.

Withnail and I is a carefree, buddy movie. The characters are frustrated, unemployed actors, lusting for the spotlight while living in squalor. It's a kind of high-class version of the 1980s comedy, *The Young Ones*. Grant is very dramatic and camp, while McGann is the fresh lamb being led to the slaughter – yet somehow surviving.

Although both McGann and Grant loved filming the movie and, over 20 years later, have many good things to say about it, it is a film for a certain age group (late teens/early 20s), and which, if it counts among your favourite films at that time, you will reminisce about fondly, but not watch religiously, for the rest of your life. For this reason, *Withnail and I* will always be classed as a cult movie and just a little too genreless to be labelled a great film. People either love it or hate it.

McGann's other significant piece of film work is the classic

SF movie, *Alien 3* (1992). There was much anticipation regarding the conclusion to the *Alien* trilogy; the first two movies in the series were nothing short of SF classics and fans believed the third film would fit nicely into this prestigious sequence. In fairness, with the previous movies having the indelible touches of Ridley Scott and James Cameron respectively, the third film had a tough act to follow and, unfortunately, failed to deliver.

Alien 3 was probably the most disappointing – or simply the worst – movie in the *Alien* franchise. There was a big media build-up regarding how good the computer-generated aliens were in the film, but the public's complaints that they couldn't see the creatures too well because of the dark corridors and recesses in which they hid contradicted that claim.

And what of Paul McGann's part in the movie? McGann is an outcast, a deranged prisoner. Unfortunately, his role was severely edited in the final movie, thus making it difficult to analyse his character properly. That said, to see such a laid-back actor become an alien-addicted psychopath showed yet another side to his versatility. What is worth mentioning here is 'The Assembly Cut', which is a segment of the movie restored for the Blu-ray set of the *Alien* series, and showcases a more rounded interpretation of McGann's character – but still nothing like the thorough Director's Cut of *Aliens*, so it simply adds to the frustration.

Alien 3 was almost certainly a worthwhile project for McGann to be part of, for experience's sake, but it didn't give him the artistic licence he might have hoped for.

Doctor Who – The Movie (1996) is the third outing for the Time Lord on the big screen (well, actually, it was a TV movie with a far bigger budget than the show was normally accustomed to). The target market was clearly the American one (it was made by Fox, after all) but, unlike the early *Star Trek* movies, the baggage of the TV series encroached too much; as a consequence, only a true fan of the show would be impressed by references to the Daleks and understand the history of the Master and Time Lords.

Combine the above with a very average script and you have the downside of the film encapsulated. There was too much to absorb, too much legacy to understand. The film should have been a self-contained entity but even the reason for regeneration wasn't credible: the TARDIS appears, San Francisco gangsters shoot at it and the Doctor, completely unaware, just steps out of the TARDIS and is gunned down in a complete lack of perception. This is probably why Russell T. Davies decided not to have a regeneration scene at the beginning of the new millennium *Doctor Who*. To justify it and make it credible needs to take at least 15 minutes of story time from the outset. A Sylvester McCoy story with a regeneration scene at the end (perhaps during the Doctor and Master's Dracula and Van Helsing fight scene in the movie) could have been more credible, and awarded at least 10 minutes back to the overall story development time.

The upside of *Doctor Who – The Movie* is the interaction between Paul McGann and Daphne Ashbrook (Dr Grace Holloway), who really do hit it off on screen.

McGann is the young, dashing Doctor, full of energy and passion, but not in a James Bond type of way. Yes, he does steal a kiss from Grace and one would hope that it would be the beginning of a wonderful relationship but sadly, no.

Since Sydney Newman laid down the law in 1963, the Doctor doesn't do guns. He might be streetwise as far as the Daleks are concerned, but not to run-of-the-mill thugs from the USA, and his thirst for excitement has never diminished:

Grace: Why did you do that?
The Doctor: To liven things up!

Doctor Who – The Movie

Paul McGann reinvented the Doctor. Unfortunately, many influential people failed to see this and the fans were deprived of what would have been a highly invigorating and influential interpretation of the Doctor. If we are simply to judge McGann on his first appearance alone, then we must concur that he would definitely be up there with William Hartnell and Christopher Eccleston as one of the great debut Doctors, because his first story includes an excellent debut acting performance.

Paul might not have been the McGann to play the Doctor, as his brother Mark also went for the part, but the interpretation of Paul McGann's Doctor was impressive, albeit fleeting.

So, has *Doctor Who* had an adverse effect on Paul McGann's career?

No. McGann still dabbles in the show, he still attends the conventions and meets the fans, all of whom have much respect for him, but he manages to play many other parts without people remarking that 'he used to be Doctor Who' – one of those great key roles being Lieutenant Bush in *Hornblower* (1998–2003).

Hornblower was one of the very best period mini-series made by the ITV regions. Ioan Gruffudd starred as the main character, Horatio Hornblower, the hero of C. S. Forester's classic Napoleonic adventure stories. Gruffudd was supported by an excellent cast, which included Robert Lindsay (*Give Us a Break*) as Admiral Sir Edward Pellew, Paul Copley (*Matthews*), Sean Gilder (*Styles*) and, for four out of the eight episodes, Paul McGann as Lieutenant William Bush.

What is most endearing about McGann's role is the dignity

and total dedication to his friend and commanding officer Horatio Hornblower.

Lavishly shot and wonderfully acted, *Hornblower* was a classic series that sadly didn't get the opportunity to showcase the bigger – better – novels in C. S. Forester's series, mainly because of the cost of each episode. But it is a classic adventure series that showed that the ITV regions could create as good a period drama as the BBC – Jeremy Brett's *Sherlock Holmes* probably being the very best example of that.

In 2011 McGann appeared in *New Tricks*, a TV drama series that followed the work of the fictional Unsolved Crime and Open Case Squad (UCOS) of the Metropolitan Police. Led by Detective Superintendent Sandra Pullman, it is made up of retired policemen, including the acting talents of James Bolam, Alun Armstrong and Dennis Waterman. McGann played DCI James Larson in a role he was well suited for, but like Doctor Who, wasn't exercised enough.

Paul McGann deserves a quality regular TV role; he has established himself as an actor of depth and class from the *Monocled Mutineer* to *Hornblower*, but he has always been on the periphery of fame and close association with a key role, even though more than capable of holding his own.

Doctor Who hasn't restricted his career in any way; it's probably provided some respite between other parts. But even then he was probably the most unused screen Doctor Who, albeit quite likely the catalyst for the show's most successful comeback.

'I was only Doctor Who for six weeks.'

Paul McGann

CHAPTER TEN

THE FIRST DOCTOR REVISITED

WILLIAM HARTNELL QUIT *Doctor Who* when the strain of the shooting schedule became too much for him. It would be his last great role in an impressive career. Whether Hartnell was ever seriously considered to play the Doctor in the two Dalek movies is unclear (*Doctor Who and the Daleks*; *Daleks' Invasion Earth: 2150AD*); but the films set a trend that would last the next 50 years: impersonating the first Doctor.

Hartnell's last curtain call came in 1973 while playing the first Doctor again in the Jon Pertwee story, 'The Three Doctors'. Pertwee said in an interview that the only time he met Hartnell during the 10th Anniversary celebrations was during a publicity photo shoot prior to filming. He said that 'Bill' Hartnell was very ill and he was never seen on set, which was true. Hartnell's scenes were shot in private with dummy cards for him to read on the floor in front of him. It must have been a return that he was pleased to do, albeit in a compromised way, as he believed so much in the programme.

If one considers that Hartnell was not fit in 1965 to continue *Doctor Who* or to star in either of the two movies

(1965 and 1966 respectively), imagine how poor his health was in 1973.

For the films, Peter Cushing took on the grandfather figure, but not totally based upon Hartnell's portrayal of the Doctor. Where Cushing got the moustache from is anyone's guess, but it's an interpretation he kept for the second film and, strangely, adopted in a similar way in 1976 when playing an altogether different professor in the movie *At the Earth's Core*.

For anyone under the age of ten, the Dalek films were thrilling, as they showed the Doctor's nemesis in full technicolour. However, for older viewers there was more value in the dark and grainy TV counterparts of these films, 'The Daleks' and 'The Dalek Invasion of Earth', starring William Hartnell and a more modest BBC budget.

It was a year after Hartnell's death that Trevor Martin played the Doctor on stage in 'Doctor Who and the Daleks – Seven Keys to Doomsday'. On this occasion, the producers didn't want to cast outgoing actor Jon Pertwee in the role, nor for that matter incoming actor Tom Baker; they wanted their own Doctor.

Martin had previously played a Time Lord in Patrick Troughton's last story 'The War Games', as one of the three Time Lords who sentenced the Doctor to exile on Earth. But why did he have to wear a clown-sized bow around his neck and check trousers, not dissimilar to William Hartnell's Doctor Who costume? The producers stated that they wanted their Doctor to be a mixture of all the Doctors who had come before, including Peter Cushing, but with Martin's long white hair, the resemblance to Hartnell was most prominent.

'Doctor Who and the Daleks – Seven Keys to Doomsday' was written by outgoing scriptwriter Terrance Dicks and Martin enjoyed the show immensely, stating that he had been in less technical productions that had suffered more problems with visual effects. But the show was short-lived; with IRA bombs disrupting London life, the production wasn't well attended and sadly, it had to close.

The third time Hartnell's interpretation of the Doctor was imitated was perhaps the most deliberate, in the 20th Anniversary Special 'The Five Doctors'. To begin with, Richard Hurndall's role was to be much smaller than what it was, but when Tom Baker declined to take part in the story, Hurndall's part was expanded. Unfortunately Hurndall died of a heart attack five months after the story was broadcast. He was 73 years old and, like many of the actors playing the Doctor, he is more widely known for his short time as the Doctor than for any other role in his acting career.

The first Doctor continues to be cast. In the 50th Anniversary year, *Harry Potter* actor David Bradley (school caretaker Filch) didn't just play the first Doctor, he actually played William Hartnell too. Already familiar with *Doctor Who* through his role in the Matt Smith story, 'Dinosaurs on a Spaceship', he jumped at the chance to take on the role of William Hartnell in a one-off special about the creation of the series to celebrate the 50th Anniversary.

Like Hurndall, Bradley will be remembered for his role in *Doctor Who*, but like Peter Cushing and his Hammer Horror roles (and his part in the very first *Star Wars* movie) Bradley will also be remembered for his role in *Harry Potter*.

William Hartnell's Doctor will continue to be important to *Doctor Who*, because it is his interpretation that has provided the benchmark that all other interpretations are to be judged against. He was the *original* and therefore the one who demands the most respect from the *Doctor Who* community, because no other Doctor has ever been officially imitated and they are not likely to be (OK, maybe some shy lookalikes in 'The Name of the Doctor').

Grand stories such as 'The Three Doctors' and 'The Five Doctors' are now a thing of the past. There is more credibility in the chance meeting, such as 'The Two Doctors', or the way in which David Tennant and Matt Smith are brought together for the 50th Anniversary.

Colin Baker observed that he didn't really look the part anymore, and maybe that has instilled a different way of celebrating key *Doctor Who* anniversaries nowadays. Perhaps this is a good example of how the show is still evolving, with so many of the traditional values/celebrations no longer relevant or practical anymore. Who really wants three men in their seventies looking nothing like they did in their heyday, and three more look-alike actors taking on the roles of the deceased Doctors? Perhaps some people do, but it doesn't make for a credible show.

'The Five Doctors' took us to the edge of reason with one look-alike and another Doctor included only by using previously unreleased footage. So no chance of an 'Eleven Doctors' then? Let's see what the future holds with regard to CGI techniques worthy of the Doctor himself. It would be great to see William Hartnell in full-colour in a lavish feature-length story, 'The Name of the Doctor' really anticipating future technological promises to come.

'As swiftly and silently as a shadow, Doctor Who's Space and Time ship, *TARDIS*, appeared on a succession of planets each as different as the pebbles on a beach, stayed awhile and then vanished, as mysteriously as it had come. And whatever alien world it was that received him and his fellow travellers, and however well or badly they were treated, the Doctor always set things to rights...'

From the Prologue to *Doctor Who and the Crusaders*

David Whitaker

CHAPTER ELEVEN

CHRISTOPHER ECCLESTON

'What a piece of work is man.'

Hamlet
William Shakespeare

CHRISTOPHER ECCLESTON and Billie Piper are responsible for bringing *Doctor Who* back in the new millennium and making it a household name all over again.

It seems, in retrospect, that Eccleston was given a hard time for not sticking to the show for longer than an introductory year. Rumour has it that he only signed a one-year contract, but it is clear that he would have been offered a renewal due to the popularity of the programme.

Eccleston told *Doctor Who Magazine* that he emailed Russell T. Davies upon hearing that the show was making a comeback, and he wanted to be considered for the main role because of Davies's involvement. But what happened during that first year for him to suddenly change his mind? It surely wasn't the pressure of work; Eccleston was an experienced actor. Could it have been a slight fear of the love, adoration and total euphoria of the legions of *Doctor Who* fans? Eccleston wasn't a SF fan, he was a level-headed Northerner who played football and hung out with the lads while growing up. He didn't know about the intensity of the so-called *Doctor Who* anoraks (the 'Whovians'), particularly those fans – both new and old – who would be overwhelmed by the show's reinvention and his interpretation of the leading role.

Eccleston has been given a hard time by the fans who consider him a 'lightweight' (a phrase used by one of the ex-Doctors in my presence on hearing that he had quit) for leaving without much of an explanation. His track record was impressive and he certainly had enough quality work behind him not to be swallowed up and typecast by the show.

There was an element of Jon Pertwee about his interpretation of the Doctor: he could be deadly serious, he could get angry, but he could also be warm-hearted and amusing. Eccleston brought the action back into the show, something I'm sure Paul McGann would have done, if given the chance.

Eccleston's Doctor provided a blueprint that David Tennant would build upon. He introduced the programme to a whole new generation. Yes, those children would shout 'Exterminate' in the playground, but they would also chant 'Mummmmmmyyyy, are you my mummy?' Some of the scares the new show had to offer were just as terrifying as those memorable scenes from the original series. And older fans still enjoyed the programme. What really worked for them was the faithful blue police box – the TARDIS, a more sinister version of what was recognisably the same old theme tune, and, most importantly, the Time Lord with two hearts and more love and compassion for the human race than any other alien in SF history.

Again, like Pertwee, many of Eccleston's stories centred round the Earth but, unlike Pertwee, he had to deal with modern girls and modern families, resulting in more than one amusing 'domestic' incident. So was the Doctor romantically linked again? The Doctor actually dances with Rose Tyler (Billie Piper) and we appreciate that she is in love with him; but that love is, as ever, strained and unfulfilled. It's Jo Grant all over again, but this time the Doctor doesn't drive off in Bessie. He stands his ground; he lets the relationship move on until, during the era of David Tennant's Doctor, he loses her and has his heart – or hearts – broken by their parting ('The Parting of the Ways').

There has been much to learn about the Doctor emotionally since the programme came back. The return of Sarah Jane Smith (Elisabeth Sladen) during the Tennant years was a bittersweet moment. She admits that she has been in love with him and has waited for his return. She tells him that she thought he had died, and he delivers the killer blow, saying that he had lived and everybody else had died. And there lay the loneliness of the Doctor, the doomed romantic that he is. The Time Lord who wants a relationship with a human woman but knows it cannot happen, knows that it wouldn't last long, because she wouldn't live as long as him (echoes of *Highlander* here). And so it seems the Doctor simply breaks the hearts of many an adventurous woman on his travels. It is part of his curse. So suddenly we understand more about the Doctor on an emotional level; in fact, more than we came to realise throughout the whole of the original series. Put the CGI and other great things about the new show to one side, and look at the emotions that have streamed out of the TARDIS doors since its comeback.

The Doctor has disciples nowadays, a group of eclectic

companions who follow him religiously. It's not just the odd companion that comes and goes; it's a group of people who come in and out of his life to join his clan, to dance to his merry tune. The Doctor is still the Pied Piper, his cave – the TARDIS into which no one apart from the initiated can follow – is still the doorway that leads to the land of magical dreams. When Eccleston poked his head back out of the TARDIS door at the end of the first episode and asked Rose Tyler if she was coming with him, she instantly ran straight in to be transported to another world from which she might never have returned, so powerful is the Doctor's charm.

It was Christopher Eccleston who started the ball rolling with the new series of *Doctor Who*. He was the next generation William Hartnell, a man of mystery all over again – an intergalactic loner with no home planet, but on a gallant crusade to rid the universe of evil.

With such an attractive Doctor at the helm of the TARDIS, a lot of women swooned, just as they would again when David Tennant took over for his four-year stint. But with only one solitary year as the Doctor, did the show have any impact on Eccleston's career, or him personally? Possibly not. He found work immediately after *Doctor Who* and with equal plaudits. Christopher Eccleston could perhaps be described as a jobbing actor and one who will turn his hand to a wide variety of roles. Where his predecessor would find it difficult to let go, he didn't. He was professional enough to stand back and say, 'I've done enough.' So how did it all start for Eccleston, and how has his career developed over the years?

Christopher Eccleston was born on 16 February 1964 in Little Hulton, near Salford, Lancashire. He was educated at Salford Technical College and, by his own admission, was not a model student, being too much in love with

Manchester United Football Club and television to take his studies seriously.

At the age of 19, he had to make a decision: either continue with the football, at which he wasn't exactly brilliant, or take his acting seriously.

Inspired by BBC2's drama *The Boys from the Blackstuff*, Eccleston went on to train at the Central School of Speech and Drama. He wanted to pursue his love of gritty roles centred round the Midlands and North of England (*Kes*, and *Saturday Night and Sunday Morning* being good examples). However, it was Shakespeare and Chekhov that he worked at first, the staple of any serious future acting career.

At the age of 25, Eccleston joined the Bristol Old Vic for *A Streetcar Named Desire*. This was perfect casting for him, and his confidence grew as he went on to perform in several other plays around that time.

Like his *Doctor Who* predecessor Tom Baker, Eccleston found some periods of unemployment and worked on a building site to earn his money, but his big break came in 1991 when he took the lead in the film *Let Him Have It*. He played Derek Bentley, a slow-witted guy who falls in with a group of small-time criminals.

The film is based upon a true story and details how Bentley was hanged (28 January 1953) for a crime he didn't commit. Bentley was held by a policeman after an abortive break-in and called out to his 16-year-old friend Chris Craig, 'Let him have it,' meaning that Craig should surrender the gun he was carrying. Craig apparently read this request the wrong way, believing that Bentley had asked him to kill the policeman, which he duly did. Craig was imprisoned while the unarmed 19-year-old, Bentley, was hanged.

Eccleston plays Bentley wonderfully, showcasing the young

man's goodness and innocence against a society that had no time for him.

Shortly before being hanged, Bentley dictates a letter to his guard (Michael Elphick). Eccleston shows through the despair of the character, how simple and inexperienced of life's horrors Bentley really was. The guard knows this, praising Bentley for his letter, which the doomed man just manages to sign at the bottom.

Let Him Have It is a powerful and poignant story. Although Bentley has now been officially pardoned (his case had a radical influence on the British legal system), the film serves as a testament to the different levels of influence and corruption within the criminal and judicial world and why hanging wasn't always – or shouldn't have been – the answer.

Eccleston's next career highlight was *Shallow Grave* (1994). This was his first project with director Danny Boyle, his second being *28 Days Later* (2002).

Shallow Grave would be Ewan McGregor's first film. Eccleston plays an accountant called David and the role shows clearly that he can be something other than rough and ready. It was a good 'growing' film for him as an actor – but the best was yet to come.

Later the same year, he took the part of Nicholas 'Nicky' Hutchinson in the BBC drama *Our Friends in the North* (1996). Over nine weeks, Eccleston gave a performance second to none, working alongside Daniel Craig, Malcolm McDowell, Gina McKee and Larry Lamb in a landmark in 1990s television.

Our Friends in the North had the public divided. Some people thought the series was contrived and patronising, while others saw it as inspired and a pastiche of modern-day Britain. Perhaps the series was too honest, perhaps it hit home too much, exposing the hurt felt in certain parts of Britain which the general viewer didn't want to acknowledge. Eccleston certainly believed in his part and played his extremist and egotistical role to the hilt, which leaves a bitter taste – and rightly so.

Hard-hitting roles suddenly became Eccleston's staple, none more so than in *Hillsborough* (1996) and *The Second Coming* (2003).

Hillsborough is Jimmy McGovern with his heart on his sleeve. Sometimes he can lose direction, but not so here. Eccleston took his part well. You don't have to be a fan of Liverpool Football Club – or even a football fan – to feel the weight of the terrible tragedy that took place at Hillsborough in that FA Cup semi-final.

Hillsborough was proof – if proof were needed – that current tragedies could be dramatised without facing public outcry. There was a genuine need by society to understand what had happened at that football match and to ensure that it never happened again. Eccleston likes being involved with high drama, and also with important dramas depicting real-life issues that shaped the society we live in today.

Let Him Have It was the first time we saw this, *Hillsborough* a worthy second. After that dreadful day, fences were taken down at football matches and crowds respected the decision, bringing a greater awareness and responsibility to the game of football – a game Christopher Eccleston once considered as a career. Yes, this dramatisation meant much to him, and it clearly showed in his powerful performance.

The Second Coming (2003) was written by Russell T. Davies, and the writer/producer would come to fully appreciate Eccleston's skills as an actor by the end of it. The story follows the story of Steven Baxter (Eccleston), an ordinary Northern man, and how he comes to realise that he is the son of God and full of the power of miracles – but is the modern world ready for him?

Shown over two episodes on ITV (after being turned down by Channel 4 and the BBC), it provided a rare taste of pure serial quality. *The Second Coming* is a perfect representation of how the modern world couldn't cope with the reality of Jesus Christ being something other than just part of an ancient faith. Where society demands answers in the modern world Steven Baxter had none to give. This provoked extra suspicion and hatred by those who didn't believe or, conversely, those who believed too much. Baxter is unsure if what he is doing is right. He doesn't understand what *he* should be doing, let alone anyone else around him; he is an uncertain Christ figure.

The Second Coming questioned the need for religion in the modern world. It highlighted its importance to different people and therefore its ability to cause conflict, war and death on a huge scale. The series was stark and gritty in its basic message and provided the sound base that Eccleston and Russell T. Davies would build on with the return of *Doctor Who*.

In 2001, Eccleston appeared alongside Nicole Kidman in *The Others*. Directed by Alejandro Amenábar, this chilling ghost story of a mother-of-two's realisation that her house is haunted is both intriguing and captivating.

Grace (Kidman) has plenty of psychological baggage to endure inside her unsettling house, and the return of her husband (Eccleston) from the Second World War compounds that. Then she finds that her daughter Anne has been conversing with the dead.

The Others succeeds because of the unease and tension the director brings to the movie, with the aid of the key actors. The children's aversion to sunlight, combined with the choice of lighting and colour bring an extra dimension to the film, even though the story is a tried and proven one.

Eccleston wasn't a fan of *Doctor Who*. He said that he had seen it in passing while growing up, but it was Davies and the work they had achieved before *Doctor Who* that had attracted him to the part and he played it for as long as any other serialisation, just for a one-off season.

On taking the role of the Doctor, he explained (to chat-show host Jonathan Ross) that the Doctor was known as 'a posh part' and that he was 'not going to be everybody's cup of tea'. He also explained to Ross that when he pictured the Doctor he saw Patrick Troughton (a Doctor also favoured by Matt Smith). He also explained that Jon Pertwee and Tom Baker were the other two Doctors he was most aware of.

One could say that Eccleston had a bit of a chip on his shoulder regarding the 'posh' accent of the previous Doctors; indeed, he mentioned that a Mancunian now had the prime BBC slot – himself – while two Geordies had the prime ITV slot – Ant and Dec.

Eccleston's Doctor could handle himself. He looked the part. No longer a cosmic hobo and/or an eccentric professor, he was a no-nonsense fixer of hostile extra-terrestrial activity, a kind of Jon Pertwee figure in street clothes.

His first story 'Rose' sees him battle against an old *Doctor Who* foe, the Autons (the Nestine Intelligence from the Pertwee years). Fast paced and filled with incident, it was the perfect introduction to the new-look show. Billie Piper was the ideal modern girl to be the new *Doctor Who* companion, so suddenly the show was off on a brand-new rollercoaster.

Some viewers thought it amusing that the show had come back, and so successfully too. Some old fans were flabbergasted that it was now considered 'cool' (or as certain children called it 'sick' – meaning cool), when it used to be strictly for SF anoraks. But it was well made, it had a quality budget, production team and, of course, a quality selection of regular actors. When John Barrowman turned up in 'The Empty Child', women swooned. With all tastes catered for through Eccleston, Piper and Barrowman, *Doctor Who* was suddenly sexy.

One of the great achievements of the new series was the self-contained story. In the old days, *Doctor Who* was made up of a set of 25-minute episodes (normally spread over a month – four episodes), but nowadays the stories were started and finished in no more than two 50-minute episodes (many being one solitary episode long). The reason for this was explained by the show's producer, Russell T. Davies: because life was lived at a much faster pace in the new millennium, people were not prepared to wait four weeks to see a whole story. He was right and the season finale, which took in many recurring themes – and some sub-themes – throughout the season, made for a strong and satisfying conclusion. The very fact that the Daleks were involved – many of them, in fact more than ever before – was an added thrill for the long-term fans.

The season finale, 'Bad Wolf'/'The Parting of the Ways', was a breath-taking piece of television. *Doctor Who* was getting five stars right across the board from critics and, when Rose Tyler is captured by the Daleks, the Doctor – not unlike a chivalrous knight in shining armour – tells her that he is coming to get her amid a horde of Dalek protests, top viewing figures were achieved. Russell T. Davies had pulled off the perfect comeback: the cast were household names, the show had completely regenerated into something new and quite special... and then Christopher Eccleston announced that it was time to go.

Virtually everyone was shocked, but Eccleston didn't look back.

After he left *Doctor Who*, it was announced at the Cannes Film Festival that he was to star in a Lynda La Plante-produced SF romantic comedy, *Double Life*. This sent the message that Eccleston hadn't dismissed the SF genre. One might have thought that his career would have changed direction after *Doctor Who* but this wasn't strictly true – not immediately anyway.

In 2005, Eccleston provided the commentary for *Best Ever Muppet Moments*. Diversely, he also appeared on stage at the Old Vic Theatre in London in *Night Sky*. This one-night play also featured Navin Chowdhry, David Warner, Bruno Langley, Saffron Burrows and David Baddiel.

It was announced on 20 December 2005 that Eccleston would star as Christopher Marlowe in Peter Whelan's *The School of Night*, an inspired piece of casting – but alas, the production was cancelled on 6 January. This setback didn't turn Eccleston away from the Elizabethan genre, though. In May 2006, he appeared as the narrator in the Lowry Theatre (Salford) production of *Romeo and Juliet*. This showcased Eccleston working with actors with learning difficulties in his hometown. This return to his roots and concern for those less fortunate is a side of him that is rarely appreciated, which is a shame as he is quite a misunderstood person in that respect. Indeed, his depth of feeling – as an actor and human being – made him the BBC Breakfast narrator of the tsunami disaster, for which he flew out to Indonesia (December 2005). Eccleston was the perfect choice to explain how people were rebuilding their lives after the tragedy of Boxing Day 2004.

In 2006 he starred in *Perfect Parents*, an ITV drama written and directed by Joe Ahearne, who had directed him in *Doctor*

Who. In 2007 he played a more obscure role, as the Rider in a film adaptation of Susan Cooper's novel *The Seeker: The Dark is Rising*: A young man's life is changed when he realises that he is the last in a line of immortal warriors dedicated to fighting the forces of darkness. It was a fun role, which proved that Eccleston could let his hair down amidst the more heavyweight roles.

Eccleston travelled back across the Atlantic to take part in *New Orleans, Mon Armour* (2008). He then played a character called Claude in the episode 'Godsend' in NBC's *Heroes*.

In 2009 he starred opposite Archie Panjabi in the short film *The Happiness Salesman*. He then went on to win an International Emmy Award for his part in Episode One of the BBC drama *Accused* (2010). Eccleston played a lapsed Catholic in the dock for committing adultery. Each episode detailed a different person and their reasons for being in the dock, in what were deep and sensitive parts. Once again, he was working with Jimmy McGovern and produced one of his most impressive performances yet.

2010 was a good year for Eccleston, as he also gave a commanding performance as rock genius John Lennon in the BBC4 film *Lennon Naked* (2010). Made as part of Fatherhood season, the film focused on how Lennon's childhood haunted his adulthood. He starred alongside Naoko Mori (who played Yoko Ono), who had appeared with him in *Doctor Who*.

Eccleston's interpretation of Lennon instantly captivated his audience with perfect voice and mannerisms. The way he understood the humiliation of Lennon's very public reunion with his father (played by Christopher Fairbank) shows his sensitivity as an actor; and then his portrayal of the way Lennon treated Julian, his son from his first marriage, horrifies the audience.

Lennon Naked was a true-to-life play showcasing a very

personal side of John Lennon's life. Although Lennon was happy to castigate his father, he couldn't see how, or wasn't prepared to do anything, to save his own son from the same hurt of a broken marriage and the scars of a fatherless youth, as he himself had been subjected to.

Eccleston's portrayal of Lennon was of a man so wrapped up in his own troubled mind – but rushed through life by the people around him – he couldn't see or discriminate the moral dilemmas of his personal life.

Lennon Naked was one of the finest interpretations of the icon of a generation that was John Lennon. The script was specific, the music score made up of the original songs and there was even real footage of The Beatles to link together the key moments in Lennon's life. It was quality stuff.

In 2011 Eccleston played Joseph Bede in a seven-part drama for BBC2 called *The Shadow Line*. The first episode was screened on 12 April 2011 at BAFTA's Princess Anne Theatre in Piccadilly, and was followed by a Q&A session, which featured Eccleston.

The Shadow Line is a great story showing how the police and the criminal underworld have different ways of investigating the same murder case, crossing many a moral line along the way. It was an excellent series that deserved a follow-up; but sadly one wasn't commissioned.

On 31 December that year Eccleston played Pod Clock in a marvellous adaptation of Mary Norton's children's classic *The Borrowers* (BBC1).

The Borrowers, like most children's classics, had been done before, but new technology in special effects really adds to the thrills and Eccleston's version is one of the most memorable. His interpretation of Clock is that of a stern father and really reflects the original story well.

In July 2012 he starred in the political thriller *Blackout* for the BBC, while during the same month he played Creon in *Antigone* at the Royal National Theatre, where critics called his part 'charismatic' and 'intense', which describes his special blend of acting quite crisply.

It appears that *Doctor Who* hasn't restricted Eccleston's career at all. If it has done anything, it has opened a previously closed door of SF, which now stands proudly open to provide a little respite from the more serious roles he undertakes. Also, it may have persuaded him to take the odd lighter role to balance those intense and dark roles.

But let us return to the reasons why Eccleston left *Doctor Who*. In June 2010 he explained: 'I didn't enjoy the environment and the culture that we, the cast and crew, had to work in. I wasn't comfortable.'

This is explanation enough, as it exposes the very private – but highly talented – actor that Eccleston is. John Barrowman implied in his autobiography that David Tennant fitted into the *Doctor Who* family more than Eccleston had. This takes nothing away from what was a fabulous performance from Eccleston, as he himself qualifies: '...the most important thing is that I did it, not that I left. I really feel that, because it kind of broke the mould and it helped to reinvent it. I'm very proud of it.'

The BBC released an apology after insinuating that Eccleston had found the series gruelling and feared being typecast, which indeed he didn't, and wasn't. He treated *Doctor Who* just as any other part he had taken – professionally, passionately and originally, then he moved on dispassionately to concentrate on many other roles in diverse genres. In this respect he really does emulate his predecessor Patrick Troughton, especially with regard to Troughton's natural reluctance to giving too many interviews: isn't it indeed wrong for a character actor to reveal his own personality to the general public? Doesn't it make acting so much harder to do if people know you as a person and not just the character in front of them on screen?

'I durst the great celestial battles tell,
Hundred-hand Gyges, and had done it well.'

Elegia I
Christopher Marlowe

CHAPTER TWELVE

DAVID TENNANT

'Time travel is increasingly regarded as a menace. History is being polluted.'

Life, the Universe and Everything
Douglas Adams

DAVID TENNANT WAS born David John McDonald on 18 April 1971 in Bathgate, West Lothian. He grew up in Ralston, Renfrewshire. His father was Alexander 'Sandy' McDonald, the local Church of Scotland minister. David had two older siblings, Blair and Karen, six and eight years his senior.

The young David attended Ralston Primary School and Paisley Grammar School, before earning a bachelor's degree from the Royal Scottish Academy of Music and Drama.

He always had aspirations to become an actor (from the age of three) and, not unlike many other children growing up in the 1970s, he wanted to be Doctor Who. He managed to meet Tom Baker at a book signing in Glasgow and his single-mindedness seemed to persist right through to the role he made his own – just like his multi-coloured-scarfed mentor – for a whole new generation after the show was re-launched in the new millennium.

When joining Equity, David found that he couldn't use his own name, as there was already an actor called David McDonald and so, inspired by a writer at *Smash Hits* magazine (and front-man of pop group the Pet Shop Boys), he used the surname, Tennant.

It wasn't long before Tennant started to get roles on Scottish TV, one of his first being in an anti-smoking advert for Scottish TV. Extremely young, he played a teenager called Jim who is a smoker; but one of his gang refuses to buckle to the pressure of her peers to join in. It's a good short film (5 minutes in duration).

One of his most famous Scottish parts was as an over-the-top transvestite barmaid in *Rab C. Nesbitt*. From this unusual start, he was noticed by the BBC and began to receive roles, albeit small ones to begin with.

Ever keen on the theatre, Tennant kept up the pace by treading the boards alongside his TV and occasional film work. His energy and natural enthusiasm shone through at all times and he became quite prolific. Years later, actors such as John Barrowman and Billie Piper would comment on Tennant's fun side, despite the hard workload on *Doctor Who*. This was sometimes discussed in comparison to his more serious predecessor Christopher Eccleston, which was a shame as Eccleston was an entirely different type of actor.

In 2000, Tennant appeared in the first episode of the new *Randall and Hopkirk (Deceased)*, alongside Vic Reeves, Bob Mortimer and Tom Baker. The episode was called 'Drop Dead' and he played emotionally unwell character (Gordon Stylus), who even wears a wedding dress in the episode.

His next significant role was in *Foyle's War* (2002). He

played Theo Howard in a story about an investigation into a young evacuee's death from a booby trap in a summerhouse, after a Conscientious Objector dies in his cell after losing his appeal at court. Two unrelated subjects they may appear to be, but a judge appears to be the catalyst for much of what went on.

Foyle's War was significant on a personal basis as well as professional, as actress Sophia Myles also appeared in Tennant's episode (Sophia would later play Madame de Pompadour in the *Doctor Who* story 'The Girl in the Fireplace'). Although never in the same scene together, Tennant did catch up with the actress on set, and they started dating before playing alongside each other in *Doctor Who*.

Tennant's short films for the BBC are quite watchable. *Sweetnightgoodheart* (2001) is a ten minute short film in which he tries to tell his girlfriend he wants to split up but ends up proposing. Another ten minute short film, *Traffic Warden* (2004), showed his capacity for comedy and farce, as well as an ability to play the romantic lead – anticipating *Casanova* (2005), his breakthrough TV role the following year.

Casanova was the start of Tennant's professional journey to *Doctor Who*. Released in 2005, it was written by the man who would bring back the enigmatic Time Lord, Russell T. Davies. Directed by Sheree Folkson and produced by Red Production Company for BBC Wales in association with Granada Television, the show was three episodes long and told the story of the flamboyant 18th-century Giacomo Casanova, based upon his 12-volume memoirs. The comedy drama also featured Peter O'Toole as the old Casanova, looking back over his life, and Matt Lucas, as a Venecian duke.

The show's veracity and offbeat humour made it an unusual hit, highlighting Russell T. Davies's talents and teaming him with executive producer Julie Gardner, with whom he would work on *Doctor Who* later that year.

Tennant's next role of note was in *Harry Potter and the Goblet of Fire* (2005). It was in this film that we saw his darker side, perhaps anticipating traits (in anger, at least) of his tragic *Hamlet*, still four years away. He played Barty Crouch Jnr, who is disguised as Professor Moody to begin with. In a scene that appears much more painful than a Time Lord's regeneration, he transforms from the professor to his normal self. Crouch is a highly charged, sweating delinquent, with no redeeming features. Tennant said of his role, 'It's fun to be a baddy. To do a bit of moustache twisting.' And he certainly played it with passion.

Although his part was minor, there was a fair bit of Harry Potter name dropping in one *Doctor Who* episode, 'The Shakespeare Code', where the Doctor admits to being a fan himself: 'Wait till you read book seven. I cried!' he says, almost coyly. He then brought the episode finale to a climax by shouting out a Potter spell and saying 'Good old JK', name-checking *Potter* author JK Rowling.

Tennant adored his role in *Harry Potter and the Goblet of Fire*. He stated that he would never be in anything as big again. He wasn't being modest: Tennant was in awe of the size of the crowd at Leicester Square for the premiere, just as he would be for the premiere of the next movie, *Harry Potter and the Order of the Phoenix*, where he stated that he now felt part of the Harry Potter family. By then, though, there was another family he was already a major part of.

In *Doctor Who* he did much running and jumping around, and if we look back at his humble beginnings as a TV actor, he was running around even then (see *Sweetnightgoodheart*). It's the madly adventurous/subtly romantic roles that seem to attract him and, in that way, he is perhaps a little typecast. Even his *Hamlet* was a bit of an aerobics exercise, but a damn good one nevertheless.

Doctor Who was the right thing at the right time for David Tennant. It enhanced his career by putting his talents firmly in the public eye, and he managed to do other work at the same time, in order to keep his career travelling in the right direction and battle the threat of typecasting.

Tennant exploded onto the scene as the Doctor. Although undergoing a difficult regeneration, he manages to save the world yet again in his first story, 'The Christmas Invasion', albeit losing a hand in the process.

Tennant took a short film of watching his screen debut at his parents home in Scotland. Lasting no more than five minutes the short film shows his aunt and parents watching the show on Christmas Day and passing comment on Boxing Day. It's a wonderful insight into the beginning of a *Doctor Who* legend.

There was no lean period when Tennant took over the role. *Doctor Who* had only been on air for a year and people were still reeling from Christopher Eccleston's shock departure. Tennant was accepted and, from the moment that he told Rose Tyler's mother to be quiet, his popularity grew and grew.

Like Pertwee and Manning before them, Tennant and Piper truly got on, both on camera and off. Their friendship was obvious and something Piper mentions herself in her autobiography, *Growing Pains*. When John Barrowman joined the regular cast, the camaraderie became more intense and a special team started to form, including Piper's on-screen mother, father and estranged boyfriend. Put all that together with the return of Sarah Jane Smith (Elisabeth Sladen) and K9, and there was certainly a big and quite brilliant regular cast working on the show.

Doctor Who – like pop music – was suddenly a community movement. Boy bands, girl bands, street people, groups of people coming together to express themselves, it was all very millennium and something rock genius David Bowie anticipated in interview (from as early as 1993, so it shouldn't have been a shock). Solo artists were not the norm and the Doctor needed a fuller TARDIS, or at least people he could call upon – sometimes by intergalactic cell phone – in times of trouble.

During a break from *Doctor Who*, Tennant appeared on Ainsley Harriott's *Ready Steady Cook* with his father Sandy (who took a non-speaking part as a footman in the Agatha Christie-inspired *Doctor Who* episode 'The Unicorn and the Wasp'). Their appearance on the long-running and popular cookery show resulted in a great Scottish episode: haggis, neeps and tatties became the order of the day for Sandy – with, of course, some quality Scotch broth alongside. David's less adventurous chicken and rice won the day, however... perhaps because the audience was crammed with *Doctor Who* fans.

Naturally, Sandy got his own back throughout the show, talking about his son's formative years. It became clear that Tennant had always wanted to be an actor, even taking the leading role in his very first school production, and then the defining moment when he played an important part in a TV anti-smoking advertisement.

Sandy had clearly thought about his selection of food for *Ready Steady Cook*. What he had selected were foods the 'poorer Scottish families' had to live on in the past, and his love of his own country's culture was refreshing and interesting. The very fact that the money David won on the show went to a hospice in Paisley (close to where he went to school) was the perfect end to a highly endearing episode of the cookery series.

Tennant knew by this time that *Doctor Who* had changed his life. Of course he was living the dream, his childhood dream. He even mentioned that the Cybermen would be back in his second season, along with K9. His natural enthusiasm for *Doctor Who* overshadowed his more fragile moments in the kitchen opposite his father. At one stage, the audience laughed at his best efforts, upon which he declared, 'The audience are laughing at me!' But it was all done in good taste, and his dad was on hand to show who was the more competent cook, rather than best actor.

As Tennant's era as the Doctor continued, so too did the plaudits. The transition from Eccleston to Tennant was seamless in as much as the quality continued; no one was on a learning curve. Stories such as 'Army of Ghosts' and 'Doomsday', which detailed the end of the Doctor and Rose's relationship, made way for more classics, such as 'The Shakespeare Code', 'The Family of Blood' (featuring Charles Dickens' great-great-grandson Harry Lloyd as Jeremy) and the poignant 'Planet of the Ood'.

Tennant embraced each story with relish. There's no denying that he loved his four years as the Doctor; it's there in every performance. He lived the part, and that really came across to his fellow actors and the watching audience. Billie Piper described him as 'David Ten-inch' with a laugh and a cuddle, while John Barrowman (Captain Jack) spoke highly of him and his humour and companionship, both on screen and off. It appeared that the good ship TARDIS under the command of David Tennant was always in happy mode. John Simm (the Master) actually stated that part of the reason why he wanted to play the Master was to act alongside him. High praise indeed from the accomplished actor of *The Lakes* and *Life on Mars*, but he meant every word of it; and 'The Sound of Drums'/'Last of the Time Lords' was one of the great stories of the new millennium *Doctor Who*.

'Whatever you do, don't blink.'

The Doctor

Then came the story 'Blink', a masterpiece of gothic suspense that clearly proved you didn't need the Doctor in the show all the time to rivet and scare the audience – just a sensational idea, great actors and more scares than an army of Daleks.

Bernard Cribbins enjoyed his time reacquainted with the Doctor and the TARDIS, going over the top in the space-gun scene in Tennant's very last story, 'The End of Time', but that summed up the Tennant years perfectly: scary fun.

In 2005 Tennant performed at the Theatre Royal, Bath, and the Lyceum Theatre, Edinburgh, in John Osborne's *Look Back in Anger*. He took the part of Jimmy Porter. The latter performance was recorded by the National Video Archive of Performance for the Victoria & Albert Museum Theatre Collection. It was the yearning for more serious roles that made him consider how long he would live the dream of being the Doctor.

Along with *Ready Steady Cook*, Tennant appeared in another BBC2 show, *Who Do You Think You Are?* (27 September 2006). The programme explored both his Scottish and Northern Irish ancestry. His maternal great-great-grandfather, James Blair, was a prominent Ulster Unionist member of Derry City Council after the partition of Ireland. He was also a member of the Orange Order, which appeared not to sit well with Tennant, but he was fascinated by what he found out about his ancestors on the show.

In 2007 Tennant starred in *Learners*, a BBC comedy drama

written by and starring Jessica Hynes (who had appeared in the two-episode *Doctor Who* story 'Human Nature'/'The Family of Blood'). Tennant played a Christian driving instructor who becomes the focus of a young student's obsession.

When Tennant picked up the award for Outstanding Drama Performance at the National Television Awards in October 2008, he also announced to an unsuspecting TV audience that he would be leaving *Doctor Who*. There was an instant wail of disappointment from his many fans. But perhaps his way of dealing with his decision to depart was the right one. He didn't let rumours slip out and he spoke directly to camera – to the fans – by satellite link during the interval of the RSC's *Hamlet* and announced his departure and the reason that he couldn't do it forever. He then gave them over a year to get used to the idea. It was the best and most noble thing to do.

Tennant adored playing the Doctor. On *The Graham Norton Show* (9 November 2009), he said that he enjoyed every minute of it, that he loved getting up and going to work every day. He also explained that if he didn't leave then, he would never leave the series and they would one day have to bring him out in a bath chair (which is almost the same thing as he said when making the original announcement of his departure at the National Television Awards).

However, quitting the most successful show on television was a tough decision to make for Tennant. *Doctor Who* had been such an incredibly popular show during his reign; he didn't want the bubble to burst. Personally, he wanted to quit while he was in front and not have to face the day when he would say, 'Oh no, not Daleks again!'

It would appear that he did peak with his penultimate story, 'The Waters of Mars', which broke viewing-figure history for a *Doctor Who* story in the United States. Also,

Tennant's last story hit the 10 million mark in the UK over Christmas 2009 and New Year's Day 2010.

Although bitterly disappointed, his fans accepted the decision to go. Tennant had taken a few serious roles while playing the Doctor, including that of a man who recovers from a serious head injury in a road accident (*Recovery*, which I will discuss presently) and, of course, his stint in Stratford-upon-Avon playing, most notably, *Hamlet*, but he wanted to do much more. And so he left in the New Year's Day special.

Tennant returned to the real world with a bit of a crash. He found that – certainly in America – he had to audition again, which was something he didn't have to do in the UK while playing the Doctor. Indeed, the Doctor had his privileges and the BBC had been rightly criticised for picking the same actors for their programmes time and again. This didn't happen outside its protective bubble and Tennant knew and embraced this challenge.

Although filled with trepidation, Tennant made the brave step away from the show and, so far, he has done well. Of course, he will always be the Doctor to a whole generation of *Doctor Who* fans, but then again, the same thing applies to all his predecessors – and probably successors too. The last scene he filmed saw him hanging from a wire in front of a blue screen, not the emotional regeneration into Matt Smith's Doctor. He recalled in *Doctor Who Magazine* that, after his regeneration scene, he left the studio alone while Matt Smith continued filming. He went home and revised his lines for the following day. Such is an actor's lot.

When the final episode was completed, Tennant was given a box of *Doctor Who* goodies, including his sonic screwdriver, something he considered so precious that he refused to keep it at home as he feared burglary.

Being the Doctor was something Tennant adored and, like most of his predecessors, he quit while he was ahead, but he did face some bitter moments. While shooting the Christmas 2007 Special 'Voyage of the Damned', his mother, Helen, passed away. In an interview with *Doctor Who Magazine*, he admitted that, although the working day wasn't difficult, going home and learning lines on his own was 'trickier' – surely an understatement from one of the celebrity patrons of the Association for International Cancer Research?

Tennant managed to fit in other TV work during short breaks in *Doctor Who*, probably the most important of which was *Recovery* (2007). He played Alan Hamilton, a hardworking man with a loving family who is knocked over in the street by a van travelling at high speed. He suffers brain damage and the 90-minute TV drama documents his slow and painful recovery.

Sarah Parish plays Tennant's wife, Tricia Hamilton, in the drama, and she goes through every type of emotional rollercoaster as her husband fights to regain his mind, body, family and dignity. Tennant said of the story, 'You can't really imagine what it must be like to be married to somebody who becomes a different human being [through brain injury],' but that's indeed what happens in the drama. One minute Tennant's character is fine, the next he is playing with a woman's breasts at a party and not aware that what he is doing is wrong, to his wife's total shock and embarrassment.

Recovery showed Tennant as a serious character actor, not just a Doctor Who with lots of CGI behind him. Was that the way Tennant looked at it? No, probably not, but he knew that he needed to play a variety of other roles in order to progress his career and continue to enhance his reputation as a quality actor. He was still quite young as an actor, with many years stretching ahead of him in a variety of different roles, or so he would hope.

As we have seen throughout this book, especially with the first four Doctors, *Doctor Who* never goes away. In one shape or form the actor returns. Tennant has already come back in a two-part story in *The Sarah Jane Adventures* (2009), and of course the 50th Anniversary special (with Billie Piper). There has been talk once again about another *Doctor Who* movie, and no one is better placed to take on the role than Tennant. Once upon a time Jon Pertwee talked about a *Doctor Who* movie, but the backers wanted an American actor to play the lead, so time will tell.

So what about life after *Doctor Who*?

Even before his last episode was aired, Tennant had become the CBeebies *Bedroom Stories* reader over Christmas 2009 with five stories. More importantly, he was signed to star as Rex Alexander, a Chicago litigator who, following a panic attack, coaches clients to represent themselves in the NBC drama pilot, *Rex is Not Your Lawyer*.

Christmas 2009 was a bumper one for Tennant on the BBC. Not only was Part One of his final *Doctor Who* story aired, but he also took an amusing role in *Nan's Christmas Carol* (Catherine Tate) and then there was the BBC version of the RSC's *Hamlet*.

Including most of the original cast, the TV *Hamlet* was a lavish affair, with its spy cameras, two-way mirrors and exotic camera angles.

'How is it that the clouds still hang on you?' Patrick Stewart's opening words to Tennant's Hamlet sum up the stark loneliness of the self-wounding prince we first meet. But then Hamlet denies his sorrow with vigour, only to spill his bitter-torn heart on the floor when alone.

Tennant's Hamlet is full of emotion. Passionate, with an at

times vicious delivery, he brings out the child in the young prince. The way he embraces his good friend Horatio directly after his first soliloquy is childishly over-happy, in comparison to the devastated prince-alone two heartbeats earlier.

The reason Tennant received rave reviews for his stage *Hamlet* in Stratford-upon-Avon was because *Doctor Who* fans suddenly saw what the actor was capable of – and, like the critics, they were blown away.

It was right that the BBC showed *Hamlet* the same Christmas as Tennant's last *Doctor Who* story. The production clearly showed that the show couldn't keep an actor of his calibre in the same suit forever when he was capable of so much more. And he needed stretching. *Love's Labour's Lost* was good, but a small role; *Hamlet* was an exceptional lead.

For me, the modern glitzy sets, suits and ties in *Hamlet* stifle the performance. There is always a dark, depraved starkness about the period *Hamlet*, and Tennant showed this with a classical interpretation. In short, the modern look took something away from the period piece, but not the performances.

While other actors seem happy to gently walk through their lines with polite perfection, Tennant painstakingly lived – and indeed thought through – every word.

Hamlet was his giant leap away from *Doctor Who*. It should not have come as too much of a surprise, though. For 15 years, Tennant trod the boards, appeared in a variety of TV character roles and indifferent film parts; but it was *Doctor Who* that made him a household name, and *Hamlet* – and possibly *Recovery* (2007) – took him forwards as a potentially great actor who was once Doctor Who, an actor the adult female audience would follow without question (a love-interest Pied Piper, no less).

For Tennant, work continued to flow in 2010. He provided a voice in the film *How to Train Your Dragon* and was reunited with the *Casanova/Doctor Who* Red Production Company for a four-part TV serial *Single Father*, which was also well received.

Single Father was an 'emotionally powerful yet funny' BBC drama, made by the Red Production Company through BBC Scotland. Written by Mick Ford (*Ashes to Ashes*), it followed the life of a photographer called Dave (Tennant) with the seemingly impossible task of bringing up four children alone. Tennant said of the role, 'I feel very lucky to have been sent the script. When I read what Mick Ford had written, I was desperate to be part of the project. And to be working with Red Production Company again makes me very happy indeed.'

In 2011 Tennant starred in quite a different BBC2 film: *United*, which told the story of the 'Busby Babes', the Manchester United football team who lost their lives in the Munich air disaster. He played coach/assistant manager Jimmy Murphy in a very good interpretation of the tragic story. The role was quite divorced from anything else he had done before, but was still heart-felt in what was a notable production.

2013 saw Tennant appear in two very different dramas: *The Politician's Husband* (BBC2) and *Broadchurch* (BBC1). Both series would be acclaimed, but the former drama played second fiddle to the latter. In *The Politician's Husband* Tennant played the less than likeable Aiden Hoynes. Although he liked playing villainous roles, to do his bit of 'moustache twisting', audiences preferred him either in the romantic lead or that of an anti-hero, and that's where *Broadchurch* came in.

Broadchurch was an eight-part drama written by *Doctor Who* and *Torchwood* writer Chris Chibnall. Tennant played Detective Inspector Alec Hardy as part of an impressive cast that included Olivia Colman, Will Mellor and Arthur Darvill as the town priest. Chibnall said that the drama had 'scale and intimacy' and that the characters' lives were 'laid bare'.

This was quite true. Every single character – including Tennant's – had complexities and any one of them might have been the murderer in this riveting whodunit. The show really caught the viewing audience's imagination, with the final episode clocking up an impressive 10 million viewers (similar to audiences for *Doctor Who*). The BBC quickly decided to commission another season of the drama.

Later in the year, despite his *Doctor Who* comeback to celebrate the show's 50th Anniversary, Tennant was back with the RSC, most notably taking the main role in *Richard II* for the winter season in Stratford-upon-Avon.

But life had not been all work for Tennant. He married Peter Davison's daughter, Georgia Moffett ('The Doctor's Daughter') on 30 December 2011. Their daughter Olive was born 30 March 2011, and Tennant adopted Georgia's son Tyler from a previous relationship in September before they tied the knot at the end of the year. On the birth of their child, he said: 'It feels an important thing to do and I'd hate to miss out on it. I'm only 38, but my parents had had three kids by this age and I have had none yet.'

'Call me but love, and I'll be new baptiz'd.'

Romeo and Juliet
William Shakespeare

Tennant took some time out with his new family and the media backed away. Yes, there was the obligatory photo of the couple with baby carriage, but by-and-large they were left alone.

He started turning up the momentum of his career again

(2012/13) with *Broadchurch*, the RSC and, of course, *Doctor Who*. And *Doctor Who* will always run alongside Tennant's career, a happy indulgence rather than an Albatross around his neck. The sheer volume of diverse work that he does will allow *Doctor Who* to find its place within his career. In that way he is not unlike Jon Pertwee, who had many important and popular roles scattered across his lengthy career.

So what happened to Doctor Who after David Tennant left?

Enter Matt Smith, the youngest actor to take on the iconic role.

Smith certainly had a mountain to climb following Tennant. He wasn't the sexy hero, so deadly serious and heroic, nor so comic and reassuring. He was a 26-year-old actor with much less experience, but still had plenty of plaudits. Some of the female audience who liked the 'eye candy' of David Tennant (and even Christopher Eccleston) saw Smith spit during his first scene in the TARDIS and instantly dismissed him.

The Doctor was enigmatic. He didn't eat, drink, swear – or spit. Also, this chap looked a little geeky, or was he a tad too preppy?

Audiences were passing judgement before they even saw him perform properly. It was as though the odd couple of minutes they saw of him in the TARDIS as it plummeted to Earth were enough for them to know exactly what this Doctor was going to be like, and they didn't approve.

As *Doctor Who* has shown us over the years, you can write off an actor but you cannot write off the character. No matter how good the last actor was, the Doctor – those essential ingredients – still existed, and each actor had those ingredients firmly sown in him... so Smith took a deep breath and gave it his all.

The show moved on, the Tenth Doctor became history, and

on 3 April 2010, with an awesome new opening sequence and music, a new executive producer and travelling companion, *Doctor Who*, the programme – not just the Doctor himself – regenerated into another entity entirely.

> "Tis as easy as lying; govern these ventages… give it breath with your mouth, and it will discourse most eloquent music.'
>
> *Hamlet*, Scene II

CHAPTER THIRTEEN
MATT SMITH

'…I wished him [Matt Smith] great success, and he left. As soon as he disappeared down the hall, I turned to the others in the office and said, "I feel as if I just cheated on David [Tennant]."'

I Am What I Am
John Barrowman

PERHAPS ONE THING Matt Smith had going for him was the fact that, to all intents and purposes, he was an unknown actor and the youngest person ever, at 26, to play the Doctor. That said, he had to follow the most popular Doctor to date (according to *Dr Who Magazine* readers), so no pressure then.

As we cannot hop forward in time to see how the show affected Smith's career as an actor, what we can do is analyse his immediate contribution against his previous work and understand how seriously he – and the rest of the production team – took the new Doctor.

As far as the show was concerned, favourite aliens were brought back for Smith's first season as a kind of safety net. Fans young and old would at least tune in to see the Daleks,

Silurians and Cybermen. And then there were the Weeping Angels from one of the most popular episodes in the show's history, 'Blink' (voted the second-best story of all time by *Doctor Who Magazine* readers). Steven Moffat, creator of the Weeping Angels, was now executive producer, and the one thing he promised audiences was greater chills not unlike the gothic days of former producer Philip Hinchcliffe (during Tom Baker's era), but it didn't quite work out that way.

Smith's first season wasn't all chills and darkness, but it did have a feast of monsters in its two-part grand finale, which included Daleks, Cybermen, Sontarans and the promise of an appearance – albeit never seen – of old favourites, the Draconians. These things would help the ratings if nothing else, but surely Matt Smith wasn't ruled out as a credible Doctor because of the success of David Tennant?

Of course not. The part is greater than the actors who have played it, but even Patrick Troughton thought no one could follow William Hartnell and, of course, millions of fans believed no one could follow Tom Baker (and some still think that); but actors do follow, and all of them have a blue police telephone box and a familiar theme tune. Along with two hearts and a fondness for red-headed human females (on *The Jonathan Ross Show* in March 2010, when asked about Karen Gillan, Smith said, 'She's a ten'), there's always proof that life goes on after the death of a Doctor. So how did Matt Smith occupy his first 25 years on Earth and suddenly find himself at the controls of the TARDIS?

Matthew Robert Smith was born in Northampton on 28 October 1982. He attended Northampton School for Boys, where he became head boy. Unlike many of his predecessors, acting wasn't his first love: it was football. Smith started out playing for his local team Northampton Town in their under-

11s and under-12s squads. He then progressed to Nottingham Forest and played in their under-12s, 13s and 14s. He finished his short football career playing for Leicester City's under-15s and 16s before he had to give up due to a back injury.

While other people give up acting for a second career, Smith gave up football for an acting career. Having kept his hand in, he did well to fall into work. This was largely due to his drama teacher, who signed him up as the tenth juror in *Twelve Angry Men*. Smith said of him: '[Mr Hardinham] encouraged me and I found it [acting] was something I enjoyed. I did an A-level in drama, without any particular aspirations at the time of becoming an actor.'

He then turned down the opportunity to go to a drama festival afterwards – something his teacher had arranged – but he was persuaded to join the National Youth Theatre in London.

His first role was in T. S. Eliot's *Murder in the Cathedral* (2003), for which Lyn Gardner of the *Guardian* singled him out as giving 'an exceptionally mature performance as the Archbishop'.

The following year, he would play in *The Master and Margarita* and *Fresh Kills*, both of which would earn him plaudits – *Fresh Kills* being his first professional performance.

The National Youth Theatre's interpretation of *The Master and Margarita* ran from 23 August to 11 September 2004, and was adapted for the stage by David Rudkin at the Lyric Theatre, Hammersmith, and directed by John Hoggarth. Smith was one of a 36-strong cast, and the production was 3 hours 10 minutes in duration, which some felt was overlong. A handful of actors were highlighted for their performances, such as Tom Allen, who played the sinister black magician Woland, supported by the 'seriously camp' Smith as Bassoon.

Smith played the 16-year-old Eddie in *Fresh Kills*, which *Variety* gave a rather poor review. Although he wasn't mentioned, the cast were accused of making 'heavy work' of the American working-class accents. Years later, Smith would adopt a Southern American accent for his narration of the audio book *The Runaway Train* (*Daily Telegraph*, 24 April 2010), which he did uncannily well.

On the Shore of the Wide World was a co-production by the National Theatre and the Royal Exchange Theatre, Manchester. At 2 hours 40 minutes, the company should have had plenty of time to convey the meaning of the piece, but audiences left a little baffled. *Variety* mentioned Smith once, saying that his character Paul Danzinger was 'crudely conceived'. Of course, not all reviews are good and Smith had to accept that, if you can't stand the heat, you should get out of the kitchen; but it appears that the heat wasn't a problem as he then took the part of Lockwood in Alan Bennett's *The History Boys* at the Lyttelton Theatre, London.

The play, which focuses on the lives of a group of bright young sixth-formers in a northern school looking for a place at Oxford or Cambridge, was another long one (2 hours and 45 minutes) but it was universally well received by theatregoers and critics alike. Within the quality cast, Smith excelled, and it was no coincidence that later that year he landed his first TV role in *The Ruby in the Smoke*.

Smith co-starred alongside Billie Piper and, although a little scattergun in its interpretation of Philip Pullman's original novel, the actors took their parts well, as they would the following year in *The Shadow in the North* and *The Secret Diary of a Call Girl* (Smith appearing in only one episode of the latter).

It seemed that Smith worked very well with Piper, which is

a little ironic considering that they missed each other in *Doctor Who*.

Smith's first West End role came in 2007 with *Swimming with Sharks*, acting alongside Christian Slater and Helen Baxendale at the Vaudeville Theatre, London. He took the part of Guy, personal assistant to devilish movie-maker Buddy Ackerman (Slater), and received much praise.

He was then shortlisted as an 'outstanding newcomer' in the *Evening Standard* Awards after his performance as Danny Foster in BBC2's political drama *Party Animals* (2007), which together with *Swimming with Sharks* really highlighted him as a young man with promise, and soon *Doctor Who* beckoned.

When Smith learned that he was to be David Tennant's replacement as the Doctor, he said that he paced around the room for three days. 'It does weird things to you,' he confessed in a promotional interview. He went on to admit that keeping the whole thing a secret was extremely hard, and that he had to tell someone – his father – who was 'flabbergasted' and started to talk about Tom Baker. But his grandfather could remember even further back.

On *The Jonathan Ross Show* (26 March 2010, a week before Smith's first episode was broadcast on 3 April 2010), he explained that he told his family that he was to be the new Doctor on Christmas Eve. Imagine the joy of telling your parents that you've just landed the biggest part on television, that you will be immortalised in TV history. Put all the past behind you, those small roles, those character-building roles, those roles that were good and respected in the business – 'Now I'm Doctor Who.'

When the dust settled, Smith had about six months to build the character of his Doctor Who. A time he called 'empowering' (*The One Show*), when nobody knew the secret, not even an actress who asked him point blank what his next role would be.

Smith decided that he would 'be brave' with the part, and try and put as much enthusiasm into it as his predecessors. In fairness, there was no point in copying the extremely popular David Tennant – his Doctor had to be a complete break from what children had come to know as the Doctor.

At the time of the promotional round of interviews before his first episode, Smith had only read two scripts but was incredibly excited about his future as the Doctor, not unlike those who had gone before him. He would later admit on *Jonathan Ross*, 'My Doctor becomes more assured as the series goes on.'

In one of his first stories (Episode 6) 'Vampires of Venice', he pulls out what looks to be an OAP bus pass with a colour photo of William Hartnell on it. The moment lasts only a couple of seconds, but the true fan immediately picked up on it. The message was clear: the legacy was there, the show went on.

Steven Moffat took great care with the building of the new Doctor's character, spending the first third of the opening story, 'The Eleventh Hour', introducing his character and that of his companion, Amelia 'Amy' Pond. The first episode was one hour long as a consequence, but Moffat's decision was vindicated when the *Daily Mail* reported that eight million people had watched it, making Smith an instant success.

It quickly became apparent that Smith liked spitting; he had done this as soon as he was regenerated from David Tennant's Doctor and now he was trying a variety of foods in his first story to see what he liked. After spitting most of them out, he settled for fish fingers dipped in custard.

Once Smith had won over the little girl serving him his fish fingers in custard – and over 35 per cent of the TV watching population – a fast-paced episode ensued and suddenly everyone was captivated by the new Doctor. But the second episode, 'The Beast Below', didn't meet with as much praise from the fans' point of view. Although the reviewers were keen to give the show four or five stars, the story – what there was of it – confused most of the audience, but that was soon sorted by the third episode: the Daleks were back (God bless Terry Nation and the neurosis of Tony Hancock), but this time they were making the tea and working for Winston Churchill.

The Doctor isn't fooled by their tricks and exposes the Daleks' mothership on the dark side of the moon. Suddenly, all hell breaks loose and Spitfires travel into outer space to attack the ship in a *Star Wars IV – A New Hope* type of way.

At the end of the story, a new-look Dalek is created and they escape to fight another day. A sinister crack on the wall appears throughout these early episodes to promise a grand finale of some substance. But for the moment it wasn't just the Spitfire attack that was evocative of the X-Wing fighter attack on the *Death Star*. Back in Smith's second story there was a chute that left them in an 'underground sewer' – a creature's mouth; more than one fan made a connection to *Star Wars*, and then there was a further moment that mirrored – to many – Princess Leia's message inside R2D2: 'Help me Obi-wan, you're my only hope'.

It was only when the Weeping Angels returned in their own two-episode story that Smith truly arrived as the Doctor, emulating the dress and style of the first three Doctors. Yes, he was – or rather *is* – a throwback to the old-style Doctor Who, so in a way he played it safe (a posh Doctor once more!).

So much was expected of Matt Smith's Doctor, and the show was battered with so much criticism by the general public – not the critics – it was almost as though they were in denial at the end of David Tennant's Doctor, but Smith weathered the storm.

His character was more erratic than his new series predecessors, basing part of it on Patrick Troughton's interpretation of the Doctor, but as Smith revealed on *The One Show* (1 April 2010), he had based part of his character on Einstein too, building in a wacky eccentricity not uncommon to any great professor. It was also on *The One Show* that he apologised to 'six million viewers' for saying 'crap'. He was almost certainly forgiven by most, due to the building excitement he felt for his first episode, less than two days later (6.20pm, 3 April 2010) – D-Day indeed, when millions of children went to bed fearing the crack in the bedroom wall, even if there wasn't one there.

With a new TARDIS interior, sonic screwdriver, companion and an excellent variation of the theme tune, the Doctor was back again to do battle with the evil of the universe. With Moffat in control, the scare voltage would be put up a notch, as that was what he did best. And the very fact that Matt Smith instantly made a success of the part, especially with the younger viewers, was proof positive that the programme would continue – as Tom Baker once put it – to 'run and run and run'.

Although Smith did many interviews in the run-up to the new series, and even toured the country like a politician seeking votes from a multitude of fans, he couldn't have planned better publicity than being arrested at the airport for carrying an offensive weapon.

The *Telegraph* reported on 31 March 2010 that he was stopped while passing security at Heathrow Airport en route for Belfast. The X-ray machine showed what looked like a weapon in Smith's pocket, when in actual fact it was his sonic screwdriver. He normally kept it on his person so that he could practise with it wherever he went and had broken four before his first episode had been screened.

Smith politely told airport staff that he was the Doctor, but they didn't seem to understand until he showed them some promotional *Doctor Who* memorabilia.

Only the Doctor could get arrested at Heathrow for having a sonic screwdriver, something that simply *has* to be written into the show.

'I have a wonderful journey in front of me.'

Matt Smith

So how did Smith cope with his first season as Doctor Who? Simply, he let the audience make up their own minds. There was resistance to begin with, because David Tennant was so popular, but as the weeks went on and the stories unfolded – along with the season sub-plot – hearts and minds were won over and, everybody realised, it was the same old Doctor.

Smith's interpretation was old school, or rather public school, but that was the eccentric character we were used to. The Doctor's companion, Amy Pond, wowed many a teenage boy – and probably his father too – and had that feisty presence we had come to expect from the Doctor's female companions. Matt Smith and Karen Gillan made a great team, and people began to appreciate that. Along with some excellent scripts, which brought back Silurians, Cybermen and Daleks (to name but a few), the show proved yet again that time moves on and there's always someone ready to take your place.

Arthur Darvill played Karen Gillan's boyfriend/husband (Rory) in the show and spent most of the time as second fiddle to the Doctor in her affections, but he did manage several very heroic scenes and when the duo eventually left the show, they were reunited forever, with a headstone marking their grave site after they had died of old age in USA-past.

Some of the most noteworthy moments in Matt Smith's tenure as Doctor Who were Vincent van Gogh's reaction to how his paintings were appreciated by future generations ('Vincent and the Doctor') and of course the showing-off of his teenage football skills ('The Lodger').

Smith readily accepted the mantle of the 50th Anniversary Doctor Who. A new companion was introduced, Clara Oswald, played by Jenna-Louise Coleman, who was apparently picked by series producer Steven Moffat because she could talk even more quickly than Smith.

In the run up to the second part of the 2012 season (March–May 2013, to create a long season of adventures for US distribution), there was heavy criticism of the BBC for not doing enough to celebrate the show's most significant anniversary. The BBC made statements and even Smith himself gave television interviews to reassure fans that there would be much to enjoy. A special feature-length drama about the genesis of the programme had been commissioned with David Bradley (of *Harry Potter* fame) as William Hartnell. There was also a 50th anniversary story that would be shown in 3D. Then it was announced shortly before the first story of 2013 (30 March) that David Tennant and Billie Piper would return for the special 50th anniversary adventure, but fans were still keen to hear if other former Doctors had been approached to take part in the festivities. However, Colin Baker and Sylvester McCoy had had nothing to say when interrogated by Chris Evans earlier in the month when the former *Doctor Who* stars bade farewell to Television Centre during its last-ever live broadcast.

When attention turned to the obligatory *Doctor Who* Christmas Special, rumours began to spread about Matt

Smith's departure from the show. This started more speculation about how long the programme would endure after Smith's demise as the main character. The Doctor was only meant to have 13 lives, which meant that only two more actors could take up the mantle. And who would be next? Yet again the guessing game was suddenly underway.

But was Smith in a rush to leave? Like David Tennant, some slack was built into his busy *Doctor Who* schedule in order for him to take on other parts. Three dramas released during his first couple of years as the Doctor (before the 50th anniversary) were quite diverse: *Womb* (2010), *Christopher and His Kind* (2011) and *Bert & Dickie* (2012).

Smith starred alongside the sensual Eva Green in *Womb*, playing Green's lover who suddenly dies, but she finds that he can be cloned and decides to have the resulting baby. The years pass and, as the child grows up, he comes to terms with the fact that she has only nurtured him in order to have her lost love back.

There is something alarmingly predictable about the plot, but Green's character is absorbing and Smith's performance is powerful.

Christopher and His Kind is a film documenting writer Christopher Isherwood's trip to Berlin 1931 to partake of free love in a poor man's *Cabaret*-style story. Smith takes his part well, donning an appropriate upper-class accent and carefree abandon in what is an inevitable story of unrequited love and in complete contrast to his role in *Doctor Who*.

To coincide with the 2012 Olympics, Smith appeared in *Bert & Dickie* (2012). The story was based partly on a true tale about the last British Olympics staged in London shortly after the Second World War. Smith plays Bert Bushnel, a working-class oarsman who is desperate for Olympic success,

THE DOCTORS WHO'S WHO

but he is teamed with an over-privileged journalist who irritates him beyond compare: Richard 'Dickie' Burnell, played by Sam Hoare.

In the end Bushnel and Burnell find common ground when discussing modifications to their boat, which could place them in a winning position and fulfil their joint Olympic dream.

The film is gentle and nicely made, but as short interviews with Smith and Hoare showed, filming had its hiccups: Smith and Hoare managed to capsize their boat during rehearsals. Although the camera crew maintained straight faces throughout the whole process, the leading actors felt slightly deflated.

Back to *Doctor Who*, and series seven was one of the most anticipated by the fans because it led up to the 50th anniversary story, with a cliffhanger end that introduced veteran actor John Hurt as the Doctor (another twist in the huge cliffhanger that promised the true identity of the Doctor on 23 November 2013).

Smith *did* announce his departure from the show at the end of the season (prior to the 50th anniversary story), citing Hollywood's need for English actors of some eccentricity. Regardless of what he does next, he will be forever known as the Doctor who took fans through the 50th anniversary. So, did he make it a success? Were the fans eventually happy with the stories?

No hardened fan would be totally happy with a *Doctor Who* season. There is too much variety nowadays, something for everyone rather than one-size-fits all. Some fans – more so than the critics who loved series seven – believed the end of certain stories to be a little rushed. This is probably a fair observation, because although the return of the Martian Ice Warriors ('The Cold War') was popular with everyone, the last third of the story hurtled to a quick conclusion with a Martian rescue vessel saving the day and a very poor line about hitching a lift to the South Pole.

Perhaps more unforgiveable was the obvious comparison to the *Alien* movie; another heart-on-sleeve influence from the production team. Throughout Moffat's era there were obvious comparisons to various *Star Wars* scenes. Mature fans would pass this off as him perhaps wanting to tie in with familiar American themes in order to encourage greater kinship with US fans (hence a Wild West theme in the 2012 part of the season). But despite some frustrations, the 2013 portion was a triumph. Stories such as 'Journey to the Centre of the TARDIS' and 'Nightmare in Silver' created lots of thrills, while the season finale, 'The Name of the Doctor', brought us a colourised William Hartnell to delight young and old fans alike. But after such a high-profile season, Smith knew he had reached his peak and so went onto pastures new.

He had managed to fit in a Hollywood movie, *How to Catch a Monster*, directed by Ryan Gosling, and had taken other interesting parts on British TV, as we have witnessed, so it was time to move on and make way for the twelfth Doctor...

'I think we have to give children more credit. Children are always going to engage with the story in a slightly different way to adults, but I tell you this, I bet you they pay more attention. The science is mad and complicated and brilliant. It's *Doctor Who*! If it's too easy, what's the point?'

Matt Smith

From 'Who's a Clever Boy Then?' Radio Times, 30 March–5 April 2013

CHAPTER FOURTEEN

PETER CAPALDI

'Like the Doctor himself, I find myself in a state of utter terror and delight.'

Peter Capaldi on becoming Doctor Who

IN A SPECIAL TV SHOW hosted by Zoe Ball on Sunday, 4 August 2013, Peter Capaldi was announced as the 12th Doctor Who. By that weekend Capaldi had already been made the hot favourite to land the part by the bookmakers and, by the Monday morning, every national newspaper had him on their front page. 'Peter Capaldi is the latest actor entrusted with the sonic screwdriver and keys to the TARDIS,' *The Times* declared.

It seemed that, with every regeneration, more hype and anticipation has gripped the nation. To have a programme dedicated to the naming of the new Doctor Who was unprecedented. When Patrick Troughton took over there was no fanfare – only confusion about the new idea. But, in 2013, during the 50th anniversary year of the programme, the event was an acceptable and exciting part of the *Doctor Who* legacy.

And what of Peter Capaldi himself?

It was as if time was repeating itself; the older man was back. At 55, Capaldi was the same age as William Hartnell when he started the show all the way back in November 1963.

Even the very conservative newspaper *The Times* let its hair down to greet the new Doctor (its leading article carried the subtitle 'Ooo Ooo Ooo, Wee Ooo Ooo') and proclaimed: 'If James Bond represents how Britain is seen by the world, perhaps Doctor Who represents how the country prefers to see itself.'

The comparison between the two greatest of Britain's fictional exports is an interesting one; they both have ways of reinventing themselves – changing their leading actors – and it is always with quite some fanfare. Of course, both the Doctor Whos and James Bonds are influenced by their times as far as the story content is concerned; but none of them, no matter how long ago, look dated. Like the rock star David Bowie, they each have a certain way of looking timeless. For James Bond this is somewhat easier, as evening suits will never go out of fashion; but celery and an over-long multi-coloured scarf is a completely different issue.

Peter Douglas Capaldi was born in Glasgow – he is to become the third Scot to take the controls of the TARDIS – on 14 April 1958, the day after Peter Davison's seventh birthday. As his surname suggests, his father came from Italian stock (his grandfather had moved to Scotland between the two world wars of the 20th Century), while his mother hailed from Killeshandra, County Cavan, Ireland.

Peter was educated at Teresa's Primary School in Glasgow's Possilpark district, north of the River Clyde. From there he moved to Bishopbriggs in East Dumbarton, where he attended St Matthew's Primary School. His love of performing shone through even at this early age as he put on a puppet show for his peers. He stated in interview that he was taken to the theatre at a young, impressionable age and marvelled at all the blood and make-up; and that's when the acting bug got him.

Peter later attended St Ninian's High School in Kirkintilloch, where he became a member of the Antonine Players, who performed at the Fort Theatre, Bishopbriggs. Around this time he found time to write to the *Radio Times* about a favourite TV show of his – *Doctor Who*. His sweet letter expressed his wish that the show could have a special edition to celebrate the 25th anniversary. He was 15 years old at the time, and how could he imagine that he would be invoved in the culmination of the 50th anniversary of the world-famous TV show he so admired? But, like his Scottish predecessor David Tennant, his *Doctor Who* dream would come true.

While attending the Glasgow School of Art, he became the lead singer in a punk rock band called Dreamboys – the drummer was future comedian Craig Ferguson. The assumed quiet, young *Doctor Who* fan, clearly had something of a rebellious side, as interested as he must have been in rock, but he was also becoming more serious about a career as an actor.

Capaldi's first role was in *Living Apart Together* (1982). This 1980s Scottish comedy film featured pop star B A Robinson as Ritchie Hannah, a second-rate musician who returns to his native Glasgow only to have his wife walk out on him. Capaldi's part is small, as a love interest to Ritchie's wife in a small selection of scenes. An underwhelming debut it may be; but the movie is something of a Scottish cult classic, now available on DVD in a lovingly restored edition by Park Circus.

The second movie that Capaldi was involved in was much more impressive. Again with a very strong Scottish connection, *Local Hero* (1983) has the honour of starring Holywood legend Burt Lancaster in one of his last great roles, and it also has the luxury of an iconic theme tune by Mark Knopfler (Dire Straits), which has been used relatively often on television over the years.

Calpadi plays the gangly and awkward Oldsen, whose job it is to assist a Texan oil billionaire's scout (Mac, played by Peter Riegert) to build a refinery along the beautiful Scottish coastline; but when the Texan turns up (Burt Lancaster) he changes his mind, sending Mac home and sharing a dream of a scientific institute with Oldsen, who has fallen under the spell of a beautiful scientist called Marina (Jenny Seagrove). The final moments of the film sum up the message of the film completely: Mac, now home in America, looks out at skyscrapers in the night, with their lights on and business still being done at all hours. Then we cut to the beautiful highland village, in the daytime, with nobody answering the telephone: money isn't everything.

Local Hero was written and directed by Bill Forsyth, whose earlier movie *Gregory's Girl* won a BAFTA. *Local Hero* would also win a BAFTA and, although a light comedy, it was a much more important movie than *Gregory's Girl*. Forsyth was good at finding home-grown talent (both films being shamelessly Scottish) and John Gordon Sinclair and Peter Capaldi respectively were excellent choices of leading actors.

In 1984 Capaldi took a role in the very straight ITV series *Crown Court*. The episode he was in was called 'Big Deal' and Capaldi plays Eamonn Donnelly, a flame-haired rockabilly artist who gives evidence to support his manager. The result is hysterical, as Eamonn is clearly out of his depth and of no use whatsoever to his frustrated manager. Looking more like Eddie Tenpole Tudor than a quality witness, this one is well worth searching the internet to watch.

A year later Capaldi appeared in long-running TV series

Minder, which starred George Cole as small-time conman Arthur Daley and Dennis Waterman as Arthur's minder Terry McCann. Capaldi's episode (Series 6, Episode 2) was called 'Life in the Fast Food Lane', where he plays a larger-than-life Scot called Ozzie, whose personality Arthur finds unnerving: 'I can see why they built Hadrian's Wall,' Arthur says dryly, when confronted with the prospect of having Ozzie as a passenger in his car.

Through the years Capaldi has played a large number of supporting roles, rarely losing his Scottish accent to play them. Like the two other Scottish Doctor Whos, he appeared in Scottish comedy series *Rab C Nesbitt*. Capaldi's role was a little more sedate than that of his Doctor Who counterparts, playing a street preacher called John who gets heckled by Nesbitt.

But life wasn't completely filled with supporting roles and bit parts. In 1985 he starred as one of The Beatles in the TV movie *John and Yoko: A Love Story*. Although centred around the relationship of John and Yoko, the movie includes the impact that relationship had on The Beatles, to the extent where John Lennon asks the rest of the Fab Four for a divorce so he can marry Yoko Ono.

Capaldi himself played George Harrison, known to many as 'the quiet one' in the band. But George's deep-thinking ways detect the growing relationship between John and Yoko very early on; and he knew he couldn't do too much about it. The way Capaldi presents this, without saying too much at all, is simply great acting.

Like the other actors, Capaldi plays one of the most iconic musician's of all time and, although he doesn't get the voice quite right, he looks the part in what is a well-scripted and emotional film.

Capaldi played manservant Azolan in the award-winning

movie *Dangerous Liasions* (1988). The movie starred Glenn Close, John Malkovitch and Michelle Pfeiffer in some of their finest roles. Capaldi is quite under-rated as Malkovitch's stooge; he sees everything but is powerless to interfere. His underplayed role is a perfect balance to the chaos of Close and Malkovitch, and won him much respect.

Another under-rated performance was in 1992 in the TV series *Early Travellers in North America*. Capaldi appeared in several episodes playing iconic Scottish writer Robert Louis Stevenson. Capaldi's lean figure and long features, along with his native accent, helped him make the part a notable one, but it was sadly ignored and quite lost today.

In 1993 Capaldi joined the *Comic Strip* team in the episode 'Jealousy'. Capaldi opens the show in a balaclava climbing over a house to spy on his wife (Jennifer Saunders). Harry (Capaldi) is a jealous husband who is destroying his marriage through a twisted interpretation of his wife's social calendar.

'Jealousy' unfourtunately isn't the most memorable of Comic Strip episodes. It has its moments; but it is quite dark and unsettling, and one cannot but worry about the twisted mind of poor Harry. Capaldi turned his hand to directing in 1995 with the film *Franz Kafka's It's a Wonderful Life*, for which he won the BAFTA Best Short Film. The following year it tied with short American film *Trevor* for the Oscar for Live Action Short Film. Capaldi's film detailed the frustrations of the writer (Kafka) when writing his most famous novel *Metamorphosis* and truly showed his talents behind the camera for a quality one-off film.

In 1996 Capaldi appeared in the BBC serialisation of Iain Banks's bestselling novel *The Crow Road*. The screenplay, by Bryan Elsley, was an excellent interpretation of Banks's intricate novel of family secrets and mysteries; so much so that

Banks himself confessed of the screenplay: 'Annoyingly better than the book in far too many places.' Was this comment from Banks too kindly? In fact, no, as he explained to me in 1999: 'I was nervous to begin with. I wondered what the BBC had done to my book, but as I watched it I became very happy with it. I thought the cast were excellent.'

The Crow Road was a milestone for many people – author and actors alike. It also started a good relationship between Banks and Capaldi in the respect that the actor started to narrate some of Banks's audio books and appeared in a radio play of Banks's musical novel *Espedair Street* (1988), alongside John Gordon Sinclair (*Gregory's Girl*).

Capaldi played Uncle Rory in *The Crow Road*, one moment happy family member, the next moment restless spirit. Like the book, the TV series is formed of a central story with many flashback scenes, as the mystery of Rory's disappearance is unravelled. The cast, including Joseph McFadden, Bill Patterson, Stella Gonet, David Robb, Dougray Scott and Valerie Edmond, were all really involved with their characters Banks stated that when he visited the set, he could see their passion for the character interaction which was more than he could recall from his novel.

The Crow Road ranks as one of Capaldi's most memorable performances, alongside his stunning – and quite surprising performance – in *Torchwood*.

Capaldi played John Frobisher in 'Torchwood: Children of Earth' in 2009. The role was not a light one. *Torchwood* was considered to be a more adult-themed interpretation of Earth-based *Doctor Who* adventures, with Captain Jack (John Barrowman) continuing his role from the Christopher Eccleston and David Tennant years of *Doctor Who*.

Capaldi played a straight-laced civil servant whose world

comes crashing down when he is faced with a terrible decision: give his children up to an alien intelligence or take their lives instead. It is an incredibly powerful episode of the show, and one in which Capaldi gives an amazing performance – not unlike his role as tough-guy head-of-news Randall Brown in series two of *The Hour*. Perhaps the most memorable scene is when Brown learns of the death of his daughter. The anger and despair is perfectly balanced to the point where you actually feel great sympathy for the character.

Capaldi was only the second Doctor Who to ever appear in the programme before taking on the lead role (Colin Baker being the first). He appeared as Roman Caecilius, an artistic, caring husband and father (like the actor himself) in 'The Fires of Pompeii'; which also included Karen Gillan before she took on the regular role of companion Amy Pond.

David Tennant was the Doctor, with Catherine Tate as companion Donna Noble, in what was nothing short of an excellent episode, mixing in some traditional *Doctor Who* themes (ancient sisterhoods and mythical monsters) with some stunning CGI moments. But Capaldi's interpretation of the Doctor was still just over five years away. In the meantime he would conclude his role as foul-mouthed spin Doctor Malcolm Tucker in the BBC series *The Thick of It*.

'I'm off to deal with the fate of the planet.'

Malcolm Tucker
The Thick of It

The Thick of It entertained TV audiences over the course of eight years with four amusing seasons (2005, 2007, 2009 and 2012), and mainly through Capaldi's outrageous character Malcolm Tucker, who was just an exaggeration of a real politician. Some said that he was an interpretation of Tony Blair's spin-doctor Alistair Campbell; but Campbell wouldn't have got away with Tucker's escapades. His trip to Washington was as hysterical as his episodes in London. Malcolm Tucker really made an impression on the public and the media alike, so much so that jokes of bad language in the TARDIS were rife when it was announced that Capaldi would become Matt Smith's replacement.

Some may have thought that Capaldi was an interesting and not obvious choice for the Doctor; but many around the programme *did* think he was an obvious choice. It was clear the programme would be taken in a new direction with Capaldi at the controls of the TARDIS, perhaps even reverting back towards the first Doctor, but Steven Moffat was excited about the new direction of the show and the scripts that had already been written ahead of the announcement of Capaldi succession.

Rarely had an established actor taken on the role. The early Doctors were well-established of course, but most of the others were all fairly young when taking on the role. So Capaldi brought the show almost full circle during its 50th year. It was an interesting concept; but how would Capaldi look? How would he act? What effect would the Doctor have on his career? The age-old questions raised themselves once more, but this self-confessed *Doctor Who* fan relished the idea on setting out in the TARDIS with his faithful companions and whole new menagerie of monsters and megalomaniacs.

The *Doctor Who* adventure continued; and so did Capaldi's career outside the show. Like the other new millennium Doctor Whos, Capaldi managed to undertake other projects at the same time as committing to the world's longest running science fiction series. While the early Doctors had to commit, priesthood-like, to the cause of *Doctor Who*, their later counterparts didn't and the fear of typecasting diminished somewhat. In 2012, while winning Best TV Comedy Actor Award yet again for Malcolm Tucker in *The Thick of It*, he managed to be a part of two Hollywood movies, one with Angelina Jolie (as the king of the fairies in *Maleficent*), and one with her husband Brad Pitt (in the zombie movie *World War Z*), commenting that the duo were very warm and friendly and had watched the box set of *The Thick of It* over one weekend in order to learn how to swear. Capaldi said that he couldn't confess to be friends with the famous Hollywood couple but was amazed by how friendly and open they were for a married couple so famous.

Doctor Who had come at an amazing time in Capaldi's career. He had achieved so much and was experiencing the height of his Hollywood limelight at the same time as being the Doctor, assuring the world that his career was as fresh and exciting as it ever was, and in fact, possibly more so.

'It's an incendiary combination: one of the most talented actors of his generation is about to play the best part on television.'

Steven Moffat on the announcement of Peter Capaldi becoming the 12th Doctor

CONCLUSION

'But lips where smiles went out and in –
There was no guessing his kith and kin!'

The Pied Piper of Hamelin
Robert Browning

A SHOW THAT ENDURES over 50 years must have something magical
– and sustainable – about it. *Doctor Who* doesn't have a cult
following, it has a broad and diverse following. It is today, as
it has always been, family entertainment and if the younger
ones get scared, the older ones will reassure. For generations
of British TV audiences, *Doctor Who* was an integral part of
growing up. A mysterious man – a Pied Piper – who you know
very little about, but nonetheless follow religiously.

The Pied Piper analogy is a strong one. Look at the Doctor's
many companions: they follow him, care for him, dance with
him – love him. But he is an isolationist, the boy who never
grew up, the man who can only watch people grow old and die,
a man who can never really love a human woman.

He is the Pied Piper, just as William Hartnell described

himself while playing the Doctor; just as Patrick Troughton depicted the Time Lord, with pipe and all; just as Jon Pertwee described himself; just as Colin Baker dressed, and the very role Sylvester McCoy performed on stage before taking on *Doctor Who* and bringing back that air of mystery. And what about Tom Baker's pied scarf? Television viewers dance to the merry tune, but is it a merry tune, or something more sinister?

As Queen Victoria stated to Christopher Eccleston's Doctor, there is something evil about him – the Time Lord – and, perhaps there is something evil about the Pied Piper too. This is something that is echoed in *The Sarah Jane Adventures* when she confronted clowns and similar fairy-tale images. It's as though, in an acting sense, the Pied Piper wears the two faces of variety theatre, the happy and the sad, and can quickly change between the two; surely that sums up the Doctor and his tetchy mood swings?

In 'Black Orchid', a two-part Peter Davison story, the Doctor wears a harlequin suit and mask – very Pied Piper-esque – and evil adopts the same costume too. Yes, there is something sinister about the Doctor, something that makes the actor playing him a little superior. Maybe this was the 'twist' Sydney Newman was looking for when developing the character all those years ago. We seem – as in all good stories – to get more from less. The fact that we don't know certain aspects of a character's make-up allows our imaginations to run riot; and when the critic is at odds with himself, the artist is in accord with himself (to misquote Oscar Wilde).

So the Pied Piper continues his merry dance, with hordes of TV companions and generations of real-life children behind him, happy to dance and play, and continue the legend that is *Doctor Who* into his fifth decade, more popular and sophisticated now than he has ever been. And yes, we follow the Piper into his cave – the TARDIS – because he promises a life of happiness and excitement, but is it always?

What happens when the tune stops? When the Piper puts down his pipe, exhausted, and the rock rolls back and those who danced have all disappeared? What lies beyond that rock? Is there a happy land where only children play; the child inside us all? Is that why adults continue to watch *Doctor Who*, to regain their youth, locked away in the mountainside of maturity? Or is it the secret yearning of the human race to dream of wandering amongst the stars in search of... what exactly? The question to the answer 'forty-two' perhaps, or maybe the reassurance that life goes on after death?

Sarah Jane waited but grew old and disillusioned before the Doctor returned. Time is relative to him, but not to the girl – or girls – who waited.

Doctor Who will one day stop forever. The Doctor – like every mortal creature – will have to die, like the original actors who have played him, such as William Hartnell, Patrick Troughton, Jon Pertwee and Peter Cushing; actors with incredible careers surrounding that iconic part. The part they played for little over four years at most, but a part that has endured and remained in public memory for decades after they cease to be Doctor Who.

If someone watches *Brighton Rock* now, they will note that William Hartnell was Doctor Who. If they watch *The Omen*, they will note that Patrick Troughton was Doctor Who. And if they watch *Worzel Gummidge*, it will again be noted that the brilliant Worzel was also Doctor Who. The actor – despite great roles – will always be pulled back to that brief period where the universe was his oyster and he could knock on any family door in the nation at teatime on a Saturday afternoon and be invited in. And there is the Pied Piper effect on adults. We tell children never to talk to strangers, never to take sweets from strangers, but if Tom Baker's Doctor offered you a jelly baby, would you take it? Conversely, if Christopher Eccleston's Doctor threw open the TARDIS door and asked, 'Coming with me?', would you run inside and let that stone slip back?

Of course you would. The uniqueness of the show makes it special, and makes the lead actors immortal for ever more; and that raises the question after all this time – is it the immortality of the character that gives immortality to the actors? Yes, perhaps it is. But the price of that immortality will always be that all their other work pales into insignificance in comparison to *Doctor Who*. Their epitaph is posthumous typecasting. As the grandparents die, more children are born and then the memories and careers of those past Doctors will fall away. The old movies will cease to be in demand and the only thing that the *Doctor Who* actors will be remembered for is being the Doctor.

So, did typecasting get them in the end or not?

I sincerely hope that this book has addressed the injustice that will continue to build around the careers of the actors who have played the Doctor, because their careers are vitally important to the historical make-up of British TV, cinema, theatre and radio. All those actors are wonderful in many different ways, and the committed *Doctor Who* fan will not cease the costly and time-consuming quest for a full set of autographs – surely the centrepiece of any great *Doctor Who* collection?

Doctor Who is full of British eccentricity – even though it was conceived by Sydney Newman, a Canadian – and while turning a stream of eclectic actors into TV legends, the Time Lord for the present continues his pioneering journey through time and space and that's exactly where we want him: fighting the most evil creatures in the universe and making children's minds more fertile along the way.

Amid the horrors of everyday life, children still need the Doctor, for he is their guardian angel, the theme music his piper's tune, and once the music stops and the TARDIS door opens, a happy and exciting new land awaits. But the adults dance into that land too, to do battle with the many different evils in the universe. The Doctor, like Robert Browning's brilliant poem, is for young and old alike.

'And folks who put me in a passion,
May find me pipe to another fashion.'

The Pied Piper of Hamelin
Robert Browning

PART TWO
THE LEGACY

'A lot of people have said it, and it's perfectly true to say that any actor who's cast as Doctor Who has to be a one-off. He had to be somebody where the mould had been broken, so that you'd never come across another actor quite like him.'

Robert Holmes
Doctor Who scriptwriter

CHAPTER ONE

ACTORS'
CREDITS

WHAT FOLLOWS IS a detailed guide to the work of the actors who have played Doctor Who. Although extensive, I do not claim this to be complete. I have checked official sources, including film archives, official websites of the actors involved and cross-referenced all that information with additional reference material (theatre programmes, handbills, DVD/video cast lists) in private collections. I believe the end result is a good reflection of what each actor achieved in his career. It clearly shows how much of a career the actors had outside of *Doctor Who* and also the importance of those roles in British theatre, television and cinema history.

I haven't included every voice-over or narration, but a small selection of the most important are highlighted, apart from advertisements, which are not documented at all. Also, when an actor has appeared in a series, where possible, I have tried to identify the names of individual episodes.

Some inconsistency was found regarding release dates for films, as the copyright date (year of filming is not necessarily the year of release) was quoted in many archives rather than the release date. The copyright date was largely, though not necessarily, the year prior to release, so I had to make a judgement as to what year to document as a 'release date'. The UK title is used for individual films and/or its foreign title if a foreign film. Additionally, a more general US title is given, if it makes it clear that the film is a sequel.

I have tried to include as many radio shows as possible, especially for Jon Pertwee who did much work there, but the main thrust is film and TV.

Finally, I didn't include dates and locations for theatre appearances because a lot of early information – from the 1960s and before – doesn't exist, especially for touring companies and appearances in repertory theatre. So what you have here is a useful guide that highlights, at a glance, the strong body of work each actor completed outside of *Doctor Who*.

WILLIAM HARTNELL

FILMS:

The Unwritten Law (1929)

School for Scandal (1930), *Man of Mayfair* (1931), *Diamond Cut Diamond* (1932), *Say it with Music* (1932), *That Night in London* (1932), *Follow the Lady* (1933), *I'm an Explosive* (1933), *The Lure* (1933), *Seeing is Believing* (1934), *The Perfect Flaw* (1934), *Swinging the Lead* (1935), *While Parents Sleep* (1935), *Old Faithful* (1935), *The Guv'nor* (1935), *The Shadow of Mike Emerald* (1935), *La Vie Parisienne* (1935) [aka *Parisian Life*, 1936], *Crimson Circle* (1936), *Nothing but Publicity* (1936), *Midnight at Madame Tussaud's* (1936), *Farewell Again* (1937), *They Drive by Night* (1938), *Too Dangerous to Live* (1939), *Murder Will Out* (1939).

They Came by Night (1940)*, *Freedom Radio* (1941)*, *Flying Fortress* (1942), *They Flew Alone* (1942), *Suspect Person* (1942), *Sabotage at Sea* (1942), *The Peterville Diamond* (1942), *The Goose Steps Out* (1942), *The Bells Go Down* (1943), *The Dark Tower* (1943), *Headline* (1943), *San Demetrio London* (1943), *The Way Ahead* (1944), *The Agitator* (1945), *Strawberry Roan* (1945), *Murder in Reverse* (1945), *Appointment with Crime* (1946), *Temptation Harbour* (1947), *Odd Man Out* (1947), *Brighton Rock* (1947), *Escape* (1948), *Now Barabbas was a Robber* (1949), *The Lost People* (1949).

Double Confession (1950), *The Dark Man* (1951), *The Magic Box* (1951), *The Ringer* (1952), *The Holly and the Ivy* (1952), *The Pickwick Papers* (1952), *Will Any Gentleman?* (1953), *Footsteps in the Fog* (1955), *Josephine and Men* (1955), *Doublecross* (1956), *Private's Progress* (1956), *Tons of Trouble* (1956), *Yangtse Incident: the Story of HMS Amethyst* (1957), *Hell Drivers* (1957), *The Hypnotist* (1957), *Dates with Disaster* (1957), *On the Run* (1958), *Carry On Sergeant* (1958), *Shake Hands with the Devil* (1959), *The Mouse that Roared* (1959), *The Night We Dropped a Clanger* (1959), *Strictly Confidential* (1959), *The Desperate Man* (1959).

And the Same to You (1960), *Jackpot* (1960), *Piccadilly Third Stop* (1960), *Tomorrow at Ten* (1962), *This Sporting Life*

(1963), *Heavens Above!* (1963), *To Have and to Hold* (1963), *The World Ten Times Over* (1963), *Tomorrow at Ten* (1964).

*uncredited and unconfirmed.

THEATRE:

The Merchant of Venice (1926), *She Stoops to Conquer* (1926), *Julius Caesar* (1926), *As You Like It* (1926), *Hamlet* (1926), *The Tempest* (1926), *School for Scandal* (1926), *The Merchant of Venice* (1926), *Macbeth* (1926), *Good Morning, Bill* (1927), *Miss Elizabeth's Prisoner* (1928), *Monsieur Beaucaire* (1928), *Hamlet* (1928), *School for Scandal* (1928), *The Merchant of Venice* (1928), *The Man Responsible* (1928), *The Lad* (1928), *Good Morning, Bill* (1928), *A Bill of Divorcement* (1928/9), *77 Park Lane* (1929).

The Ugly Duchess (1930), *The Man Who Changed His Name* (1931), *The Young Idea* (1931), *The Man I Killed* (1932), *Too Good to be True* (1932), *Just Married* (1933), *While Parents Sleep* (1934), *Behold We Live* (1934), *Good Morning, Bill* (1934), *The Brontës* (1934), *Eliza Comes to Stay* (1934), *Counsellor at Law* (1934), *Apron Strings* (1934), *Pursuit of Happiness* (1934), *Nothing but the Truth* (1934), *Indoor Fireworks* (1934), *Lord Richard in the Pantry* (1935), *Mr Faintheart* (1935), *The Maitlands* (1935), *It Pays to Advertise* (1935), *The Ghost Train* (1935), *Charley's Aunt* (1935), *White Cargo* (1935), *A Little Bit of Fluff* (1935), *The Ghost Train* (1936), *Someone at the Door* (1937), *Paganini* (1937), *Take it Easy* (1937), *Power & Glory* (1938), *Happy Returns* (1938), *The Second Man* (1939), *Faithfully Yours* (1939).

Nap Hand (1940), *What Ann Brought Home* (1940), *Brighton Rock* (1943).

What Ann Brought Home (1950), *Seagulls Over Sorrento* (1950 and 1954), *Treble Trouble* [aka *Home and Away*] (1955), *Ring for Cathy* (1956).

The Cupboard (1961), *Puss in Boots* (1967), *Brothers and Sisters* (1968).

TV:

Douglas Fairbanks Jnr Presents, 'The Auction', Season 3, Episode 28, 25 May 1955; *London Playhouse*,'The Inward Eye', Season 1, Episode 7, 10 November 1955; *The Errol Flynn Theatre*, 'The Red Geranium', Season 1, Episode 13, 1955; *The Army Game*, Season 1, Episode 1, 19 June 1957, Season 2, Episode 3, 3 January 1958; *Probation Officer*, Season 1, Episode 28; *The Flying Doctor*, 'The Changing Plain', Season 1, Episode 9, 1959; *Dial 999*, 'The Killing Job', Season 1, Episode 1, 6 July 1958, '50,000 Hands', Season 1, Episode 16, 1959.

Kraft Mystery Theatre, 'The Desperate Men', Season 1, Episode 11, 23 August 1961; *Ghost Squad*, 'High Wire', Season 1, Episode 4, 30 September 1961; *The Plane Makers*, Season 1, Episode 15, 20 May 1963; *The Edgar Wallace Mystery Theatre*, 'To Have and to Hold', Season 4, Episode 9, July 1963; *Tomorrow at Ten*, 1964; *No Hiding Place*, 'The Game', Season 10, Episode 2, 23 March 1967; *Softly, Softly*, 'Cause of Death', Season 3, Episode 13, 4 January 1968; *Crime of Passion*, 'Alain', Season 1, Episode 6, 27 April 1970; *Doctor Who*, 'The

Three Doctors', Season 10, Story 6 (4 episodes, 30 December 1922, 6 January 1973, 13 January 1973, 20 January 1973).

WILLIAM HARTNELL'S DOCTOR WHO:

Season 1
Pilot episode (1episode), 'An Unearthly Child/The Tribe of Gum' (4 episodes total), 'The Daleks' (7 episodes), 'The Edge of Destruction' (2 episodes), 'Marco Polo' (7 episodes), 'The Keys of Marinus' (6 episodes), 'The Aztecs' (4 episodes), 'The Sensorites' (6 episodes), 'The Reign of Terror'(6 episodes).

Season 2
'Planet of the Giants' (3 episodes), 'The Dalek Invasion of Earth' (6 episodes), 'The Rescue' (2 episodes), 'The Romans' (4 episodes), 'The Web Planet' (6 episodes), 'The Crusade' (4 episodes), 'The Space Museum' (4 episodes), 'The Chase' (6 episodes), 'The Time Meddler' (4 episodes).

Season 3
'Galaxy 4' (4 episodes), 'Mission to the Unknown' (one-off episode not featuring the Doctor), 'The Myth Makers' (4 episodes), 'The Dalek Master Plan' (12 episodes), 'The Massacre of St Bartholomew's Eve' (4 episodes), 'The Ark' (4 episodes), 'The Celestial Toymaker' (4 episodes), 'The Gunfighters' (4 episodes), 'The Savages' (4 episodes), 'The War Machine' (4 episodes).

Season 4
'The Smugglers' (4 episodes), 'The Tenth Planet' (4 episodes).

PATRICK TROUGHTON

FILMS:

Escape (1948), *Hamlet* (1948), *Badger's Green* (1949), *Cardboard Cavalier* (1949).

Chance of a Lifetime (1950), *Treasure Island* (1950), *Waterfront* (1950), *The Woman With No Name* (1950), *The Franchise Affair* (1951), *White Corridors* (1951), *The Black Knight* (1954), *Richard III* (1955), *The Curse of Frankenstein* (1957), *The Moonraker* (1958).

The Phantom of the Opera (1962), *Jason and the Argonauts* (1963), *The Gorgon* (1964), *The Black Torment* (1964), *The Viking Queen* (1967).

Scars of Dracula (1970), *Frankenstein and the Monster From Hell* (1974), *The Omen* (1976), *Sinbad and the Eye of the Tiger* (1977).

THEATRE:

After the Second World War, Patrick Troughton returned to the theatre. He spent some time at the Amersham Repertory Company, the Bristol Old Vic and the Pilgrim Players at the Mercury Theatre Nottingham. Little is known about his various appearances. He did play Adolf Hitler on stage in *Eva Braun* and he appeared a couple of times with William Hartnell, apparently once as an understudy.

TV:

Hamlet (1947), *King Lear* (1948), *RUR* (1948).

Kidnapped (1952) (5 episodes)
'The Brig Covenant', 'Red Fox', 'The Flight in the Heather', 'The Quarrel', 'Back to Shaws'.

Robin Hood (1953) (6 episodes)
'Gathering the Band', 'The Abbot of St Mary's', 'Who is Robin?', 'The Silver Arrow', 'A King Comes to Greenwood', 'The Secret'.

Misalliance (1954).

Clementina (1954) (6 episodes)
'For the Sake of a Throne', 'A Man Needs His Friends', 'The Night of the 27th', 'The Road to Italy', 'For Love of a Queen', 'The End of a Journey'.

The Scarlet Pimpernel (1956) (10 episodes)
'The Elusive Chauvelin', 'Something Remembered', 'The Sword of Justice', 'Sir Andrew's Fate', 'The Ambassador's Lady', 'The Christmas Present', 'The Flower Woman', 'The Imaginary Invalid', 'Antoine & Antoinette', 'A Tale of Two Pigtails'.

The Count of Monte Cristo (1956) (3 episodes)
'Marseilles', 'The Portuguese Affair', 'The Island'.

Kidnapped (1956), Lilli Palmer Theatre 'The End of Justice' (1956).

Sword of Freedom (1957) (4 episodes)
'Vespucci', 'The Tower', 'The School', 'The Ambassador'.

Assignment Foreign Legion (1 episode) 'The Conquering Hero' (1957), *Precious Bane* (1957) (6 episodes), *The New Adventures of Charlie Chan* (1 episode) (1958), *Queen's Champion* (1958), *Ivanhoe* (1 episode) 'The Kidnapping' (1958), *The Rebel Heiress* (1958), *William Tell* (1 episode) 'The Golden Wheel' (1958), *The Flying Doctor* (1 episode) 'A Stranger in Distress' (1959), *Dial 999* (2 episodes) '50,000 Hands', 'Thames Division' (1959).

The Cabin in the Clearing (1959) (4 episodes)
'Friends and Foes', 'Ordeal By Fire', 'The Desperate Plan', 'The Break Out'.

The Scarf (3 episodes) (1959), *The Naked Lady* (1 episode) (1959), *The Moonstone* (1 episode) (1959), *Interpol Calling* (1 episode) 'The Thirteen Innocents' (1959), *H. G. Wells' Invisible Man* (1 episode) (1959), *The History of Mr Polly* (2 episodes) (1959), *Three Green Nobles* (1 episode) 'The Painter' (1959).

BBC Sunday Night Theatre (6 episodes) (1950–59)
'The Family Reunion' (1950), 'Adventure Story' (1950), 'Lines of Communication' (1952), 'Midsummer Fire' (1955), 'The White Falcon' (1956), 'Maigret and the Lost Life' (1959).

Law of the Plainsman (1 episode) 'The Matriarch' (1960).

The Splendid Spur (6 episodes) (1960)
'The King's Messenger', 'The Road to the West', 'Bristol Keep', 'The Godsend', 'Joan of the Tor', 'The End of the Gleys'.

The Four Just Men (2 episodes) 'The Night of the Precious Stones', 'The Moment of Truth' (1959 and 1960).

The Adventures of Robin Hood (8 episodes) (1959–60)
'The Friar's Pilgrimage' (1956), 'The Dream' (1957), 'The Blackbird' (1957), 'The Shell Game' (1957), 'The Bandit of Brittany' (1957), 'Food For Thought' (1957), 'Elixir of Youth' (1958) 'The Bagpiper' (1960).

Paul of Tarsus (2 episodes) 'The Feast of Pentecost', 'To the Gentiles' (1960), *Danger Man* (2 episodes) 'The Lonely Chair', 'Bury the Dead' (1961 and 1962), *International Detective* (2 episodes) 'The Marion Case', 'The Martos Case' (1960 and 1961), *Maigret* (1 episode) 'Raise Your Right Hand' (1961), *Compact* (1 episode) 'Efficiency Expert' (1962).

Sir Francis Drake (3 episodes) (1961–62)
'Doctor Dee' (1961), 'Drake on Trial' (1962), 'The Bridge' (1962).

Wuthering Heights (1962).

BBC Sunday Night Play (2 episodes) (1960–62)
'Twentieth Century Theatre: The Insect Play' (1960), 'Sword of Vengeance' (1962).

Man of the World (1 episode) 'Death of a Conference' (1962), *The Sword in the Web* (1 episode) 'The Alibi' (1962), *The Old Curiosity Shop* (11 episodes) (1962–63), *Lorna Doone* (1 episode) 'A Summons to London' (1963), *No Cloak – No Dagger* (1963), *Espionage* (1 episode) 'He Rises on Sunday and We on Monday' (1963), *The Sentimental Agent* (1 episode) 'The

Scroll of Islam' (1963), *Crane* (1 episode) 'Man Without a Past' (1964), *The Midnight Men* (1 episode) 'The Man From Miditz' (1964), *Detective* (1 episode) 'The Loring Mystery' (1964), *The Third Man* (1 episode) 'A Question in Ice' (1964).

Smuggler's Bay (5 episodes) (1964)
'On the Beach', 'A Reward of Fifty Pounds', 'The Auction', 'In the Vault', 'A Death and a Discovery'.

Thorndyke (1 episode) 'The Old Lag' (1964), *HMS Paradise* (1 episode) 'Thar's Gold in Them Thar Holes' (1964), *Artist's Notebooks* (1 episode) 'William Hogarth (1697–1764)' (1964), *The Indian Tales of Rudyard Kipling* (1 episode) 'The Brokenhurst Divorce Case' (1964), *Sherlock Holmes* (1 episode) 'The Devil's Foot' (1964), *The Wednesday Play* (1 episode) 'And Did Those Feet?' (1965), *A Tale of Two Cities* (10 episodes) (1965).

No Hiding Place (4 episodes) (1959–65)
'The Stalag Story' (1959), 'Two Blind Mice' (1960), 'Process of Elimination' (1961), 'The Street' (1965).

David Copperfield (1 episode) 'The Long Journey' (1966), *Armchair Theatre* (1 episode) 'The Battersea Miracle' (1966).

ITV Play of the Week (3 episodes) (1962–63)
'Freedom in September' (1962), 'The Misunderstanding' (1965), 'The First Thunder' (1966).

The Saint (2 episodes) 'The Romantic Matron', 'Interlude in Venice' (1966), *Adam Adamant Lives!* (1 episode) 'D For Destruction' (1966).

Paul Temple (1 episode) 'Swan Song for Colonel Harp' (1970).

The Six Wives of Henry VIII (5 episodes) (1970)
'Catherine of Aragon', 'Anne Boleyn', 'Jane Seymour', 'Anne of Cleves', 'Catherine Howard'.

ITV Playhouse (1 episode) 'Don't Touch Him, He Might Resent It' (1970).

Dr Finlay's Casebook (7 episodes) (1962–70)
'Snap Diagnosis' (1962), 'A Test of Intelligence' (1964), 'The Doctor Cried' (1964), 'The Control Group' (1965), 'A Little Learning' (1965), 'Crusade' (1966), 'Dust' (1970).

Little Women (4 episodes) (1970), *Doomwatch* (1 episode) 'In the Dark' (1971), *On the House* (1 episode) 'The Secret Life of Charlie Cattermole' (1971), *Thirty-Minute Theatre* (2 episodes) 'Give the Clown His Supper', 'Jilly' (1965 and 1971), *Out of the Unknown* (1 episode) 'The Chopper' (1971), *The Persuaders!* (1 episode) 'The Old, the New, and the Deadly' (1971), *Softly, Softly* (2 episodes) 'Best Out of Three', 'Better Than Doing Porridge' (1966 and 1971), *The Goodies* (1 episode) 'The Baddies' (1972).

A Family at War (9 episodes) (1970–72)
'Line in Battle' (1970), 'The Gate of the Year' (1970), 'The Breach in the Dyke' (1970), 'The War Office Regrets' (1970), 'Salute the Happy Morn' (1971), 'The Thing You Never Told Me' (1971), 'Take It On Trust' (1971), 'This Year, Next Year' (1971), '... Yielding Place to New' (1972).

Jason King (1 episode) 'That Isn't Me, It's Somebody Else' (1972), *The Befrienders* (1 episode) 'Fallen Star' (1972), *The Protectors* (1 episode) 'Brother Hood' (1972), *Colditz* (1 episode) 'The Traitor' (1972), *Whoops Baghdad!* (1 episode) 'Ali and the Thieves' (1973), *Ego Hugo* (1973), *Hawkeye, the Pathfinder* (5 episodes) (1973), *Stars on Sunday* (1 episode) 'Glories of Christmas' (1973), *Special Branch* (1 episode) 'Alien' (1974), *Village Hall* (1 episode) 'The Magic Sponge' (1974), *Sutherland's Law* (1 episode) 'Who Cares?' (1974), *Jeannie: Lady Randolph Churchill* (2 episodes) 'Lady Randolph', 'Recovery' (1974), *Thriller* (1 episode) 'The Devil's Web' (1975), *Churchill's People* (1 episode) 'Silver Giant, Wooden Dwarf' (1975).

Z Cars (4 episodes) (1964–75)
'Inside Job' (1964), 'Pressure of Work' (1973), 'Squatters' (1975), 'Eviction' (1975).

The Sweeney (1 episode) 'Hit and Run' (1975), *Crown Court* (2 episodes) 'Pot of Basil', 'Will the Real Robert Randell Please Stand Up' (1974 and 1975), *Our Mutual Friend* (1 episode) (1976), *Survivors* (1 episode) 'Parasite' (1976), *Angels* (1 episode) 'Decision' (1976), *Lorna Doone* (5 episodes) (1976), *Warship* (1 episode) 'Robertson Crusoe' (1977), *Yanks Go Home* (1 episode) 'The Name of the Game' (1977), *Van der Valk* (1 episode) 'Accidental' (1977), *BBC2 Play of the Week* (1 episode) 'The Sinking of *HMS Victoria*' (1977), *Treasure Island* (4 episodes) (1977), *A Hitch in Time* (1978), *Space 1999* (1 episode) 'The Dorcans' (1978), *The Feathered Serpent* (12 episodes) (1976–78).

The Devil's Crown (4 episodes) (1978)

'Bolt From the Blue', 'The Flowers Are Silent', 'Tainted King', 'To the Devil They Go'.

Edward and Mrs Simpson (3 episodes) (1978)
'The Decision', 'Proposals', 'The Abdication'.

The Famous Five (1 episode) 'Five Run Away Together' (1979), *The Onedin Line* (1 episode) 'The Suitor' (1979), *Suez 1956* (1979), *All Creatures Great and Small* (1 episode) 'Hair of the Dog' (1980), *Only When I Laugh* (1 episode) 'Where There is a Will' (1980).

Bognor (6 episodes) (1981)
'Unbecoming Habits: Part 1 – Collingdale's Dead', 'Unbecoming Habits: Part 2 – Balty Tom', 'Unbecoming Habits: Part 3 – The Cross Country Monk', 'Unbecoming Habits: Part 4 – Lord Dismiss Us', 'Unbecoming Habits: Part 5 – Keeping Up With the Jones', 'Unbecoming Habits: Part 6 – Making a Bog of It'.

John Diamond (1981), *BBC2 Playhouse* (1 episode) 'The Pigman's Protege' (1982).

Nanny (5 episodes) (1981–82)
'A Pinch of Dragon's Blood' (1981), 'Other Peoples' Babies' (1981), 'Ringtime' (1982), 'Ashes to Ashes' (1982), 'A Twist of Fate' (1982).

Shine on Harvey Moon (1 episode) 'The Course of True Love' (1982), *Foxy Lady* (2 episodes) (1982), *The Cleopatras* (1 episode) '100 BC' (1983), *King's Royal* (1982–83), *Jury* (1983), *Dramarama* (1 episode) 'The Young Person's Guide to Getting Their Ball Back' (1983).

Play For Today (4 episodes) (1976–83)
'Love Letters on Blue Paper' (1976), 'No Defence' (1980), 'PQ17' (1981), 'Reluctant Chickens' (1983).

Amy (1984), *Minder* (1 episode) 'Windows' (1984), *Swallows and Amazons Forever! The Big Six* (1984).

The Box of Delights (3 episodes) (1984)
'When the Wolves Were Running', 'Where Shall the Knighted Showman Go?', 'Leave Us Not Little, Nor Yet Dark'.

The Two Ronnies 1984 Christmas Special, Long Term Memory (1985).

The Two of Us (5 episodes) (1986)
'Proposals', 'Family Pressures', 'The Limit', 'Cracks in the Pavement', 'The End of the Beginning'.

Yesterday's Dreams (4 episodes) (1987), *Inspector Morse* 'The Dead of Jericho' (1987), *Supergran* (1 episode) 'Supergran and the Heir Apparent', *Knights of God* (13 episodes) (1987).

Note: Troughton played a sizable role in an 11-part adaptation of Evelyn Waugh's *Sword of Honour* on radio in 1974.

PATRICK TROUGHTON'S DOCTOR WHO:

Season 4
'The Power of the Daleks' (6 episodes), 'The Highlanders' (4 episodes), 'The Underwater Menace' (4 episodes), 'The Moonbase' (4 episodes), 'The Macra Terror' (4 episodes), 'The

Faceless Ones' (5 episodes), 'The Evil of the Daleks' (7 episodes).

Season 5
'The Tomb of the Cybermen' (4 episodes), 'The Abominable Snowmen' (6 episodes), 'The Ice Warriors' (6 episodes), 'The Enemy of the World' (6 episodes), 'The Web of Fear' (6 episodes), 'Fury From the Deep' (6 episodes), 'The Wheel in Space' (6 episodes).

Season 6
'The Dominators' (5 episodes), 'The Mind Robber'(5 episodes), 'The Invasion' (8 episodes), 'The Krotons' (4 episodes), 'The Seeds of Death' (6 episodes), 'The Space Pirates' (6 episodes), 'The War Games' (10 episodes).

JON PERTWEE

FILMS:

Dinner at the Ritz (1937), *A Yank at Oxford* (1938), *A Young Man's Fancy* (1939), *The Four Just Men* (1939).

Trouble in the Air (1948), *A Piece of Cake* (1948), *William Comes to Town* (1948), *Murder at the Windmill* (1949), *Helter Skelter* (1949), *Dear Mr Prohack* (1949), *Miss Pilgrim's Progress* (1949).

The Body Said No (1950), *Mister Drake's Duck* (1951), *Will Any Gentleman...?* (1953), *The Gay Dog* (1954), *A Yank in*

Ermine (1955), *It's a Wonderful World* (1956), *Evans Abode* (1956), *The Ugly Duckling* (1959).

Just Joe (1960), *Not a Hope in Hell* (1960), *Nearly a Nasty Accident* (1961), *Ladies Who Do* (1963), *Carry On Cleo* (1964), *I've Gotta Horse* (1965), *Runaway Railway* (1965), *You Must Be Joking!* (1965), *Carry On Cowboy* (1966), *Carry On Screaming* (1966), *A Funny Thing Happened on the Way to the Forum* (1966), *Up in the Air* (1969).

The House That Dripped Blood (1971), *One of Our Dinosaurs is Missing* (1975), *Wombling Free* (1977), *Adventures of a Private Eye* (1977), *No.1 of the Secret Service* (1977), *The Water Babies* (1978).

Deus ex Machina (1984), *Do You Know the Milkyway?* (1985).

Carry On Columbus (1992).

THEATRE:

Twelfth Night (1935), *Lady Precious Stream* (1935), *Love From A Stranger* (1938), *Candida* (1938), *Judgement Day, To Kill A Cat, Goodbye Mr Chips, Night Must Fall* (1942), *George and Margaret* (1942), *HMS Waterlogged* (1944), *Waterlogged Spa* (1946), *The Breadwinner, A Funny Thing Happened on the Way to the Forum* (1963), *There's A Girl in My Soup* (1966), *Oh Clarence, Irene, Super Ted* (1985), *Worzel Gummidge* (1989), *Dick Whittington* (1989), *Aladdin* (1990–91) (1991–92), *Scrooge – The Musical* (1992–93) (1993–94), *Who Is Jon Pertwee?* (1995).

TV:

Toad of Toad Hall (1946).

Ivanhoe (1 episode) 'The Swindler' (1958).

The TV Lark (1963)
Note: this series came between Season Four and Season Five of
the radio show *The Navy Lark* and consisted of the same crew
(unlike the movie, which only included Leslie Phillips from the
original cast). Only titles for the first seven of the 10 episodes
have been traced: 'Opening Night', 'Advertising Drive', 'The
Party Political Broadcast', 'Back to Portsmouth', 'Serial
Programming, 'The African Incident', 'Yours or MINE!!!'

A Slight Case of... (1 episode) 'The Enemy Within' (1965),
Mother Goose (1965), *The Avengers* (1 episode) 'From Venus
With Love' (1967), *Beggar My Neighbour* (1 episode) (Season
1) (1967), *Jackanory* (10 episodes) 'The Green Witch', 'The
Talking Cat', 'The Enchanted Children', 'The Clock That
Wasn't There', 'Who is Tom Tildrum?' (1966) 'Little Grey
Rabbit's Washing Day', 'Little Grey Rabbit and the Weasel',
'Little Grey Rabbit Goes to the Sea', 'Little Grey Rabbit Makes
Lace', 'Little Grey Rabbit's Birthday' (1967).

Whodunnit (1974–78), *Four Against the Desert* (1975), *The
Goodies* (1 episode) 'Wacky Wales' (1975).

Worzel Gummidge (1979–81)
Series 1: 'Worzel's Washing Day', 'A Home Fit For Scarecrows',
'Aunt Sally', 'The Crowman', 'A Little Learning', 'Worzel Pays
A Visit', 'The Scarecrow Hop'.

Above: Sylvester McCoy starred as the next Doctor. He is pictured here with his assistant Melanie (played by Bonnie Langford). © *Rex Features*

Inset: Promotional material for a 1988 production of *The Pied Piper* starring McCoy.

Below left: Doctor Who was just a one-off character role for the versatile Paul McGann, despite also playing him in official *Doctor Who* audio adventures. © *Rex Features*

Below right: A flamboyant Peter Cushing, looking more like a modern interpretation of the Doctor in this publicity photo than the ancient professor he played on screen.

The forgotten Doctor, Peter Cushing. Although he played the Time Lord in two films in the 1960s (*above*), Cushing will always be remembered for his numerous roles in Hammer Horror films, such as 1959's *The Mummy* (*below*).

Above left: Russell T Davies, the man behind the 2005 revival of Doctor Who.

Above right: In April 2011, fans were saddened to hear of the death of the actress Elisabeth Sladen, who played Sarah Jane Smith, one of the Doctor's longest serving and most popular companions.

Below: Sladen pictured at the 2009 Welsh BAFTAs with two other Doctor Who regulars: Bernard Cribbins and Catherine Tate. ©Rex Features

Above: Christopher Eccleston was cast as the Doctor for a new generation. He left after one season, much to the disappointment of many fans. © *Rex Features*

Below: Pictured with Billie Piper – who played assistant Rose Tyler – during a break in filming in Cardiff in November 2004. © *Rex Features*

Above left: Scottish actor David Tennant was chosen to replace Eccleston in 2005. He was a phenomenal success in the role.   © *Rex Features*

Above right: With Billie Piper in 2006…   © *Rex Features*

Below left: …and Catherine Tate, who played the fiery Donna Noble.

© *Rex Features*

Below right: Sharing a joke with Freema Agyeman, who played medical student Martha Jones.   © *Rex Features*

Above: Tennant at the BAFTA Cymru Film and Television Awards in 2007, where he won the Best Actor award for *Doctor Who*. He is pictured with Eve Myles, the Best Actress winner for her performance in the *Doctor Who* spin-off, *Torchwood*.

© *Rex Features*

Below left: Tennant in the title role of the Royal Shakespeare Company's 2008 production of *Hamlet*, with Patrick Stewart. It was while he was with the RSC that he announced his departure from *Doctor Who*.

© *Rex Features*

Below right: Promotional material from *Hamlet*.

Above left: Matt Smith was chosen to play the Eleventh Doctor, the youngest actor to have ever played the Time Lord.

© *Rex Features*

Above right: Before stepping into the Tardis, Smith has acted in the West End production of *Swimming with Sharks*, which starred Christian Slater and Helen Baxendale.

Below: Although Tennant's shoes were big ones to fill, Smith proved an instant hit with fans.

© *Rex Features*

Matt Smith and Karen Gillan filming their first series of Doctor Who (*above*), and at a promotional event (*below*).   ©*Rex Features/Brian Aldrich*

Series 2: 'Worzel and Saucy Nancy', 'Worzel's Nephew', 'A Fishy Tale', 'The Trial of Worzel Gummidge', 'Very Good Worzel', 'Worzel in the Limelight', 'Fire Drill', 'The Scarecrow Wedding'.

Series 3: 'Moving On', 'Dolly Clothes-Peg', 'A Fair Old Pullover', 'Worzel the Brave', 'Worzel's Wager', 'Choir Practice', 'A Cup o' Tea and a Slice o' Cake'.

Series 4: 'Muvver's Day', 'The Return of Dolly Clothes-Peg', 'The Jumble Sale', 'Worzel in Revolt', 'Will the Real Aunt Sally...?', 'The Golden Hind', 'Worzel's Birthday'.

Super Ted (10 episodes) 'Super Ted and the Inca Treasure' (pilot), 'Super Ted and the Pearl Fishers' (1982), 'Super Ted and the Train Robbers', 'Super Ted at the Funfair', 'Super Ted and Nuts in Space', 'Super Ted and the Giant Kites', 'Super Ted and the Gold Mine', 'Super Ted and the Stolen Rocket', 'Super Ted and the Elephant's Graveyard', 'Super Ted at Creepy Castle' (1983), 'Super Ted Meets Father Christmas' (1984).

Worzel Gummidge Down Under (1987–89)
Season 1: 'As the Scarecrow Flies', 'The Sleeping Beauty', 'Full Employment', 'Worzel's Handicap', 'King of the Scarecrows', 'Two Heads Are Better Than One', 'Worzel to the Rescue', 'Salve Scarecrow', 'The Traveller Unmasked', 'A Friend in Need'.

Season 2: 'Stage Struck', 'A Red Sky in T'Morning', 'Them Thar Hills', 'The Beauty Contest', 'Balbous Cauliflower', 'Weevily Swede', 'Elementary My Dear Worty', 'Dreams of Avarish', 'The Runaway Train', 'Aunt Sally RA, Wattle Hearthbrush', 'The Bestest Scarecrow'.

The Further Adventures of Super Ted (1989), Virtual Murder (1 episode) 'A Torch For Silverado' (1992).

RADIO:

Note: It is simply impossible to list with any accuracy the number of radio appearances Jon Pertwee amassed during his career, from the odd guest appearance to the uncredited extras he provided. What follows is a listing of his major work.

Lillibulero (Ireland only), *Marmaduke Brown, Young Widow Jones, Stella Dallas, Mediterranean Merry-Go-Round* (1946), *Up the Pole* (1947–52), *Waterlogged Spa* (1948–50), *Puffney Post Office* (1950), *Pertwee Goes Round the Bend, Pertwee's Progress.*

The Navy Lark (1959–77)
Note: *The Navy Lark* spanned 18 years and 15 seasons, plus specials. Certain episodes have now been lost from the archive and anyone who can offer any help in tracing individual episodes should contact the BBC or The Navy Lark Appreciation Society. A basic guide to *The Navy Lark* follows:

Season 1: 16 episodes (1959), Season 2: 27 episodes (1959–60), Season 3: 20 episodes (1960–61), Season 4: 26 episodes (1961–62) plus Christmas Special, Season 5: 6 episodes (1963), Season 6: 19 episodes (1963–64), Season 7: 13 episodes (1965) plus Christmas Special, Season 8: 13 episodes (1966), Season 9: 20 episodes (1967), Season 10: 18 episodes (1968–69), Season 11: 16 episodes (1969–70), Season 12: 11 episodes (1971),

Season 13: 13 episodes (1972), Season 14: 13 episodes (1973), Season 15: 11 episodes (1975–76). A special final episode was broadcast in 1977.

Doctor Who Paradise of Death (1993), *The Ghosts of N Space* (1996).

JON PERTWEE'S DOCTOR WHO:

Season 7
'Spearhead From Space' (4 episodes), 'The Silurians' (7 episodes), 'Ambassadors of Death' (7 episodes), 'Inferno' (7 episodes).

Season 8
'Terror of the Autons' (4 episodes), 'The Mind of Evil' (6 episodes), 'The Claws of Axos' (4 episodes), 'Colony in Space' (6 episodes), 'The Daemons' (5 episodes).

Season 9
'Day of the Daleks' (4 episodes), 'The Curse of Peladon' (4 episodes), 'The Sea Devils' (6 episodes), 'The Mutants' (6 episodes), 'The Time Monster' (6 episodes).

Season 10
'The Three Doctors' (4 episodes), 'Carnival of Monsters' (4 episodes), 'Frontier in Space' (6 episodes), 'The Planet of the Daleks' (6 episodes), 'The Green Death' (6 episodes).

Season 11
'The Time Warrior' (4 episodes), 'Invasion of the Dinosaurs' (6

episodes), 'Death to the Daleks' (4 episodes), 'Monster of Peladon' (6 episodes), 'Planet of the Spiders' (6 episodes).

Special: 'The Five Doctors' (1983).

Note: Jon Pertwee played the Doctor in two BBC audio stories before his death on 20 May 1996. He was scheduled to take part in more.

TOM BAKER

Note: Although Tom Baker is the voice of *Little Britain*, I haven't listed everything he has provided his in-demand voice for.

FILMS:

The Winter's Tale (1968).

Nicholas and Alexandra (1971), *The Canterbury Tales* (1972), *Cari Genitori* (aka *Dear Parents*) (1973), *The Vault of Horror* (1973), *The Golden Voyage of Sinbad* (1974), *The Mutation* (1974), *The Author of Beltraffio* (1974).

The Curse of King Tut's Tomb (1980), *The Zany Adventures of Robin Hood* (1984).

Dungeons & Dragons (2000), *The Magic Roundabout* (voice only) (2005).

Saving Santa (2013).

THEATRE:

The Winter's Tale (1966), *Apple a Day* (1967), *Stand Still and Retreat Onwards* (1967), *Shop in the High Street* (1967), *Dial M for Murder* (1967), *The Reluctant Debutante* (1967), *Late Night Lowther* (1967), *A Bout in the Backyard* (1968), *Ardon of Faversham* (1968), *The Strongbox* (1968), *Hay Fever* (1968), *The Travails of Sancho Panza* (1969).

The Merchant of Venice (1970), *The Idiot* (1970), *A Woman Killed With Kindness* (1971), *The Rules of the Game* (1971), *Troilus and Cressida* (1972), *The White Devil* (1972), *Don Juan* (1972), *Macbeth* (1973), *The Trials of Oscar Wilde* (1974).

Treasure Island (1981), *Feasting With Panthers* (1981), *Educating Rita* (1982–83), *Hedda Gabler* (1982–83), *She Stoops to Conquer* (1984), *The Mask of Moriarty* (1985), *An Inspector Calls* (1987), *The Musical Comedy Murders of the 1940s* (1988).

Little Britain Live (voice only) (2006).

TV:

Dixon of Dock Green (2 episodes) 'Number 13', 'The Attack' (1968), *Z Cars*: 'Hudson's Way' (Parts 1 & 2) (1968), *George and the Dragon* (1 episode) 'The 10:15 Train' (1968), *Market in Honey Lane* (1 episode) (1968), *Thirty-Minute Theatre* 'The Victims: Frontier' (1969).

Softly, Softly 'Like Any Other Friday...' (1970), *Jackanory* 'The

Iron Man' (1972), *The Millionairess* (1972), *Arthur of the Britons* (1 episode) 'Go Warily' (1973), *Frankenstein: The True Story*, *Piccadilly Circus* (1 episode) 'The Author of Beltraffio' (1977), *The Book Tower* (22 episodes) (1979).

The Hound of the Baskervilles (4 episodes) (1982), *Jemima Shore Investigates: Dr Ziegler's Casebook* (1983), *The Passionate Pilgrim* (1984), *Remington Steele* (1984), *The Life and Loves of a She-Devil* (1986), *The Kenny Everett Television Show* (1 episode) (1986), *Roland Rat: The Series* (1 episode) (1986), *Blackadder II* (1986).

The Silver Chair Chronicles of Narnia (Parts 1 & 2) (1990), *Hyperland* (1990), *The Law Lord* (1991), *Selling Hitler* (1991).

Cluedo (Season 3, 6 episodes) (1992):
'A-Haunting We Will Go', 'Scared to Death', 'Murder in Merrie England', 'Blackmail and the Fourth Estate', 'And Then There Were Nuns', 'Deadly Dowry'.

Doctor Who: Dimensions in Time (1993), *The Diary of Jack the Ripper: Beyond Reasonable Doubt?* (narrator) (1993), *Medics* (3 & 4 episodes) (1992–95), *Have I Got News For You* (guest) (1998).

Max Bear (voice only) (2000), *The Canterbury Tales* (1 episode) 'The Journey Back' (voice only) (2000), *This is Your Life* (2000), *Alter Ego* (2001), *Top Ten TV Sci-Fi* (2001), *Fun at the Funeral Parlour* (1 episode) 'The Jaws of Doom' (2001), *Top Ten Comic Book Heroes* (2002).

Randall & Hopkirk (Deceased) (2 seasons, 10 episodes):

'Mental Disorder', 'The Best Years of Your Death', 'Paranoia', 'A Man Called Substance' (2000), 'Whatever Possessed You?', 'Revenge of the Bog People', 'O Happy Isle', 'Painkillers', 'Marshall and Snellgrove', 'The Glorious Butranekh' (2001).

Swiss Toni: Cars Don't Make You Fat (2003), *Strange* (1 episode, Season 7) 'Asmoth' (2003), *Fort Boyard* (2003), *Monarch of the Glen* (Series 6 & 7, 12 episodes), *Britain's Fifty Great Comedy Sketches* (2005), *Little Britain* (23 episodes) (narrator) (2003–06), *The Beep* (45 episodes) (narrator) (2003–06), *The Wind in the Willows* (2006), *Miss Marple: Towards Zero* (2007), *The Dame Edna Treatment* (Episode 4, Season 1) (2007), *Little Britain in America* (6 episodes) (narrator) (2008), *The Girls Aloud Party* (voice only) (2008), *Have I Got News For You* (chair) (2008).

TOM BAKER'S DOCTOR WHO:

Season 12
'Robot' (4 episodes), 'The Ark in Space' (4 episodes), 'The Sontaran Experiment' (2 episodes), 'Genesis of the Daleks' (6 episodes), 'Revenge of the Cybermen' (4 episodes).

Season 13
'Terror of the Zygons' (4 episodes), 'Planet of Evil' (4 episodes), 'Pyramids of Mars' (4 episodes), 'The Android Invasion' (4 episodes), 'The Brain of Morbius' (4 episodes), 'The Seeds of Death' (6 episodes).

Season 14
'The Masque of Mandragora' (4 episodes), 'The Hand of Fear'

(4 episodes), 'The Deadly Assassin' (4 episodes), 'The Face of Evil' (4 episodes), 'The Robots of Death' (4 episodes), 'The Talons of Weng-Chiang' (6 episodes).

Season 15
'Horror of Fang Rock' (4 episodes), 'The Invisible Enemy' (4 episodes), 'Image of the Fendahl' (4 episodes), 'The Sun Makers' (4 episodes), 'Underworld' (4 episodes), 'The Invasion of Time' (6 episodes).

Season 16
'The Ribos Operation' (4 episodes), 'The Pirate Planet' (4 episodes), 'The Stones of Blood' (4 episodes), 'The Androids of Tara' (4 episodes), 'The Power of Kroll' (4 episodes), 'The Armageddon Factor' (6 episodes).

Season 17
'Destiny of the Daleks' (4 episodes), 'City of Death' (4 episodes), 'The Creature From the Pit' (4 episodes), 'Nightmare of Eden' (4 episodes), 'The Horns of Nimon' (4 episodes), 'Shada' (6 episodes).

Note: the shoot for *Shada* was never completed due to industrial dispute at the BBC, therefore the story was never shown on television, as the studio sequences were not finished. However, BBC Video did release it in their *Doctor Who* series of videos, complete with a small script book and links provided by Tom Baker himself.

Season 18
'The Leisure Hive' (4 episodes), 'Meglos' (4 episodes), 'Full Circle' (4 episodes), 'State of Decay' (4 episodes), 'Warrior's

Gate' (4 episodes), 'The Keeper of Traken' (4 episodes), 'Logopolis' (4 episodes).

Note: Tom Baker has also taken part in the BBC audio *Doctor Who* series, reprising his role.

PETER DAVISON

FILMS:

Black Beauty (1994), *Parting Shots* (1999).

Artful Dodgers (2013).

THEATRE:

Love's Labour's Lost (1972–73), *Taming of the Shrew* (1973), *A Midsummer Night's Dream* (1974), *The Two Gentlemen of Verona* (1974), *Hamlet* (1974).

Barefoot in the Park (1981), *Cinderella* (1981), *The Decorator* (1982), *Mother Goose* (1984), *Aladdin* (1984), *Barefoot in the Park* (1984), *Cinderella* (1984), *The Owl and the Pussycat* (1986).

Arsenic and Old Lace (1991), *An Absolute Turkey* (1994), *The Last Yankee* (1995), *Dick Whittington* (1995–96), *Dial M For Murder* (1996), *Chicago* (1999).

Under the Doctor (2001), *Spamalot* (2007–08), *Legally Blonde The Musical* (2010).

TV:

Warship (1 episode) 'One of Those Days' (1974), *The Tomorrow People* (3 episodes) 'A Man for Emily' Parts 1, 2 & 3 (1975), *Love For Lydia* (7 episodes) (Season 1, Episodes 2, 3, 4, 6, 7, 8, 9) (1997), *The Hitchhiker's Guide to the Galaxy* (1 episode) (Season 1, Episode 5) 'Dish of the Day' (1981).

Holding the Fort (20 episodes) (1980–82)
'In Safe Hands', 'Jumping the Gun', 'Come to the Aid of the Party', 'Twelve Good Men and Pooh', 'After the Ball', 'Against the Grain', 'Over the Barrel' (1980), 'New Blood', 'Famous First Words', 'Over and Out', 'Under a Cloud', 'Lock, Stock and Barrel', 'A Sense of Duty' (1981), 'Feeling the Pinch', 'All Boys Together', 'A Place in the Sun', 'Under Pressure', 'One Careful Owner', 'Otherwise Engaged', 'News From the Front' (1982).

All Creatures Great and Small (65 episodes) (1978–90)
'Dog Days', 'It Takes All Kinds', 'Calf Love', 'Out of Practice', 'Nothing Like Experience', 'Golden Lads and Girls', 'Advice and Consent', 'The Last Furlong', 'Sleeping Partners', 'Bulldog Breed', 'Practice Makes Perfect', 'Breath of Life', 'Cats and Dogs', 'Attendant Problems', 'Fair Means and Fowl', 'The Beauty of the Beast', 'Judgement Day', 'Faint Hearts', 'Tricks of the Trade', 'Pride of Possession', 'The Name of the Game', 'Puppy Love', 'Ways and Means', 'Pups, Pigs and Pickle', 'A Dog's Life', 'Merry Gentlemen' (1978), 'Plenty to Grouse

About' (1979), 'Charity Begins At Home', 'Every Dog His Day...', 'Hair of the Dog', 'If Wishes Were Horses', 'Pig in the Middle', 'Be Prepared', 'A Dying Breed', 'Brink of Disaster', 'Home and Away', 'Alarms and Excursions', 'Matters of Life and Death', 'Will to Live', 'Big Steps and Little 'Uns' (1980), 1983 special, 1985 special, 'One of Nature's Little Miracles', 'Barks and Bites', 'The Bull With the Bowler Hat', 'The Pig Man Cometh', 'Hail Caesar!', 'Only One Woof', 'Ace, Queen, King, Jack', '... The Healing Touch', 'For Richer, for Poorer', 'Against the Odds', 'Place of Honour', 'Choose a Bright Morning', 'The Playing Field' (1988), 'The Call of the Wild' (1989), 'The Prodigal Returns', 'If Music Be the Food of Love', 'Knowing How to Do It', 'A Friend for Life', 'Spring Fever', 'A Cat in Hull's Chance', 'Hampered', 'Promises to Keep', 'Brotherly Love' (1990).

Sink or Swim (19 episodes) (1980–82)
'In the Beginning', 'Steve's Girlfriend', 'Croydon' (1980), 'The Turkey', 'The Car', 'The Boat', 'The Interviewer', 'Tourists', 'The Commune', 'The Folk Club', 'The Marrying', 'Ecology', 'University or What?' (1981), 'In the Pursuit of Learning', 'Nothing But Trouble', 'A Sporting Chance', 'A Slight Hankering', 'Making Amends', 'A New Departure' (1982).

Fox Tales (1985), *Anna of the Five Towns* (4 episodes) (Season 1, Episodes 1, 2, 3 & 4) (1985), *Miss Marple: A Pocketful of Rye* (1985), *Magnum PI* (2 episodes) 'Déjà Vu' Parts 1 & 2.
A Very Peculiar Practice (14 episodes) (1986–88)

'A Very Long Way From Anywhere', 'We Love You, That's Why We're Here', 'Wives of Great Men', 'Black Bob's Hamburger Suit', 'Contact Tracer', 'The Hit List', 'Catastrophe

Theory' (1986), 'The New Frontier', 'Art and Illusion', 'May the Force Be With You' 'Bad Vibrations', 'Values of the Family', 'The Big Squeeze', 'Death of a University' (1988).

Tales of the Unexpected (1 episode) 'Wink Three Times' (1988), *Kinsey* (1988).

Campion (16 episodes) (1989–90)
'Look to the Lady' Parts 1 & 2, 'Police at the Funeral' Parts 1 & 2, 'The Castle of the Late Pig' Parts 1 & 2, 'Death of a Ghost' Parts 1 & 2 (1989), 'Dancers in Mourning' Parts 1 & 2, 'Flowers for the Judge' Parts 1 & 2, 'Mystery Miles' Parts 1 & 2 (1990).

Fiddler's Three (14 episodes) (1991)
'The Scapegoat', 'Norma Dove', 'The Dark Horse', 'The Whiz Kid', 'The Velvet Glove', 'Detective Story', 'Time Out', 'The Secret File', 'The Man Most Likely to', 'We Didn't Want to Lose You' Parts 1 & 2, 'The Fiddle', 'Undue Influence', 'Cut and Dried'.

Harnessing Peacocks (1992), *Screen One: A Very Polish Practice* (1992), *The Airzone Solution* (1993), *A Man You Don't Meet Ever Day* (1994), *Mole's Christmas* (1994), *The Zero Imperative* (1994), *Molly* (1995), *The Adventures of Mole* (1995), *The Devil of Winterbourne* (1995), *Ain't Misbehavin'* (12 episodes) (two season of six episodes – 1994–95), *Jeremy Hardy Gives Good Sex* (1995), *Ghosts of Winterbourne* (1996), *Cuts* (1996), *Dear Nobody* (1997), *Scene* (1 episode), 'A Man of Letters' (1997), *Jonathan Creek* (1 episode) 'Danse Macabre' (1998), *The Stalker's Apprentice* (1998), *Verdict* (1 episode), 'Be My Valentine' (1998),

Wuthering Heights (1998), *Hope & Glory* (Season 1, Episode 1) (1999), *The Nearly Complete and Utter History of Everything* (1999), *The Mrs Bradley Mysteries* (3 episodes) 'The Worsted Viper', 'The Rising of the Moon', 'Death at the Opera' (2000), *At Home With the Braithwaites* (26 episodes) (2000–03), *Too Good to Be True* (2003), *The Complete Guide to Parenting* (2006).

Fear, Stress and Anger (6 episodes) (2007)
'The Job List', 'Sex and Friends', 'Stress and Drugs', 'Julie's Interview', 'Health and Gran', 'Menopause'.

Agatha Christie's Miss Marple 'At Bertram's Hotel' (2007).

The Last Detective (17 episodes) (2003–07)
'Pilot Episode', 'Moonlight', 'Tricia', 'Lofty' (2003), 'Christine', 'The Long Bank Holiday', 'Benefit to Mankind', 'Dangerous and the Lonely Hearts' (2004), 'Friends Reunited', 'Towpaths of Glory', 'Three Steps to Hendon', 'Willesden Confidential' (2005), 'Once Upon a Time on the Westway', 'Dangerous Liaisons', 'A Funny Thing Happened on the Way to Willesden', 'The Man From Montevideo', 'The Dead Peasants Society' (2007).

Doctor Who: Time Crash (2007), *Distant Shores* (12 episodes) (2005–08), *Unforgiven* (2009), *Al Murray's Multiple Personality Disorder* (1 episode) (Season 1, Episode 4), *Midsomer Murders* (1 episode) 'Secrets and Spies' (2009), *Micro Men* (2009), *Miranda* (1 episode) 'Teachers' (2009), *The Queen* (1 episode) (2009), *Sherlock* (1 episode) 'The Great Game' (Planetarium voiceover only) (2010).

Law & Order (17 episodes) (2011, 2013)
'The Wrong Man', 'Safe', 'Crush', 'Tick Tock', 'Intent', 'Deal', 'Survivor's Guilt', 'Immune', 'Haunted', 'Trial', 'Line Up', 'Dawn Till Dusk', 'Fault Lines' (2011), 'Tracks', 'Tremors', 'Paternal', 'Fatherly Love' (2013).

PETER DAVISON'S DOCTOR WHO:

Season 19

'Castrovalva' (4 episodes), 'Four to Doomsday' (4 episodes), 'Kinda' (4 episodes), 'The Visitation' (4 episodes), 'Black Orchid' (2 episodes), 'Earthshock' (4 episodes), 'Time-Flight' (4 episodes).

Season 20

'Arc of Infinity' (4 episodes), 'Snakedance' (4 episodes), 'Mawdryn Undead' (4 episodes), 'Terminus' (4 episodes), 'Enlightenment' (4 episodes), 'The King's Demons' (2 episodes).

20th Anniversary Special, 'The Five Doctors'.

Season 21

'Warriors of the Deep' (4 episodes), 'The Awakening' (2 episodes), 'Frontios' (4 episodes), 'Resurrection of the Daleks' (2 episodes), 'Planet of Fire' (4 episodes), 'The Caves of Androzani' (4 episodes).

COLIN BAKER

FILMS:

Zandorra (1989), *Clockwork* (1989).

THEATRE:

Plaintiff in a Pretty Hat (1969), *The Other House* (1969), *Shakespeare Cabbages & Kings, 1959 and All That, The Wizard of Oz, Green Julia, Everyman, Long Christmas Dinner, New Lamps For Old* (1969–70).

Reunion in Vienna (1971), *Caesar & Cleopatra* (1971), *The Price of Justice* (1971), *Conduct Unbecoming* (1972), *Vivat! Vivat Regina!* (1972), *Christie in Love* (1972), *A Game Called Arthur* (1972), *A Christmas Carol* (1972), *A Lion in Winter* (1973), *Guys and Dolls* (1973), *Journey's End* (1973), *Hamlet* (1973), *French Without Tears* (1973), *Move Over Mrs Markham* (1973), *September Tide* (1975), *Let's Do It Your Way* (1977), *Underground* (1977), *The Flip Side* (1978), *Trap For A Lonely Man* (1978), *Macbeth* (1978), *Odd Man In* (1979).

Dick Whittington (1980), *Doctor in the House* (1979), *Traitors* (1980), *Private Lives* (1981), *The Norman Conquest* (1981), *Stagestruck* (1981), *Goldilocks* (1982), *Suddenly At Home* (1983), *The Mousetrap* (1983–84), *Cinderella* (1984), *Aladdin* (1985), *Great Expectations – The Musical* (1985–86), *Cinderella* (1986), *Corpse* (1987), *Robinson Crusoe* (1987), *Death Trap* (1988), *Run For Your Wife* (1989), *Doctor Who:*

The Ultimate Adventure (1989), *Private Lives* (1989), *Peter Pan* (1989).

Born in the Gardens (1990), *Spider's Web* (1990), *Jack and the Beanstalk* (1990), *Privates on Parade* (1991), *Time and Time Again* (1991), *Frankie and Johnny in the Claire De Lune* (1992), *Death and the Maiden* (1992), *Dick Whittington* (1992), *Nightfright* (1993), *Peter Pan* (1993), *Not Now Darling* (1994), *Aladdin* (1994), *Peter Pan* (1995), *Fear of Frying* (1995), *Dick Whittington* (1996), *Peter Pan* (1997), *Babes in the Wood* (1997), *Kind Hearts and Coronets* (1998), *Jack and the Beanstalk* (1998), *Peter Pan* (1999), *Dick Whittington* (1999).

Love Letters (2000), *Out of Order* (2000), *Why Me?* (2000), *Snow White and the Seven Dwarfs* (2000), *Aladdin* (2001), Flare Path (2002), *Corpse* (2002), *Dick Whittington* (2002), *Corpse* (2003), *HMS Pinafore* (2003), *The Haunted Hotel* (2004), *Love Letters* (2004), *Dick Whittington* (2004), *Love Letters* (2005), *Dracula* (2005), *Snow White and the Seven Dwarfs* (2005), *Love Letters* (2006), *Strangers on a Train* (2006), *Bedroom Farce* (2007), *She Stoops to Conquer* (2007), *Dick Whittington* (2007), *She Stoops to Conquer* (2008), *Noises Off* (2008), *Jack and the Beanstalk* (2008–09).

TV:

My Wife's Sister (1954).

Roads to Freedom (13 episodes – Baker appears in 3, 5 & 6) (1970), *The Adventures of Don Quick* (Episode 2, Season 1)

(1970), *No That's Me Over Here!* (Episodes 10 & 11, Season 3) (1970), *The Mind of Mr J G Reeder* 'The Shadow Man' (Baker appears in 1 of 16 episodes) (1971), *Public Eye* 'The Man Who Didn't Eat Sweets' (Episode 9, Season 5) (1971), *Cousin Bette* (5 episodes) 'Family Angel', 'Bitter Harvest', 'Delilah and Her Handmaid', 'The House of Pleasure', 'Poor Relations' (1971), *The Moonstone* (Episode 1 only of 5) (1972), *The Man Outside* (13 episodes) (1972), *War and Peace* (4 episodes of 17), 'Name Day', 'Madness', 'Sounds of War', 'A Letter and Two Proposals' (1972), *The Edwardians* 'Daisy' (1 episode of 8) (1973), *Harriet's Back in Town* (2 episodes) (1973), *Orson Welles Great Mysteries* 'A Terrible Strange Bed' (1973), *Within These Walls* 'Prisoner By Marriage' (1974), *The Camforth Practice* 'Undue Influence' (1974), *Fall of Eagles* (2 episodes) 'End Game', 'The Secret War' (1974).

The Brothers: (46 episodes) (1974–76)
'Partings', 'Hit and Miss', 'Public Concern', 'A Big Mistake', 'The Fall Guy', 'The Self-Made Cross', 'Tiger By the Tail', 'Breakdown', 'Special Licence', 'Flight of Fancy', 'A Very Short Honeymoon', 'Big Deal', 'Package Deal', 'End of a Dream', 'The Judas Sheep', 'Jennifer's Baby', 'War Path', 'Red Sky at Night', 'A Clean Break', 'Red Sky in the Morning', 'Orange and Lemons', 'When Will You Pay Me?', 'Tender', 'The Mole', 'The Chosen Victim', 'Blood and Water', 'The Devil You Know', 'Try, Try, Again', 'The Bonus', 'Birthday', 'To Honour and Obey', 'Home and Away', 'Invitations', 'The Female of the Species', 'Manoeuvres', 'Arrivals and Departures', 'The Distaff Side', 'Cross Currents', 'Ripples', 'Celebration...', 'Windmills', 'The Golden Road', 'Out of the Blue', 'The Knock on the Door', 'The Ordeal', 'The Christmas Party'.

Blake's 7 (1 episode) 'The City at the Edge of the World' (1980), *For Maddie with Love* (1980), *Dangerous Davies: The Last Detective* (1981), *Juliet Bravo* 'The Intruder' (1982), *The Citadel* (Episode 4 of 10) (1983), *Swallows and Amazons Forever! Coot Club* (1984), *Swallows and Amazons Forever! The Big Six* (1984), *Roland Rat: The Series* (Episode 3, Season 1) (1986).

Summoned By Strangers (1992), *More Than a Messiah* (1992), *The Stranger: In Memory Alone* (1993), *The Airzone Solution* (1993), *The Zero Imperative* (1994), *Breach of the Peace* (1994), *The Stranger: The Terror Game* (1994), *Eye of the Beholder* (1995), *The Harpist* (1997), *The Famous Five* 'Five Go To Billycock Hill' (Parts 1 & 2) (1997), *Jonathan Creek* 'The Wrestler's Tomb' (1997), *The Knock* (Episodes 3, 4, 5 & 6, Season 3), *A Dance to the Music of Time* (1 episode of 4) 'Post War' (1997), *The Bill* 'Going Down' (1997), *Casualty* (2 episodes) 'Accidents Happen' (1989), 'An Eye For An Eye' (1998), *Souls Ark* (1999), *Sunburn* (Episode 2, Season 1) (1999), *The Adventures of Young Indiana Jones: Daredevils of the Desert* (1999), *The Waiting Time* (1999), *Dangerfield* 'Haunted' (1999).

The Asylum (2000), *Travel Wise* (2000), *Hollyoaks* 'The Judge' (1 episode) (2000), *Time Gentlemen Please* 'Day of Trivheads' (2000), *The Impressionable Jon Culshaw* (Episode 2, Season 1) (2000), *Little Britain* (2005), *D'Artagnan et les trios Mousquetaires* (2005), *The Afternoon Play* 'Your Mother Should Know' (2006), *Kingdom* (Episode 2, Season 3) (2009), *Doctors* (4 episodes) 'A Matters of Principle' (2001), 'Honourable Gentlemen' (2006), 'The Romantics' (2006), 'Every Heart That Beats' (2011), *Tiger Troubles*

(2010), *Hustle* (1 episode) (2010), *I'm A Celebrity... Get Me Out Of Here!* (2012).

COLIN BAKER'S DOCTOR WHO:

Season 21 cont.
'The Twin Dilemma'.

Season 22
'Attack of the Cybermen' (2 episodes), 'Vengeance on Varos' (2 episodes), 'The Mark of the Rani' (2 episodes), 'The Two Doctors' (3 episodes), 'Timelash' (2 episodes), 'Revelation of the Daleks' (2 episodes).

Season 23
'The Mysterious Planet' (4 episodes), 'Mindwarp' (4 episodes), 'Terror of the Vervoids' (4 episodes), 'The Ultimate Foe' (2 episodes).

Note: the above season comes under the heading, 'The Trial of a Time Lord'.

Additional Note: Colin Baker also took part in the BBC audio *Doctor Who* and has completed other audio dramas such as *Sapphire & Steel*.

SYLVESTER MCCOY

FILMS:

Dracula (1979).

Leapin' Leprechauns (1995), *Spellbreaker: Secret of the Leprechauns* (aka *Leapin' Leprechauns 2*) (1996).

Eldorado (2010), *Back2Hell* (2010), *Punk Strat: The Movie* (2010), *The Hobbit: An Unexpected Journey* (2012), *Highway to Hell* (2012), *The Hobbit: The Desolation of Smaug* (2013), *The Christmas Candle* (2013), *When the Devil Rides Out* (2013), *The Hobbit: There and Back Again* (2014).

THEATRE:

The Ken Campbell Roadshow 'Modern Myths' (circa 1975), *Twelfth Night* (1976), *She Stoops to Conquer* (1976).

The Secret Policeman's Ball (1981), *Pirates of Penzance* (1982), *Dracula* (1985), *The Pied Piper* (1987), *Aladdin* (1989).

Cinderella (1993), *The Government Inspector* (1993–94), *The Invisible Man* (1993–94), *Zorro: the Musical* (1995), *Life is a Dream* (1998).

The Hypochondriac (2000), *The Lion, the Witch and the Wardrobe* (2001–02), *King Lear* (2001), *The Dead Move Fast* (2001), *Live From Golgotha* (2002), *Hello Dali* (2002), *Noises*

Off (2003), *Dick Whittington* (2003–04), *Arsenic & Old Lace* (2005), *Dick Whittington* (2005–06), *A Midsummer Night's Dream* (2006), *Me and My Gal* (2006), *The Pocket Orchestra* (2006), *The Lion, the Witch and the Wardrobe* (2007), *King Lear* (2007), *The Mikado* (2008), *The Lovely Russell Concert* (2008), *Little Shop of Horrors* (2009), *Cinderella* (2010).

Other theatrical productions: *Buster's Last Stand*, *Gone With Hardy*, *Robin Hood*.

TV:

Vision On (1965).

Robert's Robots (1 episode) 'Dial C for Chaos' (1973), *Lucky Feller* (1 episode) 'Lucky Feller: pilot' (1975), *For the Love of Albert* (TV mini-series) (1977), *Tiswas* (1974–82), *Jigsaw* (1979), *All the Fun of the Fair* (1979).

BBC2 *Playhouse* (1 episode) 'Electric in the City' (1980).

Big Jim and the Figaro Club (1979–81)
'Pilot: Big Jim and the Figaro Club' (1979), 'Dung From a Rocking Horse' (1981), 'Laughing Like a Drain' (1981), 'Hearts of Oak' (1981), 'The Pursuit of Courtly Love' (1981), 'Tiny Revolutions' (1981).

Eureka (1982).

The Last Place on Earth (6 episodes) (1985)
'Leading Men', 'Rejoice', 'Foregone Conclusion', 'The Glories of the Race', 'Gentlemen and Players', 'Minor Diversion'.

No 73 (1 episode) 'Moving Space' (1985), *Dramarama* (1 episode) 'Frog' (1985), *Three Kinds of Heat* (1987), *What's Your Story?* (1988), *The Noel Edmonds Saturday Roadshow* (1 episode) (1989), *Thrill Kill Video Club* (1991), *The Airzone Solution* (1993), *Jackanory* (1979–93), *The Zero Imperative* (1994), *Frank Stubbs Promotes* (1 episode) 'Mrs Chairman' (1994), *Rab C. Nesbitt* (1 episode) 'Father' (1996), *Beyond Fear* (1997), *The History of Tom Jones, a Foundling* (4 episodes) (1997), *Destiny of the Doctor* (1998).

The Mumbo Jumbo (2000), *Do You Have a Licence to Save This Planet?* (2001), *See It, Saw It* (1 episode) 'Courage and Adventure' (2001), *Hollyoaks* (1 episode) (2002), *The Shieling of the One Night* (2002), *Still Game* (1 episode) 'Oot' (2004), *Mayo* (1 episode) (2006), *The Bill* (2 episodes) '010', '457' (2002 and 2006), *Great Performances* (1 episode) 'King Lear' (2008), *Doctors* (1 episode) 'The Lollipop Man' (2008), *Casualty* (2 episodes) 'Life and Soul', 'The Evil That Men Do' (2001 and 2008), *Al Murray's Multiple Personality Disorder* (Season 1, Episode 6) (2009), *The Academy* (2009), *The Academy Part 2: First Impressions* (2009), *The Academy: Special* (2012).

Other television: *Starstrider, Space Cadets, Today is Saturday, Wake Up Smiling, The Foot Doctor, Light in Dark Places, Hell's Kitchen, The 100 Great Kids' TV Shows*.

SYLVESTER MCCOY'S DOCTOR WHO:

Season 24
'Time and the Rani' (4 episodes), 'Paradise Towers' (4

episodes), 'Delta and the Bannerman' (3 episodes), 'Dragonfire' (3 episodes).

Season 25
'Remembrance of the Daleks' (4 episodes), 'The Happiness Patrol' (3 episodes), 'Silver Nemesis' (3 episodes), 'The Greatest Show in the Galaxy' (4 episodes).

Season 26
'Battlefield' (4 episodes), 'Ghost Light' (3 episodes), 'The Curse of Fenric' (4 episodes), 'Survival' (3 episodes).

PAUL MCGANN

FILMS:

Withnail & I (1987), *Empire of the Sun* (1988), *Snowball* (1988), *Tree of Hands* (1989), *The Rainbow* (1989), *Streets of Yesterday* (1989), *Dealers* (1989).

A Paper Mask (1990), *The Monk* (1990), *Afraid of the Dark* (1991), *Alien 3* (1992), *The Three Musketeers* (1993), *Catherine the Great* (1996), *The Hanging Gale* (1996), *Fairytale: A True Story* (1997), *Downtime* (1997), *The Dance of Shiva* (1998), *Our Mutual Friend* (1988).

My Kingdom (2001), *Queen of the Damned* (2002), *Listening* (2003), *Y Mabinogi* (voice only) (2003), *Fables of Forgotten Things* (2005), *Naked in London* (2005), *Gypo* (2005), *Poppies* (2006), *Voice From Afar* (2006), *Always Crashing in the Same Car* (2007), *Lesbian Vampire Killers* (2009), *A Little Place Off the Edgware Road* (2010).

THEATRE:

John, Paul, George, Ringo and Bert (1981), *Much Ado About Nothing* (1981), *Cain* (1981), *Piaf* (1981), *Godspell* (1981), *Oi! For England* (1982), *Yakety Yak* (1982–83), *The Genius* (1984), *Loot* (1984), *The Seagull* (1986), *A Lie of the Mind* (1987).

Sabina (1998).

Mourning Becomes Electra (2003), *Little Black Book* (2003), *The Gigli Concert* (2005), *Helen* (2009), *Sonnet 155* (2010), *The Plague* (2011), *Butley* (2011), *Grotesque Chaos* (2011).

TV:

Play for Today (1 episode) 'Whispering Wally' (1982), *Give Us a Break* (1983), *Sharpe's Rifles* (1983), *The Importance of Being Earnest* (1986).

The Monocled Mutineer (4 episodes) (1986)
'The Making of a Hero', 'A Dead Man on Leave', 'When the Hurly-Burly's Done', 'Before the Shambles'.

Screenplay (1 episode) 'Cariani and the Courtesans' (1987), *Jackanory* (1 episode) 'The Whipping Boy' (1989).

Drowning in the Shallow End (1990), *Nice Town* (3 episodes) 'Idyll', 'Unto Us a Child is Born', 'Immaculate Conception' (1992), *The Merchant of Venice* (1996), *The One That Got Away* (1996), *Breathless Hush* (1999), *Forgotten* (1999), *Nature Boy* (2000), *Fish* (2000), *Hotel!* (2001).

Hornblower (4 episodes) (2001–03)
Mutiny (2001), Retribution (2001), Loyalty (2003), Duty (2003).

My Kingdom (2001), *Sweet Revenge* (2001), *Blood Strangers* (2002), *The Biographer* (2002), *Agatha Christie's Poirot* (1 episode) 'Sad Cypress' (2003), *Lie With Me* (2004), *Twisted Tales* (1 episode) 'Txt Msg Rcvd' (2005), *Kidnapped* (2005), *Agatha Christie's 'Sleeping Murder'* (2006), *Sea of Souls* (1 episode) 'Rebound' (2006), *If I Had You* (2006), *Tripping Over* (6 episodes) (2006), *True Dare Kiss* (6 episodes) (2007), *Voice From Afar* (2007), *The True Story: Escape From Alcatraz* (2008), *Fables of Forgotten Things* (2008), *Collision* (5 episodes) (2009), *Jonathan Creek* (1 episode) 'The Judas Tree' (2010), *Luther* (2010–11), *New Tricks* (2011), *The Petrol Age* (four parts) (2012).

PAUL MCGANN AS NARRATOR:

(Due to the gravity of some of McGann's documentary narrations, it was deemed important to list some of his most memorable pieces of work.)

Dispatches: 'Hope for the Last Chance Kids', 'Cutting Edge: Leaving Home at 8', *The Making of Alien 3* (1992), *Bible*

Mysteries (3 episodes) 'Joseph and his Coat of Many Colours', 'Peter and the First Church', 'David and Saul' (1996), *The Making of Alien* (2003), *Behind the Crime* (2004), *Wacko About Jacko* (2005), *Cathedral* (2005), *Daphne Ashbrook in the UK* (2005), *Kill Me if You Can* (2005), *The Sperminator* (2005), *Foetus Snatcher* (2005), *Adopt Me, I'm A Teenager* (2005), *The Ripper Hoaxer: Wearside Jack* (2006), *Mr Miss Pageant* (2007), *World of Compulsive Hoarders* (2007), *Zero Hour* (3 episodes) 'One of America's Own', 'The Sinking of the Estonia', 'Capturing Saddam' (2006, 2007 and 2008, *The Foreign Legion: Tougher Than the Rest* (2007), *The Ties That Bind Us* (2008), *Getting A Head* (2008).

PAUL MCGANN'S DOCTOR WHO:

Doctor Who – The Movie.

Note: It must be noted that, although Paul McGann only appeared in one feature-length TV film, he did provide continuity to the series by regenerating on screen from Sylvester McCoy. McGann signed a contract for a series, but unfortunately this didn't happen because the film makers didn't believe they could make a success of the show in the United States at that time. However, his version of the interior of the TARDIS was used when the show was relaunched in the new millennium.

It must also be noted that Paul McGann has been the most prolific audio and drama Doctor Who, and that all of his appearances are available on BBC audio CDs.

CHRISTOPHER ECCLESTON

FILMS:

Let Him Have It (1991), *Anchoress* (1993), *Shallow Grave* (1994), *Jude* (1996), *Death and the Compass* (1996), *Elizabeth* (1998), *A Price About Rubies* (1998), *Heart* (1999), *eXistenZ* (1999), *With or Without You* (1999).

The Tyre (2000), *Gone in 60 Seconds* (2000), *The Others* (2001), *This Little Piggy* (2001), *Strumpet* (2001), *The Invisible Circus* (2001), *24 Hour Party* (2002), *I Am Dina* (2002), *Revengers Tragedy* (2002), *28 Days Later* (2002), *The Seeker: The Dark is Rising* (2007), *New Orleans, Mon Amour* (2008), *GI Joe: The Rise of the Cobra* (2009), *Amelia* (2009), *GI Joe 2: The Revenge of the Cobra* (2011), *Song for Marion* (2012), *Thor: The Dark World* (2013).

THEATRE:

Lock Up Your Daughters (Salford Tech), *A Streetcar Named Desire* (1998), *Woyzeck, The Wonder, Dona Rosita – The Spinster, Bent* (1990), *Abingdon Square* (1990), *Aide Memoire* (1990), *Encounters, Waiting at the Water's Edge* (1993).

Miss Julie (2000), *Hamlet* (2002), *Romeo and Juliet* (2004), *Electricity* (2004), *A Doll's House* (2009), *Antigone* (2012).

TV:

Blood Rights (1990), *Casualty* (1 episode) 'A Reasonable Man' (1990), *Inspector Morse* (1 episode) 'Second Time Around' (1991), *Boon* (1 episode) 'Cover Up' (1991), *Rachel's Dream* (1992), *Agatha Christie's Poirot* (1 episode) 'One, Two, Buckle My Shoe' (1992), *Friday On My Mind* (1992), *Business With Friends* (1992), *Roots* (1992), *Cracker* (10 episodes) 'The Mad Woman in the Attic' Part 1 & 2, 'To Say I Love You' Parts 1, 2 & 3, 'One Day A Lemming Will Fly' Parts 1, 2 & 3, 'To Be A Somebody' Parts 1, 2 & 3 (1993), *Our Friends in the North* (9 episodes) '1964', '1966', '1967', '1970', '1974', '1979', '1984', '1987', '1995' (1996).

Wilderness Men (2000), *Killing Time: The Millennium Poem* (2000), *Clocking Off* (2 episodes) 'Yvonne's Story', 'Steve's Story' (2000), *Othello* (2001), *Linda Green* (1 episode) 'Twins' (2001), *The League of Gentlemen* (1 episode) 'How the Elephant Got His Trunk' (2002), *Lost in La Mancha* (2002), *Flesh and Blood* (2002), *Sunday* (2002), *The King and Us* (2002), *The Second Coming* Parts 1 & 2 (2003), *Only Human* (1 episode) 'Bosom Buddies' (2006), *Heroes* (5 episodes) 'Chapter Twelve: Godsend', 'Chapter Thirteen: The Fix', 'Chapter Fourteen: Distraction', 'Chapter Sixteen: Unexpected', 'Chapter Seventeen: Company Man' (2007), *Perfect Parents* (2006), *The Sarah Silverman Program* (1 episode) 'I Thought My Dad Was Dead, But It Turns Out He's Not' (2008), *The Happiness Salesman* (2009), *The Beautiful Fantastic* (2010), *Lennon Naked* (2010), *Accused* (1 episode) 'Willy's Story' (2010), The *Shadow Line* (7 episodes) (2011), *The Borrowers* (2011), *Time Shift* (1 episode) 'When Wrestling was Golden: Grapples, Grunts and Grannies' (2012), *Blackout* (Series 1, episodes 1, 2 &3).

RADIO:

Chancer (1 episode) 'Jo' (1991), *Room of Leaves* (1998), *Pig Paradise* (1998).

Some Fantastic Places (2001), *Bayeux Tapestry* (2001), *The Importance of Being Morrissey* (2002), *The Iliad* (2002), *Cromwell: Warts and All* (2003), *Life Half Spent* (2004), *Crossing the Dark Sea* (2005), *Sacred Nation* (2005), *Born to Be Different* (2005), *A Day in the Death of Joe Egg* (2005), *E=mc2* (2005), *Dubai Dreams* (2005), *Wanted: Mum and Dad* (2005), *Children in Need* (2005), *This Septic Isle* (2005), *The 1970s: That Was the Decade That Was* (2006).

CHRISTOPHER ECCLESTON'S DOCTOR WHO:

Re-launched TV series.

Series I
'Rose' (1 episode), 'The End of the World' (1 episode), 'The Unquiet Dead' (1 episode), 'Aliens of London/World War Three' (2 episodes), 'Dalek' (1 episode), 'The Long Game' (1 episode), 'Father's Day' (1 episode), 'The Empty Child/The Doctor Dances' (2 episodes), 'Boom Town' (1 episode), 'Bad Wolf/The Parting of the Ways' (2 episodes).

DAVID TENNANT

FILMS:

Jude (1996), *Bite* (1997), *LA Without A Map* (1998), *The Last September* (1999), *Being Considered* (2000), *One Eyed Jacques* (2001), *Nine ½ Minutes* (2002), *Bright Young Things* (2003), *Old Street* (2004), *Harry Potter and the Goblet of Fire* (2005), *Free Jimmy* (2006), *Glorious 39* (2009), *St Trinian's: The Legend of Fritton's Gold* (2009), *How to Train Your Dragon* (voice only) (2010).

THEATRE:

The Resistible Rise of Arturo Ui (1991), *Shinda The Magic Ape* (1991–92), *Jump The Life to Come* (1992), *Hayfever* (1992), *Tartuffe* (1992), *Merlin* (1992–93), *Antigone* (1993), *The Princess and the Goblin* (1993), *The Slab Boys Trilogy* (1994), *What the Butler Saw* (1995), *An Experienced Woman Gives Advice* (1995), *The Glass Menagerie* (1996), *Long Day's Journey into Night* (1996), *Who's Afraid of Virginia Woolf?* (1996), *As You Like It* (1996), *The General From America* (1996), *The Herbal Bed* (1996), *Hurly Burly* (1997), *The Real Inspector Hound/Black Comedy* (1998), *Vassa – Scenes From Family Life* (1999), *Edward III* (1999), *King Lear* (1999), *The Comedy of Errors* (2000), *The Rivals* (2000), *Romeo & Juliet* (2000), *A Midsummer Night's Dream* (2001), *Comedians* (2001), *Push Up* (2002), *Lobby Hero* (2002), *The Pillowman* (2003), *Look Back in Anger* (2005–06), *Hamlet* (2008–09), *Love's Labour's Lost* (2008), *Much Ado About Nothing* (2010), *Richard II* (2013).

RADIO:

Nebulous (1 episode) 'Holofile 703: Us and Phlegm' (2010), *Of Mice and Men* (2010).

TV:

Dramarama 'The Secret of Croftmore' (1988), *Rab C. Nesbitt* 'Touch' (Season 3, Episode 2) (1993), *Taking Over the Asylum* (6 episodes) (1994), *The Tales of Para Handy* (9 episodes/2 seasons) (1994–95), *The Bill* 'Deadline' (1995), *A Mug's Game* (1996), *Holding the Baby* (Season 1, Episode 2) (1997), *Duck Patrol* (7 episodes) (1998), *Love in the 21st Century* 'Reproduction' (episode 1) (1999), *The Mrs Bradley Mysteries* 'Death at the Opera' (Season 1, Episode 1) (2000), *Randall & Hopkirk (Deceased)* (episode 1, Season 1) (2000), *People Like Us* 'The Actor' (Season 2, Episode 4) (2001), *Sweetnightgoodheart* (2001), *'Foyle's War' in Crime in Wartime Britain* (Episode 3) (2002), *Posh Nosh* (Episodes 3 & 8) (2003), *Trust* (Season 1, Episode 6) (2003), *Spine Chillers* 'Bradford in My Dreams' (2003), *The Deputy* (2004), *He Knew He Was Right* (4 episodes) (2004), *Blackpool* (6 episodes) (2004), *Traffic Warden* (2004), *Casanova* (3 episodes) (2005), *The Quatermass Experiment* (2005), *Secret Smile* (2 episodes) (2005), *The Romantics* (3 episodes) (2006), *The Chatterley Affair* (2006), *Recovery* (2007), *Dead Ringers* (Season 7, Episode 6) (2007), *Learners* (2007), *Top Gear* (2007), *Extras* 'Christmas Special' (2007), *Einstein and Eddington* (2008), *Derren Brown's Trick or Treat* (2 episodes) (2008), *The Sarah Jane Adventures* (2 episodes) (2009), *Hamlet* (2009), *Masterpiece Contemporary* (2009–10), *Rex is Not Your Lawyer* (2010), *Single Father* (4 episodes) (2010), *United* (2011), *This is Jinsy* (1 episode) (2011), *True Love* (2012), *The Minor Character* (2012), *Spies of Warsaw* (2012), *The Political Husband* (3-part series) (2012), *Comedy World Cup* (7 episodes as the presenter) (2012), *The Escape Artist* (2013), *Broadchurch* (2013).

DAVID TENNANT'S DOCTOR WHO:

Specials: 'Doctor Who: Children in Need', 'The Christmas Invasion'.

Series 2
'New Earth' (1 episode), 'Tooth and Claw' (1 episode), 'School Reunion' (1 episode), 'The Girl in the Fireplace' (1 episode), 'Rise of the Cybermen/The Age of Steel' (2 episodes), 'The Idiot Lantern' (1 episode), 'The Impossible Planet/The Satan Pit' (2 episodes), 'Love and Monsters' (1 episode), 'Fear Her' (1 episode), 'Army of Ghosts/Doomsday' (2 episodes).

Special: 'The Runaway Bride'.

Series 3
'Smith and Jones' (1 episode), 'The Shakespeare Code' (1 episode), 'Gridlock' (1 episode), 'Daleks in Manhattan/ Evolution of the Daleks' (2 episodes), 'The Lazarus Experiment' (1 episode), '42' (1 episode), 'Human Nature/The Family of Blood' (2 episodes), 'Blink' (1 episode), 'Utopia/The Sound of Drums/Last of the Time Lords' (3 episodes).

Special: 'Children in Need', 'Time Crash', 'Voyage of the Damned'.

Series 4

'Partners in Crime' (1 episode), 'The Fires of Pompeii' (1 episode), 'Planet of the Ood' (1 episode), 'The Sontaran Stratagem/The Poison Sky' (2 episodes), 'The Doctor's Daughter' (1 episode), 'The Unicorn and the Wasp' (1 episode), 'Silence in the Library/Forest of the Dead' (2 episodes), 'Midnight' (1 episode), 'Turn Left' (1 episode), 'The Stolen Earth/Journey's End' (2 episodes).

(Specials)
Christmas 2008 'The Next Doctor' (1 episode), Easter 2009 'Planet of the Dead' (1 episode), Autumn Special 2009 'The Waters of Mars' (1 episode), Winter Specials 2009–10 'The End of Time' (2 episodes), 50th Anniversary Special.

Animated Specials

'The Infinite Quest' (13 episodes), 'Dreamland' (6 episodes).

MATT SMITH

FILM:

How to Catch a Monster (2014).

THEATRE:

Murder in the Cathedral (2003), *The Master and Margarita* (2004), *Fresh Kills* (2004), *On the Shore of the Wild World* (2005), *The History Boys* (2005–06), *Burn/Chatroom/*

Citizenship (2006), *Swimming With Sharks* (2007–08), *That Face* (2008).

TV:

The Ruby in the Smoke (2006), *The Shadow in the North* (2007), *In Bruges* (2007), *The Street* (2007), *The Secret Diary of a Call Girl* (2007), *Party Animal* (2007), *Moses Jones* (3 episodes) (2009), *Together* (2009), *Womb* (2010), *The Sarah Jane Adventures* (2 episodes) 'Death of the Doctor' (2010), *Christopher and His Kind* (2011), *Bert and Dickie* (2012).

MATT SMITH'S DOCTOR WHO:

Series 5
'The Eleventh Hour', 'The Beast Below', 'Victory of the Daleks', 'The Time of the Angels/Flesh and Stone', 'The Vampires of Venice', 'Amy's Choice', 'The Hungry Earth/Cold Blood', 'Vincent and the Doctor', 'The Lodger', 'The Pandorica Opens/The Big Bang'.

'A Christmas Carol' (Christmas Special)
'Space', 'Time' (x2 Comic Relief specials)

Series 6
'The Impossible Astronaut/Day of the Moon' (2 episodes), 'The Curse of the Black Spot' (1 episode), 'The Doctor's Wife' (1 episode), 'The Rebel Flesh/The Almost People' (2 episodes), 'A Good Man Goes to War' (1 episode), 'Let's Kill Hitler' (1 episode), 'Night Terrors' (1 episode), 'The Girl Who Waited' (1 episode),

'The God Complex' (1 episode), 'Closing Time' (1 episode), 'The Wedding of River Song' (1 episode).

'The Doctor, the Widow and the Wardrobe' (Christmas Special) 'Pond Life' (5-part mini adventure)

Series 7
'Asylum of the Daleks' (1 episode), 'Dinosaurs on a Spaceship' (1 episode), 'A Town Called Mercy' (1 episode), 'The Power of Three' (1 episode), 'The Angels Take Manhattan' (1 episode).

'The Snowmen' (Christmas Special).

Series 7 cont.
'The Bells of Saint John' (1 episode), 'The Rings of Akhaten' (1 episode), 'Cold War' (1 episode), 'Hide' (1 episode), 'Journey to the Centre of the TARDIS' (1 episode), 'The Crimson Horror' (1 episode), 'Nightmare in Silver' (1 episode), 'The Name of the Doctor/50th Anniversary Special' (2 episodes).

Christmas Special (Christmas Day 2013) (Introducing Peter Capaldi as the 12th Doctor).

PETER CAPALDI

FILM:

Living Apart Together (1982), *Local Hero* (1983), *Turtle Diary* (1985), *The Lair of the White Worm* (1988), *The Love Child* (1988), *Dangerous Liaisons* (1988).

December Bride (1991), *Soft Top Hard Shoulder* (1993), *Captives* (1994), *Smilla's Sense of Snow* (1997), *Bean, The Ultimate Disaster Movie* (1997), *Shooting Fish* (1997), *What Rats Won't Do* (1998).

Mrs Caldicot's Cabbage War (2002), *Max* (2002), *Niceland (Population 1.000.002)* (2004), *Modigliani* (2004), *House of 9* (2005), *Wild Country* (2005), *The Best Man* (2005), *Big Fat Gypsy Gangster* (2011), *World War Z* (2013), *The Fifth Estate* (2013), *Maleficent* (2014).

THEATRE:

Dracula (1985), *Treats* (1989)
The Judas Kiss (1998)
The Ladykillers (2011-13)

TV:

Crown Court (1 Episode) 'Big Deal' (1984), *Minder* (1 Episode) 'Life in the Fast Food Lane' (1985), *Travelling Man* (1 Episode) 'Blow-Up' (1985), *John and Yoko: A Love Story* (1985), *C.A.T.S. Eyes* (1 Episode) 'Powerline' (1986), *Rab C Nesbitt* (1 Episode) 'Seasonal Greet' (1988), *Shadow of the Noose* (1 Episode) 'The Camden Town Murder' (1989), *Dream Baby* (1989), *Dramarama* (1 Episode) 'Rosie the Great' (1989). *The Chain* (4 Episodes) 'Lennox'. Vicky Elliot', 'Miss Brinkwell', 'David Lynton' (1990), *Ruth Rendell Mysteries* (3 Episodes) 'Some Lie and Some Die (Parts 1-3) (1990), *Agatha Christie: Poirot* (1 Episode) 'Wasp's Nest' (1991), *Screen Two* (1

Episode), 'Do Not Disturb' (1991), *Selling Hitler* (Season 1, Episodes 1-5) (1991), *Titmuss Regained* (3 Episodes) 'Today', 'Tomorrow', 'And the Next Day' (1991), *The Cloning of Joanna May* (1992), *Mr Wakefield's Crusade* (1992), *Early Travellers in North America* (3 Episodes) (1992), *The Secret Agent* (1992), *Micky Love* (1993), *The Comic Strip Presents... Jealousy* (1993), *Stay Lucky (*1 Episode) 'The Driving Instructor' (1993), *Prime Suspect 3* (1993), *Chandler & Co* (6 Episodes) (1994), *Runaway One* (1995), *The All New Alexei Sayle Show* (7 Episodes) (1994-95), *Giving Tongue* (1996), *The Treasure Seekers* (1996), *Lost for Words* (1996), *Delta Wave* (2 Episodes) 'The Light Fantastic' (Part 1 and 2) (1996), *Neverwhere* (5 Episodes) 'Knightsbridge', 'Earls Court to Islington', Blackfriars', 'Down Street', 'As Above, So Below' (1996), *The Crow Road* (4 Episodes) 'Prentice', 'Kenneth', 'Fergus', 'Rory' (1996), *The Vicar of Dibley* (2 Episodes) 'Songs of Praise' (1994) 'The Christmas Lunch Incident' (1996), *The History of Tom Jones, a Foundling* (Season 1, Episodes 3, 4, 5) (1997), *Psychos* (Season 1, Episode 6), *The Greatest Store in the World* (1999). *Hotel!* (2001), *High Stakes* (1 Episode) 'Dream Team' (2001), *Solid Geometry* (2003), *Unconditional Love* (2003), *In Deep* (1 Episode) 'Character Assassination: Part 1' (2003), *Fortysomething* (Season 1, Episodes 1-6) (2003), *Shotgun Dave Rides East* (2003), *Judge John Deed* (1 Episode) 'Conspiracy' (2003), *Sea of Souls* (2 Episodes) 'Seasing Double (Parts 1 and 2), *Passers By* (2004), *My Family* (1 Episode) 'Dentist to the Stars' (2004), *Foyle's War* (1 Episode) 'A War of Nerves' (2004), *Salvage* (2004), *Peep Show* (1 Episode) 'University Challenge' (2004), *The Afternoon Play* (1 Episode) 'The Singing Cactus' (2005), *Pinochet in Suburbia* (2006), *Donovan* (Season 1, Episode 3) (2006), *Midsomer Murders* (1 Episode) 'Death in Chorus' (2006), *Aftersun*

(2006), *Waking the Dead* (2 Episodes) 'The Fall (Parts 1 and 2) (2007), *Coming Up* (1 Episode) 'Brussels' (2007), *Fallen Angel* (2 Episodes) 'The Office of the Dead', 'The Judgement of Strangers' (2007), *Magicians* (2007), *Horizon* (1 Episode) 'Prof. Regan's Supermarket Secrets' (2007), *Skins* (4 Episodes), *Cold Blood* (6 Episodes) (2008), *The Devil's Whore* (Season One, Episodes 1-3), *Glendogie Bogey* (2008), *Midnight Man* (Part One-Two) (2008), *10 Minute Tales* (1 Episode) 'Syncing' (2009), *Torchwood* (Five Episodes) 'Children of Earth' (Day One-Five) (2009), *In the Loop* (2009), *Getting On* (Season 1, Episode 2) (2009), (Season 2 Episodes 2 and 6) (2010), *Bloody Foreigners* (1 Episode) 'The Untold Invasion of Britain' (2010), *Bistro* (2010), *Accused* (1 Episode) 'Helen's Story' (2010), *The Nativity* (Episodes 1-4) (2010), *The Suspicions of Mr Whicker: The Murder at Road Hill House* (2011), *The Field of Blood* (Episodes 1 and 2) (2011), *The Penguins of Madagasscar* (1 Episode) 'A Visit From Uncle Nigel' (2011), *The Thick of It* (2005-2012), *The Hours* (Season 2 Episodes 1-6) (2012), *Doctor Who* (1 Episode) 'The Fires of Pompeii' (2013), *The Three Musketeers* (TVseries) (2014).

CHAPTER TWO

LOST FROM THE VAULTS

WHAT FOLLOWS IS a list of *Doctor Who* episodes missing from the BBC archives. The BBC has spent much time and trouble recovering old stories from the William Hartnell and Patrick Troughton eras, but many episodes are still missing, feared lost forever. If any film collector has *anything* they feel may be of value to the BBC, whether clips, whole episodes or complete stories, the BBC would dearly like to hear from you. The most recent discovery of 'Enemy of the World' and 'The Web of Fear' in a Nigerian TV station store room (as publicised across the media on 12 October 2013), is proof that the search for missing stories/episodes is not a futile one.

Note regarding the Missing Episodes Guide: The number in parenthesis is the number of episodes for that story, which is then followed by the numbered episodes missing from that story. There are 97 episodes missing from the archive, which equates to 26 incomplete stories.

'Marco Polo' (7) eps 1–7; 'The Reign of Terror' (6) eps 4 & 5; 'The Crusade' (4) eps 2 & 4; 'Galaxy 4' (4) eps 1, 2, 4; 'Mission to the Unknown' (1) (note: this story does not feature the Doctor) ep 1; 'The Myth Makers' (4) 1–4; 'The Dalek Master Plan'(12) eps 1, 3, 4, 6, 7, 8, 9, 11, 12; 'The Massacre of St Bartholomew's Eve' (4) eps 1–4; 'The Celestial Toymaker' (4) 1–3; 'The Savages' (4) eps 1–4; 'The Smugglers' (4) eps 1–4; 'The Tenth Planet' (4) ep 4.

'The Power of the Daleks' (6) eps 1–6; 'The Highlanders' (4) eps 1–4; 'The Underwater Menace' (4) eps 1 & 4; 'The Moonbase' (4) eps 1 & 3; 'The Macra Terror' (4) eps 1–4; 'The Faceless Ones' (6) eps 2, 4, 5, 6; 'The Evil of the Daleks' (7) eps 1, 3, 4, 5, 6, 7; 'The Abominable Snowmen' (6) eps 1, 3, 4, 5, 6; 'The Ice Warriors' (6) eps 2 & 3; 'The Web of Fear' (6) ep 3; 'Fury From the Deep' (6) eps 1–6; 'The Wheel in Space' (6) eps 1, 2, 4, 5; 'The Invasion' (8) eps 1 & 4; 'The Space Pirates' (6) 1, 3, 4, 5, 6.

Note regarding Jon Pertwee stories: Although there is a record of every single episode featuring Jon Pertwee's Doctor, the quality of some prints is not up to scratch. Also some surviving prints are overseas edits of full-length UK episodes/stories or colourised from existing black and white stock. Therefore if anybody has prints of Pertwee episodes they are encouraged to contact the BBC to check if they have a full-length version currently missing from the Archives.

Fan Favourites: Although recovery of all *Doctor Who* episodes is a priority of fans and the BBC alike, long-term fans of the show highlight the following episodes as the greatest priority to recover: 'Marco Polo' (rated as one of the greatest historical stories ever and one the BBC poured more money into than usual, regarding sets and costumes. This 7-episode story is the only completely missing story from *Doctor Who*'s first ever season), 'The Tenth Planet' episode 4 (the whole story apart from the last episode exists in the BBC archives). Although the regeneration scene exists, the rest of episode 4 is sadly missing. 'The Power of the Daleks' (the whole story is missing from the archive, but the recovery of episode 1 is most desirable as it shows the Doctor coming to terms with his new body), 'The Dalek Master Plan' episode 12 (features a gruesome end to a *Doctor Who* companion and climax to the longest-ever story, 9 episodes remain missing).

Note regarding DVD releases: Some missing episodes have been animated and the original soundtrack – which still exists of every *Doctor Who* episode – applied to create a complete record of some stories. If at least half the story exists in the archive, there is a valid reason to 'complete' missing stories and release them on DVD, but please do not think that the missing episodes are no longer required: they are. Stories that have benefited from the animation process and therefore available on DVD are 'The Reign of Terror', 'The Invasion', 'The Ice Warriors' and 'The Tenth Planet'. Other stories planned for this process include 'The Crusade', 'The Underwater Menace', 'The Web of Fear' and 'The Moonbase'. If animated episodes were made of all these stories there would be less than 20 missing stories from the BBC archive.

Reconstructed stories: Some fans are not happy with the animation process applied to some missing stories. There are other reconstructions of missing episodes/stories, built from surviving clips and extensive photographs or photograph reconstructions. Good examples of this are episode 4 of 'The Tenth Planet' and all seven episodes of 'Marco Polo' in colour. It must be stressed that none of these reconstructions, animated or otherwise, compensate for the loss of the original episode/story, but they give a clear picture of how they were made and appeared to the original audience, 'Marco Polo' being most impressive.

Also missing from the BBC Archive: worthy of mention here is the multitude of other shows missing from the BBC archives, from Patrick Troughton's *Robin Hood* to the TV *Navy Lark*. There are also many missing early performances from legendary double acts and comedy series, such as *Morecambe and Wise* and *Steptoe and Son*. The BBC would dearly like to hear from anyone who may hold copies of these too.

CHAPTER THREE
THE LEGACY OF
DOCTOR WHO

ENDURING THE YEARS

For a programme to endure for 50 years it has to have something constantly refreshing about it, something that continues to stimulate the audiences and makes them thirst for more.

What is especially interesting about the legacy of *Doctor Who*, and before we drill down to some of the very best individual stories, is the power of key seasons.

Throughout its history, *Doctor Who* has enjoyed a string of brilliantly written and darkly portrayed stories that have enhanced its life. Listed below are the author's top five favourite seasons:

1. First Season: 'An Unearthly Child', 'The Tribe of Gum', 'The Daleks', 'The Edge of Destruction', 'Marco Polo', 'The Keys of Marinus', 'The Aztecs', 'The Sensorites', 'The Reign of Terror'.
2. Fifth Season: 'The Tomb of the Cybermen', 'The Abominable Snowmen', 'The Ice Warriors', 'The Enemy of the World', 'The Web of Fear', 'Fury From the Deep', 'The Wheel in Space'.

3. Seventh Season: 'Spearhead from Space', 'The Silurians', 'The Ambassadors of Death', 'Inferno'.

4. Twelfth Season: 'Robot', 'The Ark in Space', 'The Sontaran Experiment', 'Genesis of the Daleks', 'Revenge of the Cybermen'.

5. Fourteenth Season: 'The Masque of Mandragora', 'The Hand of Fear', 'The Deadly Assassin', 'The Face of Evil', 'The Robots of Death', 'The Talons of Weng-Chiang'.

So, what makes these seasons important? By and large they are the first complete season of the first four Doctors. There is a slight cheat for Patrick Troughton as his first season started with the last two William Hartnell stories, so the season detailed is his first *full* season.

The point is: different production crews, writers and cast are identified in all but one of the seasons listed above, even if you picked the Fourth Season instead of the Fifth. Granted Tom Baker appears in two seasons, but there are great changes between the Twelfth Season and the Fourteenth Season. Really it's not just the Doctor who regenerates, the whole programme does too, and this injects new life. To begin with, in the very first season, Verity Lambert's passion for getting it right was supreme, supported by Sydney Newman, Mervyn Pinfield, some great writers and, of course, Waris Hussein (at key moments). Lambert created a wonderful new programme. At a key moment in Patrick Troughton's tenure as the Doctor, a host of wonderful stories happened on the bounce. The Fifth Season is sometimes referred to as 'The Monster Season', and with it beginning and ending with Cybermen and including the only two Yeti stories so far and introducing the Ice Warriors, it is no wonder. But often overlooked is Patrick Troughton's doppelganger story, 'Enemy of the World', where he plays the good Doctor and the evil Salamander, in what is nothing short of a magnificent performance.

Jon Pertwee's first season enjoyed the same 'hand-over' of the old from the new, plus the programme was suddenly in colour and, thanks to the input of Malcolm Hulke, the show took on a more serious and philosophical angle, especially for stories like 'The Silurians' and 'Inferno'. 'The Ambassadors of Death' featured helicopters and the most exciting shoot-out (only rivalled by the death toll in 'The Mind of Evil' during the next season).

The first Tom Baker season – the Twelfth Season – was a radical change of direction for the character and, with the return of the Daleks and the Cybermen too, it couldn't fail to please.

Like Tom Baker's first season, his third (the Fourteenth Season), falls within that fan favourite run of stories known as 'The Hinchcliffe Years' with new producer Philip Hinchcliffe taking the darkness – gothic appeal – much further than his predecessor, Barry Letts. Some of the great lines come from the Fourteenth Season, such as: (Cardinal Borusa) 'If heroes don't exist it is necessary to invent them'; (the Doctor to the Master) 'You'll delay an execution to pull the wings off a fly'; (Robots of Death) 'Kill the humans'; and of course (Sarah Jane Smith) 'Eldrad Must Live!'

What this analysis of individual seasons clearly shows us is that the various reinventions of the show, the injection of new blood, is what keeps the programme fresh and innovative. It is something that has already happened in the new millennium *Doctor Who* in the transition from David Tennant's Doctor to Matt Smith's.

That said, one might argue that John Nathan-Turner stayed too long as producer and the show was cancelled as a consequence, but then again Nathan-Turner did so much good for the show over the years, he more than justified his reign. In fact, his first season as producer saw him change Tom Baker's outfit, change the opening titles and theme music and introduce three new companions and lose two, and of course regenerate the Doctor. So why isn't Tom Baker's last season in the top five? For some people it might be, indeed three of the author's favourite stories are in that season, but the swish music and glitzy title sequence took a lot of foreboding doom out of the show, and maybe tempered the anticipation, failing to whet the appetite as much as the eerie music that had played to audiences for the past 18 years. That and poor choices of first two stories really hammers the Eighteenth Season into seventh place (sixth place going to the Fourth Season).

By his own admission Tom Baker never liked a 'themed season' and 'The Key to Time' season, the Sixteenth Season, seems to get overlooked as a consequence. This may be a reason why Colin Baker's 'Trial of a Time Lord' season doesn't get much credit either. It is vindicated by the fact that Peter Davison's second season, the Twentieth Season, doesn't get knocked too much. Not because it is the 20th Anniversary season but because there are only three themed stories within it ('The Black Guardian Trilogy'), and they are framed by other stories. It is probably during the Twentieth Season that we begin to seen big ideas being compromised by dwindling budgets. The huge snake at the end of 'Snakedance' is embarrassing rather than scary, but from the Twenty-First Season onwards, the effects grew noticeably more daft, and that's where the original series began to lose credibility and of course, viewing figures.

When discussing the legacy of *Doctor Who*, one must recognise the opening seasons of the new millennium Doctors, and note the repetition of pattern already referred to. I don't compare the new series with the classic series, because it is unfair on both. The stunning CGI and budget of the new adventures is tarnished by the need to explain everything within 50 minutes (two episodes if you're lucky).

Doctor Who will continue to evolve and change with the times; another 50 years should see him reach the end of his second cycle of regenerations – all that's needed is an excuse to stimulate that second cycle. If the Master can get power from the Keeper of Traken and be resurrected by Black Mass, there must be some answer for the Doctor too. But perhaps the lifeline is already there. During 'The Five Doctors', the Master was offered a whole new life-cycle by the High Council of the Time Lords, so perhaps a future generation will be applauding the 100th Anniversary of *Doctor Who*. Books will probably not be physical hardbacks and paperbacks then, so if a book was produced to update this one the reader won't need to hump several telephone directories around with them, the Kindle, or its replacement, will be enough.

AN EXPLORATION OF 50 YEARS OF *DOCTOR WHO* THROUGH 50 OF ITS GREATEST STORIES

1. 'The Deadly Assassin' (Tom Baker)
2. 'Blink' (David Tennant)
3. 'Genesis of the Daleks' (Tom Baker)
4. 'State of Decay' (Tom Baker)
5. 'The Daemons' (Jon Pertwee)
6. 'The Abominable Snowmen' (Patrick Troughton)
7. 'An Unearthly Child' (William Hartnell)
8. 'The Keeper of Traken' (Tom Baker)
9. 'The Tenth Planet' (William Hartnell)
10. 'The Tomb of the Cybermen' (Patrick Troughton)

11. 'Marco Polo' (William Hartnell)
12. 'The Talons of Weng-Chiang' (Tom Baker)
13. 'The Pyramids of Mars' (Tom Baker)
14. 'The Planet of the Ood' (David Tennant)
15. 'The Caves of Androzani' (Peter Davison)
16. 'Human Nature/The Family of Blood' (David Tennant)
17. 'The Visitation' (Peter Davison)
18. 'Logopolis' (Tom Baker)
19. 'The Two Doctors' (Colin Baker/Patrick Troughton)
20. 'The Robots of Death' (Tom Baker)
21. 'The Daleks' (William Hartnell)
22. 'The Rescue' (William Hartnell)
23. 'Nightmare in Silver' (Matt Smith)
24. 'Midnight' (David Tennant)
25. 'School Reunion' (David Tennant)
26. 'The Sea Devils' (Jon Pertwee)
27. 'The Silurians' (Jon Pertwee)
28. 'The Time Meddler' (William Hartnell)
29. 'City of Death' (Tom Baker)
30. 'The Ice Warriors' (Patrick Troughton)
31. 'The Doctor's Wife' (Matt Smith)
32. 'The Time of the Angels/Flesh and Stone' (Matt Smith)
33. 'Vincent and the Doctor' (Matt Smith)
34. 'The Moonbase' (Patrick Troughton)
35. 'Planet of the Spiders' (Jon Pertwee)
36. 'The Three Doctors' (Jon Pertwee/Patrick Troughton/ William Hartnell)
37. 'Spearhead From Space' (Jon Pertwee)
38. 'Death to the Daleks' (Jon Pertwee)
39. 'The Doctor's Daughter' (David Tennant)
40. 'The Fires of Pompeii' (David Tennant)
41. 'The Time Warrior' (Jon Pertwee)

42. 'Father's Day' (Christopher Eccleston)
43. 'The Empty Child/The Doctor Dances' (Christopher Eccleston)
44. 'The Sound of Drums/Last of the Time Lords' (David Tennant)
45. 'The Celestial Toymaker' (William Hartnell)
46. 'Battlefield' (Sylvester McCoy)
47. 'Earthshock' (Peter Davison)
48. 'The Web of Fear' (Patrick Troughton)
49. 'The Enemy of the World' (Patrick Troughton)
50. 'Doctor Who – The Movie' (Paul McGann)

If a point is given for every story each actor has been in and half a point for each guest role he has made ('The Three Doctors'/'The Two Doctors'), the most popular doctors by importance of story content are:

1. Tom Baker (9)
2. David Tennant (8)
3. William Hartnell (7½)
3. Jon Pertwee (7 ½)
4. Patrick Troughton (7)
5. Matt Smith (4)
6. Peter Davison (3)
7. Christopher Eccleston (2)
8. Colin Baker (1)
9. Sylvester McCoy (1)
10. Paul McGann (1)

Perhaps this is an unfair way of marking popularity, especially when you consider that Paul McGann was only in one story and Christopher Eccleston only ever made one season, while

Tom Baker played the role for seven years. Despite this, the list does make sense, with the youngest Doctors mid-table and the two Doctors with the poorest budgets and scripts near the bottom. If *Doctor Who* is judged on its innovation, moral stance and good stories, as well as characters and monsters, then the best Doctors, for all-round thrills, are those highlighted in the top five of this specifically calculated list.

ANALYSIS

It is 5.15 on Saturday, 23 November 1963. The world is reeling from the news headlines: President Kennedy's assassination in Dallas the previous day and a lone gunman, Lee Harvey Oswald, accused of his murder. Closer to home news came in that Matt Busby's Manchester United had lost by a single goal to nil against Bill Shankly's Liverpool in a tough top-of-the-table football match. Later on, Liverpool's very own teenage heart-throbs, The Beatles, would play their 19th gig on their autumn UK tour in Newcastle, to the delight of their ever-growing fan-base.

It was a cold and wet evening, so not everyone chose to be out. Many families sat around the TV in anticipation of a brand-new children's TV series. It had made big news in the current edition of *The Radio Times* and was to star film actor William Hartnell, famed for his tough-guy roles in *Brighton Rock* and *Hell's Drivers*, but this time playing a completely different character: a mysterious grandfather-figure called The Doctor. The show was called *Doctor Who* and nobody either watching it or connected with it would dream that it would thrill audiences for at least the next 50 years. How could they? It was planned to run for only 52 weeks.

As soon as Ron Grainer's haunting theme tune started and the time vortex swirled for the very first time, television history was made. The title *Doctor Who* appeared and faded and the familiar figure of a policeman appeared from thick fog. A church bell chimed 3am and the gates to 76 Totters Yard, a rundown London scrap yard, creaked open, inviting you, the audience, into a bizarre new universe of possibilities. The music continued and the camera panned to a familiar sight, a Police Public Call Box, which – rather unsettlingly – hummed steadily, as if it was somehow *alive*, but of course it couldn't be... The camera lingered on the police box for a moment, the audience intrigued but unsuspecting; how could they guess that this so-familiar sight (as it was then) was a space/time capsule? But within 25 minutes, before The Beatles hit the stage in Newcastle and conversations about Communist threats on the Western world continued in the wake of the Kennedy assassination, people would know of a strange being called the Doctor, his equally intriguing 'granddaughter' Susan, and the police-box spacecraft known as the TARDIS.

The very first episode of *Doctor Who* 'An Unearthly Child' is an amazing piece of television. It works as a one-off story of alien abduction, but not from a malicious point of view, like *The X Files*. The Doctor and Susan travelled in time and space and chose London, 1963, as a place to hide and to try and lead a peaceful life, but Susan's genius in certain school lessons – and ignorance of 1960s culture – makes her teachers curious as to her home life. They decide to follow her home, to the junkyard from the beginning of the episode, and there they lose her, only to be confronted by the Doctor, a crotchety old man who appears to know more about Susan than he lets on. But Susan appears in the police box doorway and the schoolteachers, Ian Chesterton and Barbara Wright, become anxious. They push their way into the small cabinet and find themselves in a gleaming spaceship that is bigger on the inside than the outside. It is here that they learn that the Doctor and Susan are exiles from their own planet. Did they escape? It appears so. Are they criminals? It is uncertain. They appear worried that they could be exposed to the authorities, but it is an accident, a tussle between the Doctor and the programme's first hero, Ian Chesterton, that catapults them into adventures in time and space.

An early draft of Anthony Coburn's script for 'An Unearthly Child' has a more sinister twist to it regarding the abduction scene (see Chapter One). It is implied that the Doctor should actually kill Ian and Barbara (Miss Canning in the early draft). It is clear that Susan (Suzanne in the early draft) is scared of him. One line preserved from this macabre segment in the final programme is where Susan tells the teachers that he (the Doctor) won't let them go, whereupon the Doctor laughs to himself, enjoying the terror he is inflicting.

Doctor Who creator Sydney Newman correctly had the threat of murder cut from the final script: it went too far. Instead of being a man of wonder, the Doctor was suddenly a homicidal maniac, something Tom Baker's Doctor would accuse double-agent Kellman of in 'Revenge of the Cybermen' 12 years – and three leading actors – later. Newman also wanted the explanation of why the Doctor and Susan were in a junkyard in 1963 cut from the script. The point was to keep the sense of mystery implied in the title: Doctor Who? A question that existed for 50 years and was noted as the oldest question in the show's history. It is this shaping of the original script by Newman, the genius behind *Doctor Who*, that provided the most perfect starting point for the show; the firm base from which future success would be built. We further appreciate this, in a visual way, when looking at the pilot episode. It lacked polish in certain areas so Newman rejected it. Unusually, he didn't sack the producer and director responsible; he decided to give them another go. They then made the subtle changes that created the perfection that has now endured and expanded over 50 years. 'An Unearthly Child' is a classic example of understating the grand theme in order to perpetuate a legend for so long. Was this by default? No, it was what Newman wanted all along. He didn't want anyone to know who the Doctor and Susan were, and he wanted things to be totally different. No strapping into seats at the main console (see the early draft of the script), no rocket ships.

Carole Ann Ford, the actress who played Susan, didn't see the early draft script and therefore didn't understand that she wasn't the Doctor's granddaughter after all: she was a princess or queen saved by the good-hearted Doctor, who whisked her away, just as he did every other companion thereafter. If Ford had known the original intention of the scriptwriter, maybe she would have approached the character in a different way. She always maintained that she enjoyed being the Doctor's granddaughter and the very title gives her far more authority than any other travelling companion, but sadly the intention was for her never to have been part of the Doctor's family: she is an orphan, her mother and father are dead in a fabled story that started the Doctor's travels.

'An Unearthly Child' was painstakingly shaped by the writer, the creator, the producer and director, shot and reshot, in order to get things perfect and, looking back with what we now know, we can confirm that it *is* perfect. This process of writing and re-shooting wouldn't happen today; it was rare for yesterday. Newman had a vision and he knew that the young, talented and quite feisty Verity Lambert had what it took to bring that clear vision to the screen. That is why 'An Unearthly Child' is a one-episode story in itself. The story that follows is a three-part caveman story that doesn't work as well. This is probably why the first *Doctor Who* novelisation has an introduction to the characters (based upon an earlier idea called 'Nothing at the End of the Lane') coupled with the second full story 'The Daleks', the story that introduced the homicidal pepper-pots and made the show immortal. For the author of the novel not to include elements of 'An Unearthly Child' doesn't do it an injustice. The novel was written by David Whittaker, who had submitted his own idea for a first episode at the same time as Anthony Coburn – he was simply allowed to explore his alternative version of the first ever episode in his novel.

'The Daleks' is important because it proved that Verity Lambert was the right person for the programme. Newman insisted that he didn't want 'bug-eyed monsters' in the show, he wanted quality, believable scripts; he wanted to teach children about history, and to have the Doctor and his companions float around time and space to do just that. It was a lovely concept, so he absolutely exploded when he saw the Daleks for the first time, but Lambert appeased him by saying that they were humans in the future who had to live in protective casing because of high radiation. She got away with it – just – and later, Newman admitted that he was wrong to criticise her and her 'bug-eyed monsters'. He knew the Daleks were the reason for *Doctor Who*'s lasting success, not stories featuring Marco Polo or the Aztecs. The soaring viewing figures every time the Daleks appeared vindicated that. And that is the crucial point: it took the young Verity Lambert to push that envelope as far as possible. *Doctor Who* had become more than one man's dream. It was Verity Lambert's dream too, and let's not forget William Hartnell. He was thrilled to play in a children's programme, to break his typecasting and do something completely different. This was the beginning of the tight-knit *Doctor Who* family. No matter what mix has come together over the years, the actors, writers and production staff appear to bond to create a passionate, winning team. Unfortunately (or fortunately) they also seem to leave together too – a good example of this being the end of Patrick Troughton's era. When Troughton announced that he was to quit the show, both his companions (played by Frazer Hines and Wendy Padbury) did so too, creating a total cut-off point between the atmospheric black and white era at the end of the 1960s and the more heroic colour version of the show at the turn of the 1970s.

Although 'An Unearthly Child' changed the face of TV, it was a delayed reaction. It didn't happen on the evening of 23 November 1963. After The Beatles had left the stage and older Liverpool fans had been moved on after last orders, the people of Britain went to their beds more mindful of the assassination of President Kennedy the previous day than thoughts of the first ever episode of a new children's TV programme. The very fact that that first episode was repeated the following week vindicates this. It had been largely overlooked and no one was any the wiser. But it's not surprising: people weren't expecting a big deal. Even though *The Radio Times* had placed it as a future highlight in its previous week's issue and the latest issue included a profile piece about the new show, as well as mentioning it on the cover, the British public was happy to reserve judgement and indeed show indifference to cavemen, but not so those dreaded Daleks.

Dalekmania became for children what Beatlemania was for the new-found teenager. And by default, a 52 weeks TV show became a 50-plus years TV phenomenon. Very few monsters during the first Doctor's incarnation took over children's imagination as much as the Daleks. The BBC tried to push the Zarbi – through a novelisation and a story in the very first *Doctor Who* annual (1965), after their first appearance in the second season – but they never returned. In fact it wasn't until William Hartnell's very last story, 'The Tenth Planet', that we encountered foes as impressive as the Daleks: the Cybermen. And the very fact that Daleks and Cybermen are staples of the show in the new millennium proves the Hartnell years are still incredibly significant to the current culture. But great monsters are not always needed. We take the very first episode of *Doctor Who* for granted nowadays. Look upon it as a quaint, maybe a modest introduction to the world of the Doctor, but we would be wrong to think that way. The show avoided cliché. There had never been a programme with opening music like *that* before. Creepy, haunting, it altered the mindset of the watcher, clearing away the worries of everyday life to stimulate the boundless imagination of the viewer.

This mindset was also something US TV science fiction series *Star Trek* would also do well from its inception in the mid-sixties. *Star Trek* was the brainchild of Gene Roddenberry. It was an optimistic vision of the future of the human race, where Russians, Chinese and Africans would sit alongside their Western counterparts – an elite, united group, who would work to push the barriers of human knowledge and 'Boldy Go Where No One Had Gone Before'. It was perhaps the possible dream-state inspired by the liberal John F. Kennedy and Martin Luther King, although they would be assassinated for such foresight. But TV creators such as Sydney Newman and Gene Roddenberry, alongside quality writers such as Robert Bloch and Terry Nation, kept the dreams alive. Where Kennedy wanted a man on the moon by the end of the decade, visionaries were united in the deeper mysteries of the universe. Not just writers but designers were important too. The magnificent design of the starship *Enterprise* and the innovative design of the Daleks richly enhanced the popularity of each show, impressing audiences with the practical imagination at work behind the scenes, turning a writer's vision into something sophisticated. *Star Trek*, like *Doctor Who*, was all about teamwork. The Doctor and his companions, like Kirk and his crew, are the dedicated team that thwart evil, while at the same time there was a dedicated team behind the camera too.

Over the years both *Doctor Who* and *Star Trek* have tackled huge themes, even though made for a younger audience. The simple way in which *Star Trek* dealt with the issue of racism – especially at that particular time in American history (Martin Luther King and Malcolm X amidst racial disharmony) – was outstanding. It occurred in an episode titled 'Let That Be Your Last Battlefield'. Two survivors of a planet destroyed by race-riots are fighting each other to the death because one has the left side of his face black and the other has the right side of his face black. Because one is declared different by the more vindictive other, he is therefore deemed inferior and not worthy of living, but the inferior fights back. Neither creature learns from the fate of their race who have massacred themselves to genocide through racial hatred. The story is an amazing reminder of the stupidity of racism.

Doctor Who tackled racism in 'Planet of the Ood'. A race of creatures – the Ood – are persecuted and enslaved by the human race, mocked and considered inferior, but they are far from it. Internal oppression is at last overcome and the remarkable accomplishments of the Ood and their culture are at last appreciated in a heart-warming scene. The whole story has the feel of the Nazi persecution of the Jews during the Second World War, but done in such a way that children can appreciate the sadness and moral undertones to such a story

THE DOCTORS WHO'S WHO

without learning the full horror. This is good writing, and can only work when it is one step removed from real-life.

Both *Doctor Who* and *Star Trek* have ventured back to the terrible times of the Nazis, but perhaps *Doctor Who* explained the nuances of this better through one of its greatest stories, 'Genesis of the Daleks'. Written by Dalek creator Terry Nation, 'Genesis of the Daleks' showed us how the Daleks were born and the evil mastermind who created them – Davros – and the totalitarian regime that spawned their single-minded genius.

'Genesis of the Daleks' contradicted 'The Daleks' because the race that created the Daleks, the Dals, was suddenly called Kaleds (an anagram of Dalek). But *Doctor Who* has had many contradictions over the years, one of the big ones being the argument over the home planet of the Cybermen: Mondas or Telos? The audience still appears confused, even though there is a brief reference at the beginning of 'The Tomb of the Cybermen' stating that Mondas was the home planet.

Unlike a programme such as *The X Files*, *Doctor Who* can carry off certain contradictions in its legacy. It can blame alternative realities or similar races. Unfortunately there is further evidence to explain which planet the Cybermen come from (other than that related in 'The Tomb of the Cybermen'). In the novelisation of 'The Tenth Planet', creator of the Cybermen, Gerry Davis, tells us that the Cybermen came from Telos, but left the planet to inhabit the sister world of Earth, Mondas, from where the Doctor first meets them. And therein lies the irretrievable contradiction!

Regardless of the planet mix-up, the one-page 'Creation of the Cybermen' in Davis' novel is an excellent introduction to the silver metal giants that, unfortunately, the TV counterparts have never truly emulated. The new series Cybermen started by showing some of their mighty strength, but instead of being the race-that-adapted to rid themselves of disease, they were a disparate mix of races harvested from their bodies by an evil human creator. So not the Cybermen of old, but some alternative state of Cybermen that Rose Tyler would come to hate and we the viewer would look upon as nothing more than grotesques, not an advanced species.

Not so in the Neil Gaiman story 'Nightmare in Silver'. The ultimate Cyberman make-over (with the Cybermat to Cybermite transition) a breathtaking compromise between the old and the new with new-model army features. A brilliant interpretation and excellent story, with Gaiman's love of the old strip stories of *Doctor Who* blended into the story (children in the TARDIS thrilled by their adventure with the Doctor). Marvellous stuff!

The Cybermen were always a more credible extreme adversary than the Daleks. Never appearing with Jon Pertwee's Doctor, they carved their own piece of immortality through Patrick Troughton's era. 'The Moonbase' was a good story but 'The Tomb of the Cybermen' was an absolute classic, bringing in an archeological twist and therefore an air of mystery and menace. 'The Tomb of the Cybermen' truly started a mythos for the show – and the true Cybermen – that gained momentum from Troughton's time, continuing with 'The Wheel in Space' and 'The Invasion' (the latter too long in my opinion), but it would be nearly seven years before we would see them again (Tom Baker's 'Revenge of the Cybermen'). Their return was, however, excellent and showcased the fact that they were as popular as the Daleks, with just a handful of stories showcasing them against many of the pepper-pot megalomaniacs.

Rarely has there been a darkly imaginative Dalek story. Normally their presence dominates, ruining the delicate atmosphere, but stories such as 'Genesis of the Daleks' and

'Death to the Daleks' manage this through quality story, surreal sets and perfect lighting.

The ancient Exxilon city in 'Death to the Daleks' is one of the 700 wonders of the universe and provides a powerful and mysterious backdrop to the story. The Daleks are rendered powerless by the city, allowing the Doctor to deliver his chaos with dignified respect. Interestingly, while the Doctor takes on every challenge set by the city on his quest to its very heart, the Daleks adapt their weapons and bully their way through the challenges, showing clearly the greatest flaw in their make-up – a lack of empathy and with that, the inability to stop and think.

'Death to the Daleks' is important because it shows how and why the Daleks constantly fail. They are the battling French fleet tirelessly thwarted by Lord Nelson, because they don't have the strategic mindset necessary for world domination. It is the same reasoning we can apply to the Nazis and of course, the Nazi-like Kaleds in 'Genesis of the Daleks', but when the Doctor has the power to wipe them out forever – from their birth – he stops to ask himself 'Do I have the right?' Like anybody who has mused over the notion of having a time machine and travelling back in time to kill Adolf Hitler, the Doctor ponders the same question regarding the Daleks: should he destroy them? Yes, of course he should, but what about all the races that would became allies because of their hatred or fear of the Daleks? The Doctor ultimately decides that out of the Daleks' evil something good would come. Perhaps a similar thing might be said about Adolf Hitler. Maybe the horrendous crimes he perpetrated made the human race stop and think that one second more and thus avoid a Third World War, a nuclear holocaust, believing that they couldn't, as a race, stoop so low again.

Imagine talking to Hitler, reasoning with him, understanding him... It is this ominous pleasure the Doctor has with Davros –

just the two of them in a room, talking. It is probably the most memorable scene in the show's history, made more awe-inspiring because we have known Davros such a short time. But this character is awesome in voice and appearance; we immediately sense his evil genius (because of the unmatchable acting of Michael Wisher). The Doctor has an agenda, though: he needs to know if Davros is mad. He needs to justify exterminating the Daleks at their birth, albeit at the request of the Time Lords. He asks Davros if a chemical agent were created in his laboratories so powerful that it could destroy the universe, would he use it? Davros ponders the notion, not the yes or no answer – he has instantly decided yes, he just wallows in the excitement of the prospect. He takes pleasure from visualising the moment when he can hold in his hand a tiny vial where the tiniest pressure from his fingers, enough to break the glass, would destroy the universe. This excites him, makes him manic; the Doctor needs to hear no more and demands that Davros destroys the Daleks – but it doesn't happen. The past is too strong, the momentum of the creation too wide. And so the Doctor loses, but perhaps he wins by default, knowing the Time Lords were wrong and he was right to hesitate and stop the genocide of the Daleks.

This ploy of exposing the madness of scientific genius had been applied before by the second Doctor in 'Tomb of the Cybermen', when the Doctor goads the manic archeologist Eric Klieg to relish in his insane union with the Cybermen, concluding, 'Well, now I know you're mad.'

'Genesis of the Daleks', not unlike 'Tomb of the Cybermen', is one of the most moral and creative stories in the history of *Doctor Who*. That takes nothing away from the Daleks' very first story. 'The Daleks' is important because not only was it the very first Dalek story (and perhaps the one that made a success of the show), it was also the first outing for an alien race.

During the first season of *Doctor Who*, only three of the eight stories featured alien races. And although the other two stories ('The Keys of Marinus' and 'The Sensorites') had their good points, they didn't have creatures that had the command of the TV screen as much as the Daleks.

Does this mean that the more science fiction elements of the show would have been dropped in future seasons, had the Daleks not been invented? Quite possibly. The second season of *Doctor Who* included a strong presence from the Daleks, but there were more earth-based (and historical) stories. Sydney Newman's original mindset wasn't wholly ignored. There was an exception, of course: a two-episode gem entitled 'The Rescue'. This story included an incredibly scary alien that ended up being something quite different. What is really interesting about it is how the religious history of a supposed dead people is perpetrated through misrepresentation. I love this idea because it gives pause for thought as to how we treat/understand the religion and beliefs of ancient Aztec or Egyptian cultures, so perhaps through a short science fiction piece, *Doctor Who* was still teaching children about their own history. It is something we take for granted with the show nowadays, 'The Fires of Pompeii' being a classic example, where children can be taught about the great volcanic tragedy but still have time for a fire-and-brimstone monster and immense excitement into the bargain (this story is of special note because it included Peter Capaldi and Karen Gillan before they became regular cast members). It is this very aspect that keeps *Doctor Who* fresh. Every time he and his companions step from the TARDIS, past, present, future, Earth or alien worlds and situations have immense possibility and instruction.

The mindset of the programme hasn't altered after 50 years; it is still there and crucial to the programme's success. 'I've just snogged Madame de Pompadour,' David Tennant's Doctor says cheekily and children laugh with the same gusto as listening to a naughty Roald Dahl line. But it hasn't always been that way. The first true historical *Doctor Who* story was 'Marco Polo'. With lavish sets and costumes, the BBC pulled out all the stops for this historical masterpiece. Directed by Waris Hussein and written by Marco Polo expert John Lucarotti (a man hand-picked by Sydney Newman to write for the show), it became the benchmark for all future historical stories and truly echoed the spirit of what Newman wanted from the show in the first place. For that alone it must rate as the best ever – and most loyally interpreted – *Doctor Who* story.

Something that has been important to *Doctor Who* over the years is the *Doctor Who* annual. First released by World Distributors in 1965, it has stimulated interest in the programme over the Christmas holidays and other long periods of time when the show wasn't on TV. In the days before DVD (or video), the *Doctor Who* annual was the constant companion of the die-hard fan, who would be horrified not to find it in their Christmas stocking each year, not just as a filler but an important present. It says a lot about the Daleks too, who had their own annual for several years in the 1960s and 70s.

Often thought to be the best *Doctor Who* annual ever is the very first one. Its two short features regarding the character of the Doctor are insightful and intriguing. Writer Bill Strutton had a large part in writing the first annual and bringing back the Zarbi and Voords. With the latter's story 'Peril in Mechanistria', the annual really adds a bigger-budget interpretation of the worlds of *Doctor Who* – beyond the poor 1960s BBC visual effects budget, that is.

With the resurrection of the annual with the new-look

THE DOCTORS WHO'S WHO

Doctor Who of the millennium, the book allowed the writers to experiment with a story before being re-written for television. The exploits of Sally Sparrow and the Weeping Angels first appeared in Christopher Eccleston's only solo annual (2006), and suggests how the iconic story 'Blink' would have worked with Eccleston at the helm rather than David Tennant. The illustrated interpretation of Sally Sparrow is a bit of a shock in retrospect – glasses and dreadlocks rather than dimples and sparkling eyes. 'What I did on my Christmas Holidays by Sally Sparrow' is a wonderful glimpse into the growth of a great story in the writer's mind. Steven Moffat clearly shows the basis of his masterful story of the Weeping Angels, even though they are not in it. Panini's 2006 annual is a triumph. Beautifully illustrated (especially 'Doctor Vs Doctor') and excellently written, it highlights the enthusiasm of everyone associated with the Doctor's comeback in the millennium.

So were the Weeping Angels the Daleks of the new millennium and indicative of the successful comeback of the show? Not really, they had their place but much later (with David Tennant). The first season, Eccleston's only season, was a triumph and showed that you could have a big budget for *Doctor Who*, as well as great storylines. 'The Empty Child', written by Moffat, had children shouting 'Muuuummmmmyyyy' in the playground rather than 'Exterminate', but the Daleks, or Dalek, came back in a very well-scripted story that allowed us to view the new-look tank-like Dalek that was able to climb stairs (first introduced during Sylvester McCoy's reign), and show more emotions due to Rose Tyler's meddling. 'Dalek' became a fresh start for the archetypical *Doctor Who* monster. It also raised the bar of expectation when the new-look programme confronted its incredible past and what could be termed its legacy – something I still maintain it failed to embrace with regard to the Cybermen and made a mockery of with the Sontarans (see 'The Snowmen').

Myths and legends are important to storytelling and incredibly so when it comes to a show like *Doctor Who*. The way vampire myths were blended with Time Lord legend to create a rich and atmospheric story like 'State of Decay' is a good example. 'State of Decay' is often overlooked nowadays because it is part of a trilogy that comes under the 'E Space' umbrella. That said, Tom Baker's last season as the Doctor had some brilliantly imaginative stories, 'State of Decay', 'The Keeper of Traken' and 'Logopolis' being strong examples, with wonderfully atmospheric sets and excellent acting. 'Full Circle' had its moments too, but 'Meglos' perhaps overstretched things slightly, despite giving us a classic image in the cactus-faced Doctor.

Having been turned into a long white-haired OAP in the first story that season ('The Leisure Hive'), Tom Baker certainly earned his money as he prepared to bid farewell to the TARDIS. The same season, Romana and K9 left the show in the poor 'Warrior's Gate' and across four stories three new companions were introduced, thus making the busiest TARDIS crew ever assembled in the Classic Series.

'The Keeper of Traken' provided a solution to the end of a Time Lord's regeneration cycle: by stealing someone else's body. This anticipated a wonderfully chilling scene in the very next story ('Logopolis'), when Nyssa realises that the Master has not only killed her father, but destroyed her home planet too. It brought home the reality that the Doctor's companions felt when confronting the horrors that affected them in each story. People suffer because of the actions of the Doctor, for his longing for adventure, and is that justifiable? According to Queen Victoria in 'Tooth and Claw' years later, no. She saw something unpleasant in the Doctor's make-up and told him so.

Returning to 'The Keeper of Traken', the tradition of the Keeper, his Consoles, the Fosters, the grove and the Melkhar were incredible ideas that seemed plausible and real despite being very alien. From the moment the Keeper appears in the TARDIS, one knows that a very different type of adventure is about to begin. This portent of doom was also most exquisitely delivered at the beginning of 'Pyramids of Mars', when Sarah Jane witnesses a projection of evil above the TARDIS console. At first the Doctor doesn't believe it, but very soon he does. Interestingly, evil is clearly defined in each of these two stories, the manifestation in the TARDIS being the portent of immense power and something more poorly done in 'Arc of Infinity' when Omega enters the Doctor's domain.

'Pyramids of Mars' brings in ancient Egyptian gods and archeological expeditions, coupled with the notion that mankind originally came from the stars. To have a Howard Carter/Tutankhamen catalyst for a story was something fans had wished for, and when the story eventually arrived in the middle of the Hinchcliffe years (mid 1970s), it didn't fail to deliver, so is now accepted as one of the truly great *Doctor Who* stories. With its very characteristic mummies and wonderful Osiren, 'Pyramids of Mars' ticks many boxes, not least of which the sub-story of a man trying to win back his brother despite the obvious fact that he had been taken over and was just a shadow of his former self. In that respect 'Pyramids of Mars' is a very human story and, perhaps, to complement its title a little more (which it really doesn't do), has more reason to be longer than its four episodes, unlike other stories throughout the show's history (such as 'The Invasion', which only really started thrilling the audience from episode four). The 'Pyramids of Mars' had so much more to offer.

It is interesting to note that most of the stories listed in the top 50 above are standard-length stories of their day; it is important to note that story content has to hold up for the longer ones. A good example of a story enduring over six or seven weeks are those from Jon Pertwee's first ever season. 'Inferno' was good and introduced the alternative universe; but the moral implications implied by Malcolm Hulke's 'The Silurians' was amazing. Pertwee was always at his best when outraged by small-mindedness, either the Brigadier's desire to blow things up, or some other official person throwing red tape around and hindering his access to a specific project or location.

There is a marvellous cliff-hanger scene in 'The Silurians' where one of the creatures walks through a living-room door behind the Doctor. It is terrifying, not because the Doctor doesn't see the creature to begin with, but because it has just entered a child's comfort zone. It has walked into *their* living room.

Hulke continued his reptilian theme with 'The Sea Devils', a story that had large scenes shot on location and includes a much-loved shot where the Sea Devils rise from the ocean to confront the Doctor and his companion.

'The Sea Devils' was an ambitious story to pull off and indeed the Royal Navy stepped in to provide some assistance. With quality location filming, eerie music, and some fun moments with Roger Delgado's Master, it is one of the highlights of Jon Pertwee's tenure as the Doctor and certainly not overlong.

Malcolm Hulke's stories always had a high moral tone to them and in the novelisations of his work he was keen to expand upon the characters to make them appear more realistic. A good example of this is in 'The Doomsday Weapon' (based upon the Pertwee story, 'Colony in Space'). The opening chapter includes an ancient Time Lord, approximately 1,000 years old and nearing the end of his life. To write with such sensitivity about a trivial supporting character provided a rich start to an action-packed adventure novel and showed how much the writer cared about the development of his stories.

Sometimes an audience can get so much more from less. One of the very best examples of this is 'Midnight'. The story works on the premise that there is something hostile outside the ship and, although we cannot see it, we know that it's there.

'Midnight' is a very clever tale as it builds tension with an eerie wonder. We see the hinterland, we know there's something out there, but we can't see what it is, we can't feel it, we can't communicate with it; but it kills us all the same, so we are hopelessly lost. We are terrified, we are out of our depth, and so much behind the 'superior' being that we are humbled. Indeed, is the being 'superior'? What is it? Could we befriend it? Probably not; but it's the not knowing, and that's the way it ends.

The thing disappears. Suddenly we realise that we'll never know any more about the entity that conspired against the vessel. We have to carry on as normal, with no answers, no explanations, nothing, apart from the fact that there are forces in the universe we know nothing about, that are far greater than us, and that we will never be allowed to learn from. 'Midnight' is indeed a humbling story; it tells us not to take things for granted and, perhaps as importantly, not to be scared of the unknown. 'There are more things in heaven and earth than are dreamt of in your philosophy,' Shakespeare tells us, and 'Midnight' perfectly showcases the meaning behind this quotation.

Not since William Hartnell and Patrick Troughton's day has there been such foreboding from a story. In the surviving episode of 'The Abominable Snowmen', we have ancient powers locked deep in a monastery, the flickering flames and shadows in black and white; in 'The Web of Fear' we have the dark and gloomy London underground with the Yeti skulking through; we hear ancient chanting in the deserted monastery from 'The Time Meddler' and an evil creature that lurks in the caves and visits the spaceship in 'The Rescue'. All these things speak of an otherness, and evoke a deep foreboding, that uneasy place that we as human beings dare not let our senses go, not willingly; but we enjoy those feelings of fear, we wallow in them while sitting in our living room, waxing lyrical like the most self-assured armchair football supporter. But in the comfort of our living room we can explore many themes in quiet security, especially the fear evoked by a horror film or science fiction show, because those feelings are an essential part of being human, and if *Doctor Who* allows us to enjoy those feelings in the secure environment of our living room – behind the obligatory sofa or cushion – then so be it. That is the reason why we watch, it is this very feeling that makes us love *Doctor Who*.

On the subject of more from less, there is a story in which the Doctor hardly appears but is hailed one of the greatest *Doctor Who* stories ever, and that is 'Blink'. The story of the Weeping Angels and how Sally Sparrow and her friends try to thwart them with the Doctor is legendary. It's a great lesson in *Doctor Who* scriptwriting: pace, scare factor, good character development is what it's all about. Sometimes the Doctor isn't needed, but usually he is, to release the tension, to explain

THE DOCTORS WHO'S WHO

things and reassure in a 'timey-wimey' sort of way. He is the crackpot professor, the stranger that rides into town to sort things out (a Clint Eastwood anti-hero-like character). Simply, he is the Doctor who makes people better – but in what way better? Because surely some die due to his dabbling?

The Weeping Angels provide a very emotional farewell to Amy and Rory, two of the 11th Doctor's most loyal companions ('The Angels Take Manhattan'). Carving their names on a gravestone and sentencing them to life in the past, the Doctor destroys a 'happy couple' to the extent of destroying their opportunity to live in their own time. Some companions have died as a result of their time with the Doctor, most notably Adric at the end of 'Earthshock' in an extremely powerful farewell, but sometimes a fate worse than death ensues. Witness the plight of Peri, who had her body taken over by an evil creature and her mind and spirit destroyed.

The Weeping Angels have had successful stories since their first appearance, but part of their success – scare factor – is because they do not communicate face-to-face: they do it indirectly. Their voice is not their own, it is the voice of their prey and they speak in persuasive tones, like the lure of the Devil, which is both sinister and unsettling. This is done to remarkable effect in their second story, 'The Time of the Angels/Flesh and Stone'.

Sometimes *Doctor Who* wallows in darkness, a gothic horror that deals with tried and proven legends, and this enhances the mystique of the show. Stories such as 'State of Decay' are under-rated in the *Doctor Who* canon. 'State of Decay' deals with exploitation, corruption, traditional values and legends. The very idea that a castle could be a spaceship and simultaneously a giant stake is ingenious to say the least. Another great gothic story that falls within this category is 'The Daemons', from the

Jon Pertwee era. An ancient barrow is opened and a creature not unlike the Devil released to cause havoc.

Jon Pertwee rated 'The Daemons' as a personal favourite, and with its beautiful location, sinister demons and devils – as well as the Master and UNIT – it ticks many boxes, proving you don't need the biggest budget to tell a great story, you just need a great script and a dose of eeriness.

There are two stories that go even deeper within the gothic realm and place the Doctor way out of his comfort zone. Only very occasionally do we see him covered in mud, his clothes ripped, his knees scraped. Rarely do we see him actually bleed but in 'The Caves of Androzani' and 'The Deadly Assassin', we get plenty of this, and an exciting story ensues.

With 'The Caves of Androzani' the Doctor actually gives his life to save that of his companion. Effectively, he loses, but because he is a Time Lord, he escapes to fight another day, the proverbial cat with nine – thirteen? – lives. He regenerates.

'The Caves of Androzani' is also suspenseful because of the deranged masked man who hides down below the Citadel; he is, like the wicked master in 'The Talons of Weng-Chiang', a *Phantom of the Opera*-like creature. But what 'Androzani' has over 'Weng-Chiang' is gothic romance. Peri (the Doctor's companion) becomes the Phantom's (Sharaz Jek) love interest, and the Doctor doesn't just have to save her from the madman but he must also save both Peri and himself from a killer disease. In the end, it all becomes too much for him and he passes away to his next regeneration.

In 'The Deadly Assassin', the Doctor is again at full stretch. Powerful mind games send him into a schizophrenic limbo world, where he is shot at, partially drowned, blown up, run over by a speeding train and just generally terrified. For me, 'The Deadly Assassin' is the best *Doctor Who* story ever for sheer imagination and gothic appeal. It is the Doctor alone on his home planet, pitted against the Master in his new more sinister incarnation, with the Time Lords seemingly against him too. At one stage, the Master is thought to be dead, but he has only drugged himself and comes back to kill and destroy all that he surveys. The High Council of the Time Lords puts the Doctor on trial and tortures him, believing him to be the murderer of the President himself – the Assassin; but the whole thing is a set-up by the Master. Ingenious, brutal and incredibly imaginative, 'The Deadly Assassins' showcases some of the best scares *Doctor Who* has to offer, not dissimilar to the gothic horror of rats, disfigured madman and bleeding dolls in a foggy Victorian London, as seen in 'The Talons of Weng-Chiang'.

Both 'The Deadly Assassin' and 'The Talons of Weng-Chiang' come from an era in the Tom Baker years known as the Hinchcliffe Years, where Philip Hinchcliffe was the producer and brought a more sinister, gothic edge to the stories, not unlike Steven Moffat promised in the new-look *Doctor Who* of Matt Smith (indeed, he had vampires, Weeping Angels and a host of other great foes to draw on in his very first season).

Another impressive story from the Hinchcliffe Years is 'The Robots of Death', run-of-the-mill *Doctor Who* fodder, but great Saturday-night entertainment.

'The Robots of Death' worked Isaac Asimov's laws of robotics from *I, Robot*, not dissimilar to how 'The Daemons' played with Arthur C. Clarke's devil creatures from *Childhood's End*. Sometimes classic SF does influence current SF, inasmuch as it encourages good practice.

'The Robots of Death' is not a brilliant allegory or, for that matter, a radical script. It's a good script with its Art Deco robots and a supporting cast you actually care for – well, some of them anyway.

Louise Jameson is terrific as Leela and really comes into her own in this story, which has the obligatory mad man wanting to take over the world. A murder is committed and the Doctor and Leela turn up just in time to be the prime suspects. It's a tried and tested Agatha Christie pathway, but every time there's a subtle difference and the Doctor's way of remedying the evil in the story is both amusing and ingenious.

Doctor Who does sometimes have its poignant moments but stories that pull at the heartstrings are rare, especially those done exceptionally well. Stories such as 'Father's Day', 'Human Nature/Family of Blood' show off this theme tremendously well. In 'Father's Day', Rose Tyler (the Doctor's companion) wants to travel back in time and see her father when he was alive. But instead of just observing him, she saves his life in a road accident and releases creatures into the world that need to repair the break in time. One of the creatures eats the Doctor and it is left to Rose to right the wrong she has created. The way in which the story builds into a credible basis for Rose's parents to understand that the Doctor's Rose is actually the grown up counterpart to their babe-in-arms is nothing short of quality scriptwriting, and the poignancy evoked by the end of the episode is both tender and moving.

In the double bill 'Human Nature/Family of Blood', the Doctor toys with the mortality of being human and the horror humans bestow upon each other (the backdrop being the Great War). One of the most memorable scenes in the history of the show is Martha Jones pinning a poppy to the Doctor's lapel as the Great War veteran looks on. What brings home the underlying message are the words of the great poem 'For the Fallen', which begins, 'They will not grow old...' and indeed the time travellers haven't aged a day since they last saw the veteran as a boy about to go to war; they've simply jumped forward seconds in time, but the veteran has taken 90 Earth years to get to that moment. He sees them and is humbled by their respect, in a wonderfully poignant scene. The waste of human lives through war is also brought home, but one thing more: the Doctor's longing for true companionship. His love of human females but despair that they just don't live long enough is painfully clear. In 'Human Nature', he becomes human, falls in love and in an amazing visual projection, has children and then dies. There is something very *Highlander* about this part of the story, extremely sad but telling.

The one thing the new-millennium *Doctor Who* gives us is a sense of love captured and lost, a true sense of loneliness. The Doctor's home planet has been destroyed, there is only his adopted planet – Earth – left; but there he is nothing more than a stranger in a strange land, a Robert Heinlein exile harking back to Jon Pertwee's Doctor driving Bessie away from his beloved Jo Grant. But the reverse happens too. In 'School Reunion', we witness how a companion has to readjust to normal life after successfully leaving the TARDIS. Sarah Jane Smith never had children, she secretly longed for the return of the most remarkable man she had ever known. When he did return, it was too late for her to love him the way she longed, but she could still have more thrilling adventures with him. She forgives him and says a final goodbye, turning her back and leaving with her beloved K9 to continue her own adventures.

There's an enigma surrounding the Doctor. Will he marry and have children? In a safe way, he has – i.e. he has been when there is not the risk of commitment from the programme maker. In 'Human Nature/Family of Blood' he does so in a future mental projection of himself as a human. Of course it doesn't happen. In the story 'The Doctor's Wife', he is the metaphorical husband of the TARDIS. Although the story is still a slight cop-out, it is a dark masterpiece with Neil Gaiman's name all over it. The world of patchwork-people and a Time Lord doom-world is excellently constructed in a one-off story that, unlike many new millennium stories, doesn't appear contrived or rushed. It has depth, menace, classic scenes (a manic Ood stalking Amy and Rory deep within the TARDIS); it is full of quality thrills and chills.

In 'The Doctor's Daughter', it is a DNA-extracted daughter that emerges as his kin. Is this an on-screen science-fiction rape scene? How can it be when he quickly comes to terms with his daughter and shows great love for her? He instantly bonds with her, even though she is his opposite: she has a love affair with weapons.

The theme of the horrors of war is clear in 'The Doctor's Daughter' and ultimately, there is the loss of a loved one. So the Doctor loses another piece of himself as he gives himself to the goodness in the cosmos, a Christ-figure surrounded by his disciples (was Peter Davison's companion Turlough Judas?).

What is strange is we never learn more about the Doctor when he meets his other selves. He tends to squabble with them like a spoilt sibling. There is no reminiscence in the character's make-up. He is forward looking, which is a positive image for children. He battles terrible odds in 'The Two Doctors' and especially 'The Three Doctors', and this is where he overcomes petty squabbles with his other selves in order to get the job done. It is this very point that makes 'The Five Doctors' a lesser story. Each Doctor has an individual quest to reach the tower, so a mini *Lord of the Rings* in that respect. The Doctor doesn't pull his many selves together until the end. One could argue that the very fact that he is torn from time, in a hostile manner, prevents a fellowship occurring. Maybe it would have been too contrived, but only when the tower is reached, the quest over, do all the leaders (Doctors) and their close companions come together to provide closure – the fellowship encapsulated.

A significant flaw in 'The Five Doctors' was the absence of the fourth Doctor. He makes a cameo appearance through some previously unused (at that time) footage from the incomplete story 'Shada' (and a waxwork figure in publicity stills), but his absence is a massive disappointment to the overall story: would he have solved the final riddle rather than the first Doctor? Surely the egos of the first and fourth Doctor are the largest and would probably cause more dramatic moments than the second and third Doctors? It's an interesting concept, but sadly one we will never witness…

The first Doctor is the father figure to the other Doctors in 'The Five Doctors', and his story arcs appear to emanate that too. 'Human Nature' recalls the very first *Doctor Who* story, or an early draft of the script ('An Unearthly Child'), where Suzanne (Susan Foreman) and the Doctor explain that a race of creatures is after them to kill them and steal the TARDIS, so they must hide. The only reason the Doctor became human was to hide from terrifying creatures who want to use him and his TARDIS. In a way it is history repeating itself. In fact, could this be the race of creatures that wanted to kill the Doctor and Susan all those years ago? Nobody knows, but maybe time will tell. If Suzanne became human, that would explain a lot about her motives and calling the Doctor her grandfather. So will the Doctor have to return to the human Suzanne before she dies of human old age? Again, an interesting concept from an unfulfilled story arc within the series.

Androids are a constant in *Doctor Who*. They range from the placid, such as the unaffected VOCs in 'Robots of Death', to the totally scary androids, e.g. 'The Girl in the Fireplace' and 'The Visitation'. But one thing most have in common – indeed all of the above have in common – is that *something* or *somebody* made them do wrong. They are only scary because the person who programmed them made them dangerous.

In 'The Visitation' Nyssa refers to her deadly android assailant as a beautiful creation. And indeed he was, but the android is just an aside in one of the finest historical *Doctor Who* stories ever, a story that blended history so beautifully with alien invasion, and supporting actors as fantastically believable characters (such as Michael Robbins as Richard Mace and the delightful family at the beginning of Episode One).

Another good example of this wonderful blend of history and alien invasion is 'The Time Warrior'. This is the first time we meet the once-mighty (see new millennium *Doctor Who*) Sontarans and companion Sarah Jane Smith. The contradiction to this is the android in 'The Time Warrior', which is the most primitive looking in the show's history (early visual effects to one side).

The Autons are not really androids, but once they possess inanimate objects, they behave like the most ruthless androids the Doctor has ever encountered. Crashing through shop windows to shoot innocent bystanders in the first ever colour story 'Spearhead From Space', gave them a memorable scene that begged for their return when the show was re-launched in the new millennium (and a rare *Doctor Who* Blu-ray DVD). The problem with the re-launch story 'Rose' was that the story had too many similarities, it was just a higher budget version, and I can argue that the scare factor – not wow factor – was greater in the first Auton story.

One could stretch the android theme and suggest that the original Cybermen – those scary automatons from 'The Tenth

Planet' – are an extension of the sophistication of alien races. In a way, they are the product of a self-wounding race at odds with their own bodies and emotions and therefore turned themselves into emotionless androids. Their human hands stuck on the end of robotic arms give them a sinister look not seen in other versions of the deadly enemy. This mixture of flesh and machinery was explored further in 'The Girl in the Fireplace'.

I still believe the Cyberman have been underused in the programme; witness 'Nightmare in Silver' Cybermen, not just 'The Tenth Planet' Cybermen. And shouldn't a story to rival 'Genesis of the Daleks' be made to embrace the original concept of this self-wounding race? The same could be said of the original and utterly ruthless Sontarans. The new potato-head butler is a mockery of a savage and noble race and is more comic than dangerous.

Humour has its place in *Doctor Who*, from the Doctor's return from a Jacobean wild party to thwart the clockwork men in 'The Girl in the Fireplace', to the theatrical – and slightly pitiful – antics of Richard Mace in 'The Visitation'. Humour has always been there to counterbalance the scary bits and that certainly happened in 'The Girl in the Fireplace' and even 'The Sound of Drums' (where the Master gasses all of the British Cabinet but first puts on a gas mask and gives a choking man the thumbs-up when he tells him he's mad).

The humour shared between the Second Doctor and an alien chef in a restaurant ('The Two Doctors') while craving human flesh is of particular note, especially as it defuses a stabbing scene seconds later, but even that degenerates into a comic chase scene. Comedy is so important to *Doctor Who*. When overplayed it highlights its worst scenes; done well, it's magical.

Douglas Adams was a writer renowned for his humour, and

'The City of Death' is a masterwork, blending quality science fiction themes with historical insight and an extremely scary foe that had more than one child hiding from the terrifying alien face.

'The City of Death' used da Vinci and his Mona Lisa in a way Dan Brown wouldn't dare, and every now and then the art world crops up in the Doctor's travels. 'Vincent and the Doctor' is a great example of this. Van Gogh marvelling at the beautiful colour of Amy Pond's hair and clearly showing the curse of his lust for life is beautifully counterbalanced by the wonderfully poignant scene at the end, where van Gogh is brought forward in time to see how much he truly is appreciated. Again, another tear-jerking scene from the new millennium *Doctor Who* and allowing genius to at last see the just rewards of its pain. Now let's have John Lennon please, with David Bowie working out the spaceman direction of his work from the Doctor; yes David, there is a Starman waiting in the sky.

There has been a wealth of emotion and incident in *Doctor Who* over the years, but there is a recurring theme of death. From the natural – the Fourth Doctor falling from a great height and smashing his body ('Logopolis') – to the macabre – the Master taking over a person's body at the end of 'The Keeper of Traken', death is everywhere in *Doctor Who*. In 'The Last of the Time Lords', we look back at the Doctor's dead race, we see into the madness of the Master and see him will himself to death while the Doctor grieves over his body. In fact, in all of the stories I have discussed in this section, someone dies or, more accurately, someone is killed. It's as though someone always has to pay for the Doctor's – and his companions' – thrills. But in legend, isn't it true that any time the Grim Reaper is called up he must take a soul away with him? Is the Doctor the Grim Reaper, is he a Jesus-like figure with disciples, or is he the more sinister Pied Piper leading the children away? Evidence points to the latter more than the former.

In 'The Curse of the Black Spot,' a mysterical siren strips a pirate ship of its crew; but has the Doctor been doing that throughout his travels?

The Doctor is aware of his profound influence on people's lives and has sacrificed himself to save others many times (making him a possible Jesus-allegory), and this is part of the reason why he regenerates so quickly. At the end of 'The Planet of the Spiders' he knew that entering The Great One's cave would mean certain death, but he is not afraid to die. Like a gallant warrior he walks into trouble, to confront evil. In 'Terror of the Zygons' the Doctor might be called foolish for entering the organic spaceship of the Zygons, but he is simply saving time. The enemy has to be faced – evil must always be faced – and there is a logical reason behind his cavalier behaviour. Sometimes he uses his intellect only to thwart his opponent. A great example of this was in 'The Celestial Toymaker', where we truly respect his ability to outwit his nemesis. And perhaps it is from things like this that we acquire our deep respect for the First Doctor. He surprises us with his strength. Not his physical strength, but his inner strength: his power of mind over matter and sharp brain. And that's why he solves the puzzle at the end of 'The Five Doctors' – he is geared to solving impossible puzzles, just as he did against the dangerous and mysterious celestial toymaker.

During his seventh regeneration the Doctor surprises us with his mystique. In 'Battlefield' he seems to offer so much more than we've ever discovered about him, from the death of the Brigadier to the legacy of Merlin the Magician. The witch queen Morgaine perpetuates the King Arthur legend, again showing the divide between good and evil, and modern methods come into play as the Brigadier finally succumbs to his age and looks on as a female brigadier takes the lead at UNIT.

There is so much legacy in 'Battlefield', it really shows how rich the history of the programme was in the original series, something that is still alive and well in the new series, but should perhaps have been handled better when the Daleks eventually fought the Cybermen. Such a wonderful showdown should have enjoyed a more sophisticated outcome, but great stories cannot always be short.

The watershed for *Doctor Who* came several stories, and a few years, after 'Battlefield'. 'Doctor Who – The Movie' was a major leap into the new mindset that has endured since the show's return in the Millennium. A doctor full of life, love and passion, with a larger, new-look TARDIS, is as radical as Jon Pertwee's colour appearance and desire to drive/pilot anything mechanical, even a wheelchair in 'Spearhead From Space'.

Paul McGann may have had only one television outing as the Doctor, but despite an over-loaded script, there were ideas and scenes that were important to the ongoing *Doctor Who* legacy. Yes, kissing his companion has something of Captain Kirk's first (inter-racial) kiss on TV about it, because the Doctor didn't do things like that. Tom Baker didn't smoke or drink in front of children when he was the Doctor; he stated that the Doctor should be enigmatic and this gave him an alien-like quality that has never been replicated as well since.

In the new millennium, the Doctor gets involved in domestic issues, always seeming to upset the parents and grandparents of his feisty young companions. Life is lived at a much faster pace nowadays. Children don't want to wait 12 weeks to enjoy the whole of a Dalek master plan, they want a quality action-packed drama in two segments if – frustratingly – we must, and that was also anticipated by 'Doctor Who – The Movie'.

The *Doctor Who* legacy is populated by people who still remember seeing the very first episode on a dark and wet night, back in 1963, who remember watching episodes – stories – that no longer exist in the BBC archive. And perhaps that's where so many 'favourite stories' polls can be slightly skewed. The poll is conducted by people influenced by the Doctor they grew up with and the stories they saw. So many of the older generation talk of William Hartnell as being the best Doctor; his food dispensing machine and complete mystery as to where he came from – Doctor Who? To appreciate this original concept and ignore all the thrills and spills that have come afterwards is difficult. The eeriness, the darkness, the not knowing who this alien genius is, alongside the whispering monks, dancing flames and baffled companions of classic stories lost, echoes the thrills of a totally different show; but there is a police box, a familiar – albeit unsettling – theme, and a character we can still identify as special and not of our kind.

There are stories such as 'The Ice Warriors' and 'The Abominable Snowmen' that were so popular in the black and white series they demanded a return of the famous enemies on TV and comic strip. Other stories, such as 'The Power of the Daleks', are taken for granted because we accept them as yet another Dalek story. We cannot fully appreciate the over-powering performance of Patrick Troughton coming to terms with his new body and convincing audiences to keep watching. The second Doctor's stovepipe hat is legendary but we cannot watch him wear it in that very first adventure of his anymore. Conversely we now have an opportunity to enjoy the second Doctor's lookalike foe Salamander from 'The Enemy of the World' – a truly excellent performance if a rather strange one. Sometimes those wonderful lost stories are returned to us. The soundtracks still exist; many photographs and reminiscences of the actors are available to us too, for the ones that are still lost. Very occasionally a lost story returns to the archive (or a single episode) and oddly, these gems never cease to thrill. The return of 'Tomb of the Cybermen' was a monumental moment and rubber-stamped its position as a total classic when the latest – youngest – fans actually got to watch it. The joint return of 'The Enemy of the World' and 'The Web of Fear' in October 2013 made front page news – so important.

Doctor Who has endured for 50 years and has a rich legacy to draw from. The visual effects have improved over the years and the Doctor's face may have changed a dozen times, but the one thing that has stayed the same is the Doctor's soul, the TARDIS and that menacing theme tune that harks back to a dark night in 1963, when The Beatles was just starting out and the world mourned a great American president. The Doctor still has some mystique about him, but audiences nowadays demand complete understanding and greater thrills; tiny nuances are lost, the time to build tension cut short, because communication is *now*, via cell phone, text, email, Skype, and many other multi-media tools. Technology moves on and so does our need for *Doctor Who*. We still need the show – perhaps more so now than ever before – to stimulate imagination in the young and teach the fundamentals of good and evil. If sometimes the aliens are compromised to grotesque caricature (see the new millennium Sontarans or the Eccleston/Tennant Cybermen), we accept it is a necessary evil for the show to endure and to appeal to a whole new generation, even though some may feel that it fails artistically as a consequence.

The *Doctor Who* legacy is far from over.

'If heroes don't exist, it is necessary to invent them.'

Cardinal Borusa to the Doctor
'The Deadly Assassin'

CHAPTER FOUR

BLINK – QUALITY SCIENCE FICTION OR FLAWED MASTERPIECE?

ALTHOUGH ONE OF the best *Doctor Who* stories ever, 'Blink' includes scenes that make little sense and are only included for dramatic effect. Does this make it an edge-of-the-seat quality SF story or a flawed masterpiece?

The most important scene to analyse is the opening teaser: Sally Sparrow breaks into a deserted house and peels wallpaper from a wall to reveal a message telling her to duck by the Doctor. So dutifully – and not knowing who the Doctor is - she ducks and a rock sores over her head and bounces off the wall, supposedly thrown by a Weeping Angel; why on earth would they want to throw stones, and why would the Doctor want to warn her? It's a mystery we can't reconcile, it doesn't make any sense; but it is a great teaser and starts one of the most atmospheric stories ever.

And that's the paradox about 'Blink'. It *is* one of the best *Doctor Who* stories ever; that is not in question, what is being questioned however, is how an audience – or film maker – can allow so many inconsistancies (irrelevant scene or missing explanations) in order to invoke a higher sense of mystery and drama.

The next odd scene in 'Blink' is when Kathy Nightingale has disaapeared and Sally walks back upstairs to be comfronted by the Weeping Angels. How did they get the TARDIS key and why would it be on offer to Sally when they wanted the TARDIS themselves? Later we see them trying to get into the TARDIS in the police underground car park, so why give away the key beforehand? We are told by the Doctor on the DVD Easter Egg that the 'Angels have the phone box'; but they don't, do they?

We know the TARDIS was left outside the spooky house (Wester Drumlins) and then taken by the police to the underground car park, where all the abandoned vehicles from Dumlins are kept; so the angels didn't have the police box; but they knew where it was, and tried to get into it after giving away the key.

A little bit stupid don't you think?

Billy Shipton falls victim to the Weeping Angels in the police car park, just as quickly as when Kathy was taken; but why wasn't Sally taken as quickly? In the TARDIS key scene there is ample time for an Angel to touch Sally and send her back in time; but it doesn't happen – now that's interesting favouritism!

A lot of inconsistency is put down to the Doctor's 'timey-wimey' excuse; but how does he know that Billy would die on a certain night, the very night he would meet Sally Sparrow again, and how did he know what DVD's to put the Easter Egg on? Was it all from the pack of photos and letters Sally gave the Doctor? We are led to believe so; but it's a bit of a leap of faith surely? Would Sally put the whole stone throwing incident in there, would the Doctor go to the house and write the message on the wall and wallpaper over it? Would anyone else leave the message there if they were wallpapering such a once-quality property? At the very least, all this speculation stretches the glimmer of reality an audience will put up with in a drama. Martha Jones helped paint and decorate a house with the Doctor? Come on now!

Sally tells us that she's intelligent and feels a commitment to the Doctor and is determined to see the intricacies of her adventure through, to do her best for her dead friends (Kathy and Billy), then she has closure; and she gets it too. We trust that all the information has been given to the Doctor and he will go off and do all the background stuff (like painting and decorating) and only then the cycle is complete. Only then can she move on.

So all that happens and she gets the closure she needs and then instantly decides that she can now commit to her dead friend's brother, not only do they have their own business, they have a deep relationship. Sally can at last get on with her life and that life is with the man who found the DVD Easter Eggs.

And everyone wants to know what happens to them next...

Don't they?

The conclusion is that the general audience don't want to think too deeply about a great drama. Like the viewer of an action film, they are willing to suspend belief for a while, to escape and enjoy a fantasy outside the pattern of their everyday life, to let the story send spine-tingling shards down their back and let the chill wash all over them. And 'Blink' delievered that beautifully with characters we hardly know; but care for, and a new foe of pure quality.

So ignore the inconsistancies; just blink and you'll miss them; but the story will stay with you forever.

CHAPTER FIVE

THE PERSONALITY OF THE DOCTOR

'In my case, real life was something I was only very tenuously connected to. The hardest thing of all was to be aware that I was no longer a hero to children.'

Tom Baker's recollections on leaving *Doctor Who*
from *Who On Earth is Tom Baker?*

THIS BOOK HAS DISCUSSED the many actors who have played the role of Doctor Who in context to the rest of their careers. Each has played the character differently, but how has the character evolved over the years and how have those individual interpretations moved the character away from Sydney Newman's original conception?

The original character outline for the Doctor stated that he was a Doctor of Science and over 60 years old. It went on to say that 'He is frail-looking, but wiry and tough like an old turkey'. An odd thing to say maybe but then it goes on to state that he has 'watery blue eyes', that he is 'bewildered' and 'suspicious' and 'can be enormously cunning'. He has flashes of brilliance but can also be sometimes vague. Perhaps this describes William

Hartnell's Doctor very well, but what about Patrick Troughton? What did he add to the Doctor's complex personality?

In appearance, Troughton's Doctor was not much different to Hartnell's, with a black frock coat and check trousers. He also wore a woolly hat at times, something Hartnell's Doctor did in the very first episode, but Troughton's stovepipe hat and recorder gave him the appearance of a wandering minstrel. He also confessed to hamming up his early performances, but he was always more humorous, taking the sting out of frightening scenes with a hint of comedy.

Hartnell's Doctor always took notes, which is good practice for a scientist, but Troughton favoured his 500-year diary, using his experiences more than the acquisition of facts. In that respect, Troughton was more self-assured, worldly – or rather universally – wise, and that self-assurance generated the humour. Those 'bewildered' and 'suspicious' eyes took on more conviction, but could be almost childlike sometimes, especially when he was caught out when being a little too cunning.

Jon Pertwee's Doctor leapt into action. Extrovert – but still Edwardian in dress sense – the second Doctor's flowing clown-style pocket handkerchief turned into a frilly shirt and dashing cape. The recorder vanished and the sonic screwdriver became the instrument of choice. Where the second Doctor kept reasonably cool when confronted by ignorance, the third Doctor showed his distaste to the individual in question with outrage, often needing a mediator to calm things down (Brigadier or companion).

The third Doctor was much more physical than his predecessors. Venusian Aikido and a passion for cars, hovercraft and, well anything mechanical (even taking the TARDIS to pieces), was the order of the day. Of course throughout his first three generations the Doctor was mechanically minded, taking consoles to pieces and even robots on occasion, but with the third Doctor it was more of an excuse to get his hands dirty.

The fourth Doctor brought out more of the eccentricity of the Doctor. His long, multicoloured scarf, big eyes, curly hair and toothy grin, and, not least, his love of jelly babies and yo-yos, enhanced his nonchalance when confronted by anything remotely scary. While the third Doctor could be a little egotistical, the fourth Doctor grew quite arrogant and even sulked more than his second incarnation. His serious moments could turn to anger – not the outrage of the third Doctor but out-and-out fury.

All of the Doctor's tetchiness seemed to be tempered by his mid-lives crisis, his fifth incarnation. A mediator and methodical thinker, the fifth Doctor was the model of fair play, which was characterised in his Edwardian cricket jacket and love of the thoroughly-English game. Wearing a stick of celery had its scientific use, but certainly showed that a love of the wilder clothing of his youth was still there deep within. Unfortunately, the mid-lives crisis exploded with the sixth Doctor, outrage and argument akin to the first Doctor and multicoloured – pied – jacket emanating the fourth Doctor's scarf, screamed out for the universe to hear him and only him. But when his companion's body was taken over and her soul destroyed, he calmed down slightly, falling into retrospection and displaying a little inner darkness akin to his latter incarnations (ninth, tenth and eleventh).

The Doctor shared some of his mysterious past in his seventh incarnation. The check trousers were back and short coat, as if trying to reassure himself that he was always doing things for the greater good. Perhaps this uncertainty was echoed in his question-mark umbrella, but it certainly wasn't present in his brief eighth incarnation – a dashing, still quite Edwardian-costumed young gentleman. Suddenly with the maturity of an alien life-cycle, the Doctor courted sex-appeal. His ninth incarnation enhanced this with more trendy clothes and rough-and-ready looks. He was now totally assured and experienced at his work of saving the universe and ran round an awful lot more, but not as much as his super-sexy (so the females say!) tenth incarnation, who was full of a lust for life. That said, when he became extremely mad, he was an angry old man indeed (see his last story); but the egotistical scientist with Edwardian coat, bow tie and – of course – braces (another favourite recurring piece of clothing), returned to bring the Doctor almost back full circle because, yes, there is a glint of suspicion in his eyes, and yes, he doesn't always trust the people around him.

The Doctor has a common thread through his first 11 incarnations, in clothing and personality. We know he is the Pied Piper, the Doctor who tries to make people better and, despite all of this, all those adventures, there is still that question-mark umbrella; that question that is the oldest question of all: Doctor Who? We still don't know too much about his youth and where he came from. Some races consider him a God – his companions disciples – some consider him the 'evil one', and some people, especially Queen Victoria, despise him. In that way, thank God Charles Dickens, the man of the people, saw his merits in Victorian London, and even with a potential answer for Doctor Who? The legacy is still strong and the questions persist, such as Doctor Why?

When the Time Lords tried to save themselves against the tenth Doctor there was an enigmatic lady looking on. Nothing was said but was this the Doctor's mother? A sister? Even his child? The camera lingered but as usual the story writers didn't take a chance. The Doctor is a loner, an isolationist, not unlike the super-cool Thin White Duke of David Bowie's furtive imagination. 'For he is the outsider, and the outsider he will still,' says the philosopher, but must he always be so? Sydney Newman wanted him to be distant; but there was a granddaughter.

The new millennium Doctor is more involved in relationships, especially the companions' families, which have never been explored before. (Could you imagine the Doctor explaining himself to Jo Grant's father?) Maybe he came close in his second incarnation – he did know Victoria's father.

It is important to acknowledge that the Doctor hasn't changed much from Newman's original theme, but at the same time to expect great changes for the Doctor in the future. The programme has made radical changes through its first 50 years, but sometimes these have been subtle, not unlike the changes a baby makes when growing. *Doctor Who* will continue to move with the times, adapting to new fashions and trends but always embodying a Doctor who wants to do good and leading actors who take on the part for four or five years and find themselves part of a life-changing experience: becoming immortal in the ever-changing public eye.

'All the world's a stage,
And all the men and women merely players:
They have their exits and their entrances;
And one man in his time plays many parts…'

As You Like It
William Shakespeare
(and *Moon Boots and Dinner Suits*, **Jon Pertwee**)

FURTHER READING AND SOURCES

THE FOLLOWING TITLES are essentially the core of any *Doctor Who* book collection. They are suggested further reading for anyone interested in the genesis of the show, some of which were also used in the research for this book.

Doctor Who and the Daleks, David Whitaker (Frederick Muller, 1964).

Doctor Who and the Daleks, David Whitaker (Armada Paperbacks, 1965).

Doctor Who and the Zarbi, Bill Strutton (Frederick Muller, 1965).

Doctor Who and the Crusaders, David Whitaker (Frederick Muller, 1965).

The Dalek Pocket Book and Space Travellers Guide, Terry Nation (Panther Books, 1965).

Doctor Who and the Crusaders, David Whitaker (Green Dragon paperback, 1967).

The Making of Doctor Who (Pan Books limited-edition

hardback 1972 – the rarest Doctor Who book ever published). Laminated boards, limited release to libraries only.

The Making of Doctor Who, Malcolm Hulke and Terrance Dicks (Piccolo Books, 1972).

Doctor Who 10th Anniversary Radio Times Special (1973).

Doctor Who Holiday Special 1973.

Doctor Who Holiday Special 1974.

The Doctor Who Monster Book (originally issued with poster), Terrance Dicks (Target Books, 1975).

The Making of Doctor Who, Malcolm Hulke and Terrance Dicks (Target Books, 1976).

Doctor Who and the Daleks Omnibus (St Michael, 1976).

The Second Doctor Who Monster Book (Target Books, 1977).

Doctor Who Winter Special 1977.

Terry Nation's Dalek Special (Target, 1979).

A Day With a Television Producer (Day in the Life), Graham Rickard (Hodder Wayland, 1980).

Doctor Who – Making of a Television Series, Alan Road (André Deutsch, 1982).

Doctor Who 20th Anniversary Radio Times Special (originally issued with poster) (1983).

Doctor Who – A Celebration, Two Decades Through Time and Space, Peter Haining (WH Allen, 1983) (also available as a limited-edition leather-bound edition).

Doctor Who – The Key to Time, A Year-By-Year Record, 21st Anniversary Special, Peter Haining (WH Allen, 1984) (also available as a limited-edition leather-bound edition).

Moon Boots and Dinner Suits, Jon Pertwee (Elm Tree Books, 1984).

The TARDIS Inside Out, John Nathan-Turner (Piccadilly Press, 1985).

The Companions of Doctor Who, K9 and Company, Terence Dudley (Target, 1987).

The Gallifrey Chronicles, John Peel (Virgin Publishing, 1991).

The Nine Lives of Doctor Who, Peter Haining (Headline, 1991).

Doctor Who – The Sixties, David J. Howe, Mark Stammers and Stephen James Walker (Virgin, 1992).

Doctor Who – The Seventies, David J. Howe, Mark Stammers and Stephen James Walker (Virgin, 1994).

Classic Doctor Who – The Hinchcliffe Years, Seasons 12–14, Adrian Riglesford (Boxtree, 1995).

Doctor Who – The Eighties, David J. Howe, Mark Stammers and Stephen James Walker (Virgin, 1996).

Who's There? The Life and Career of William Hartnell, Jessica Carney (Hartnell's granddaughter) (Virgin, 1996).

I Am the Doctor – Jon Pertwee's Final Memoir, Jon Pertwee & David Howe (Virgin, 1996).

Who on Earth is Tom Baker? An Autobiography, Tom Baker (HarperCollins, 1997).

Jon Pertwee: The Biography, Bernard Bale (André Deutsch, 2000).

Doctor Who: The Scripts, Tom Baker 1974/5 (BBC, 2001).

Patrick Troughton – The Biography of the Second Doctor, Michael Troughton (Fantom Films Limited, 2013).

DOCTOR WHO ANNUALS:

1965 (Hartnell), *Invasion From Space* (Hartnell – Special Edition, 1966), 1966 (Hartnell), 1967 (Troughton), 1968 (Troughton), 1969 (Troughton), 1970 (Pertwee), 1971 – no annual, 1972 – *Countdown Annual* (featuring *Doctor Who* strips and Behind the Camera feature regarding the filming of

'The Daemons'), 1973 (Pertwee), 1974 (Pertwee), 1975 (Pertwee), 1976 (T. Baker), *The Amazing World of Doctor Who* (Special with wall chart to go with series of Typhoo Tea cards), 1977 (T. Baker), 1978 (T. Baker), 1979 (T. Baker), 1980 (T. Baker), 1981 (T. Baker), 1982 (T. Baker/Davison), 1983 (Davison), 1984 (Davison), 1985 (C. Baker). 1986–1989 *Doctor Who Holiday Annual* series of four, 2007 (Eccleston), 2008 (Tennant), 2009 (Tennant), 2010 (Tennant), 2011 (Smith), 2012 (Smith), 2013 (Smith), 2014 (Smith).

K9 Annual 1983 (World International, 1982).

The Dalek Book 1964 (Souvenir Press), *The Dalek World 1965* (Souvenir Press), *The Dalek Outer Space Book 1966* (Souvenir Press).
Terry Nation's Dalek Annual 1976 (World Distributors), *Terry Nation's Dalek Annual 1977* (World Distributors), *Terry Nation's Dalek Annual 1978* (World Distributors), *Terry Nation's Dalek Annual 1979* (World Distributors).

SOURCES:

Doctor Who and the Daleks, David Whitaker (Frederick Muller, 1964).
Doctor Who and the Crusaders, David Whitaker (Frederick Muller, 1965).
Doctor Who and the Crusaders, David Whitaker (Green Dragon paperback, 1967).
The Making of Doctor Who (Pan Books limited-edition hardback 1972 – the rarest Doctor Who book ever published). Laminated boards, limited release to libraries only.

Doctor Who 10th Anniversary Radio Times Special (1973).

The Making of Doctor Who, Malcolm Hulke and Terrance Dicks (Target Books, 1976).

Doctor Who 20th Anniversary Radio Times Special (originally issued with poster) (1983).

Doctor Who – A Celebration, Two Decades Through Time and Space, Peter Haining (WH Allen, 1983) (also available as a limited-edition leather-bound edition).

Who's There? The Life and Career of William Hartnell, Jessica Carney (Hartnell's granddaughter) (Virgin, 1996).

I Am th
David H
Who or
(Harper
Jon Per
2000).